Outsiders at Home

Discrimination against Muslim Americans has soared over the last two decades with hostility growing especially acute since 2016 – in no small part due to targeted attacks by policymakers and the media. *Outsiders at Home* offers the first systematic, empirically driven examination of the status of Muslim Americans in U.S. democracy, evaluating the topic from a variety of perspectives. To what extent do Muslim Americans face discrimination by legislators, the media, and the general public? What trends do we see over time, and how have conditions shifted? What, if anything, can be done to reverse course? How do Muslim Americans view their position, and what are the psychic and sociopolitical tolls? Answering each of these questions, Nazita Lajevardi shows that the rampant, mostly negative discussion of Muslims in the media and national discourse has yielded devastating political and social consequences.

NAZITA LAJEVARDI is an attorney and political scientist at Michigan State University. Her research has been featured in outlets including *The Atlantic, The New York Times, The Washington Post, Vox Magazine,* and *The Huffington Post.*

Outsiders at Home

The Politics of American Islamophobia

NAZITA LAJEVARDI

Michigan State University

CAMBRIDGE
UNIVERSITY PRESS

CAMBRIDGE
UNIVERSITY PRESS

University Printing House, Cambridge CB2 8BS, United Kingdom

One Liberty Plaza, 20th Floor, New York, NY 10006, USA

477 Williamstown Road, Port Melbourne, VIC 3207, Australia

314–321, 3rd Floor, Plot 3, Splendor Forum, Jasola District Centre,
New Delhi – 110025, India

79 Anson Road, #06–04/06, Singapore 079906

Cambridge University Press is part of the University of Cambridge.

It furthers the University's mission by disseminating knowledge in the pursuit of
education, learning, and research at the highest international levels of excellence.

www.cambridge.org
Information on this title: www.cambridge.org/9781108479233
DOI: 10.1017/9781108782814

© Cambridge University Press 2020

First published 2020

Printed in the United States of America by Sheridan Books, Inc.

A catalogue record for this publication is available from the British Library.

Library of Congress Cataloging-in-Publication Data
Names: Lajevardi, Nazita, author.
Title: Outsiders at home : the politics of American Islamophobia / Nazita
    Lajevardi, Michigan State University.
Description: Cambridge, United Kingdom; New York, NY : Cambridge
    University Press, [2020] | Includes bibliographical references and index.
Identifiers: LCCN 2020007141 (print) | LCCN 2020007142 (ebook) |
    ISBN 9781108479233 (hardback) | ISBN 9781108749503 (paperback) |
    ISBN 9781108782814 (epub)
Subjects: LCSH: Islamophobia–United States. | Muslims–United
States–Social conditions. | United States–Politics and governement.
Classification: LCC E184.M88 L35 2020 (print) | LCC E184.M88 (ebook) |
    DDC 305.60973–dc23
LC record available at https://lccn.loc.gov/2020007141
LC ebook record available at https://lccn.loc.gov/2020007142

ISBN 978-1-108-47923-3 Hardback
ISBN 978-1-108-74950-3 Paperback

Contents

List of Figures

List of Tables

Acknowledgements

The foundation of this book began at 8:46 a.m. EST on Tuesday, September 11, 2001. The future changed that morning, for the victims of the attacks, for the world, and for *our* country. It also changed for Muslims around the world and in America. It changed for me and my family. In the months that followed, I saw mothers at Ebnecina, the religious center we attended every week, remove their hijabs to reduce their visibility. Family friends put American flag stickers on their cars to signal their "patriotism" and to reassure "Americans" they did not pose a threat despite their brown skin, beards, and covered heads. At 14 years old, I learned that membership in the United States is not permanent. My community immediately camouflaged as they waited for the heightened scrutiny on us to dissipate.

But the focus did not dissipate. It intensified. In the months that followed, the war in Afghanistan began, and two years later the United States invaded Iraq. My parents' native Iran was squarely situated in between these two countries, and panic quickly spread that Iran was next. Anxieties surrounding US–Iran relations had already increased when President Bush referred to Iran as part of the Axis of Evil on January 29, 2002. Soon after, while I was worried about the prom and college applications, parents in our community, thinking we would not overhear, would whisper to one another about purchasing property abroad and moving out of the United States to escape the rising tide of harassment and discrimination. We heard. I heard. We internalized, and we understood that despite having felt "at home," we were never really welcome.

At UCLA, I took Lorrie Frasure-Yokley's American Suburbanization class. She incorporated the experiences of Iranian-Americans in her scholarship and in her class, and taught me that the experiences of my community are worthy of study. She showed me that research was an avenue that could be available and impactful. As a community college transfer student who was surviving off of Pell grants, I never knew that before. Two years later, while pursuing my JD at the University of San Francisco, I found myself writing about section 215 of the Patriot Act under the supervision of my constitutional law professor, John Adler. He was the first to actively encourage me to study Islamophobia, to turn down a career at the DA's office, and to be bold and get my Ph.D. This book would not exist without him.

My UCSD community has supported me tremendously, and I am grateful for them. My greatest thanks go to Zoli Hajnal and Marisa Abrajano, who encouraged me to write this book before I could ever imagine writing a second-year paper. I have always appreciated and admired them, but now that I am a faculty member and recognize how much time goes into advising, I am even more grateful, and humbled by how much of their time they offered me. Instead of a regular dissertation defense, my committee offered me my first book workshop. Marisa Abrajano, Matt Barreto, James Fowler, Zoli Hajnal, and Seth Hill helped set the foundation for what would come next in this body of work. They helped me to navigate how to establish the groundwork for a book. Steve Erie has been a unique and tremendous support to me. He attended my defense and hooded me at graduation. To this day, despite his retirement, he regularly mentors me and provides feedback on my scholarship. I am ever so grateful to him. Among my peers, Taylor Carlson, John Kuk, Debbi Seligsohn, Liesel Spangler, and Jason Wu have always been a source of support, sitting with me for hours, helping me theorize, developing research designs, working through challenges, and framing my work. They have read and re-read and re-re-read numerous drafts of this scholarship. I thank them.

As I have developed this book, Marisa Abrajano has been my most important ally, friend, and mentor. She encouraged me to write the book during my postdoc at Uppsala University. She checked in with me regularly despite our 9-hour time difference, and helped me to organize the book workshop. I appreciate, admire, and respect her. My book workshop was perhaps the single most wonderful academic experience I have had to date. Six brilliant, generous, and tremendously supportive scholars came to East Lansing for several days to offer their feedback and help me turn a first draft of my work into this book. I am very lucky to have learned from Marisa Abrajano, Lisa Garcia-Bedolla, Vince Hutchings, Jane Junn, Kassra Oskooii, and Spencer Piston. They offered me so much more than I can ever reciprocate and I sincerely thank them from the bottom of my heart.

Kassra Oskooii and I have become peers, colleagues, and friends. Our similar experiences and interests have formed the foundation of much of this research agenda, and a great deal of this manuscript is inspired by his work on political discrimination. I thank him for his unwavering and invaluable support.

Numerous friends, peers, and mentors have encouraged me, shaped my experiences in the scholarly community, and provided feedback on iterations of this work. They include: Linuz Agge-born, Brian Calfano, Youssef Chouhoud, Kristin Christenson, Loren Collingwood, Karam Dana, Sirus Dehdari, Steph DeMora, Dang Do, Stephen El-Khatib, Elizabeth Flores-Arroyo, Olle Folke, Bernard Fraga, Sergio Garcia-Rios, LaGina Gause, Sandra Håkansson, Allison Harris, Will Hobbs, Ammarah Iqbal, Amaney Jamal, Sara Kerosky, Jiyoung Kim, Seulgi Lee, Danielle Lemi, Valerie Martinez-Ebers, Jennifer Merolla, Melissa Michelson, Pär Nyman, Angela Ocampo, Sven Oskarsson, Maricruz Osorio, Mara Ostfeld, Camille Pellerin, Lauri Peterson, Johanna Rickne, Kat Schenke, Jamil Scott, Nura Sediqe, Michael Tesler, Neil Visalvanich, Hannah Walker, Bryan Wilcox, and Nicole Yadon. I thank them for this privilege.

I have a deep appreciation for my Michigan State community. Jakana Thomas has offered her friendship, feedback, and guidance over the years and has truly made me feel like I belong. Matt Gross-mann, Eric Gonzalez Juenke, Mohammad Khalil, and Ani Sarkissian have empowered me in more ways than I can count as I wrote this manuscript.

Most importantly, I thank my mother, father, and brother. Your courage, love, support, and strength have seen me through this journey. Thank you for amplifying my voice and supporting me every time I wavered. Thank you to Katie and Ava, who filled my life with hugs, kindness, and love. Arezo Yassai and I have traveled alongside one another in developing both of our manuscripts related to Muslims and Islam. She is the yin to my yang.

I dedicate this book to my grandparents: Pari, Mehry, Hossein, and Seyed Mohammad. Without their risks, sacrifices, and dreams none of this work would have come into fruition.

Bismillah.

1   A Climate of Muslim American Hostility

1.1   INTRODUCTION

Current hostility toward Muslim Americans in the American sociopolitical context is high. Such hostility, though, is nothing new, with Muslims long having been portrayed as in opposition to an elevated, democratic, and modern "West." The roots of modern-day Islamophobia in America extend all the way back to the foundations of the country, beginning with the antebellum Southern plantations, to which Muslims were brought as slaves (Beydoun, 2018, p. 49). The pervasive Islamophobia observable in the United States today is rooted in a long and complex history whereby Islam as a religion, as well as its adherents, have been constructed as inferior, barbaric, and warmongering (Beydoun, 2018; Esposito, 1999; Lajevardi and Oskooii, 2018; Said, 1979). While there have been significant demographic shifts in the group's composition since their arrival in the sixteenth century, the marginalization of Muslim Americans has been manifest to different degrees for centuries.

Despite this long history of discrimination, there is particular concern over the status of Muslims in the United States today. In the wake of the murderous events of September 11, 2001, elites publicly linked Muslim Americans with the attacks. For example, President George W. Bush, visiting the Islamic Center of Washington D.C. less than a week following the attacks, remarked:

> Like the good folks standing with me, the American people were appalled and outraged at last Tuesday's attacks. And so were Muslims all across the world. Both Americans and Muslim friends and citizens, tax-paying citizens, and Muslims in nations were appalled and could not believe what we saw on our TV screens.

These acts of violence against innocents violate the fundamental
tenets of the Islamic faith. And it's important for my fellow
Americans to understand that. The English translation is not as
eloquent as the original Arabic, but let me quote from the Koran
itself: "In the long run, evil in the extreme will be the end of those
who do evil. For that they rejected the signs of Allah and held
them up to ridicule." The face of terror is not the true faith of
Islam. That is not what Islam is all about. Islam is peace. These
terrorists don't represent peace.[1]

Notwithstanding this warning, discrimination against Muslim
Americans soared. Fifteen years later, during the 2016 presidential
election, Muslims – both foreign and domestic – were once again at
the forefront of the national discourse, garnering negative attention
in part due to targeted attacks by policymakers. Lawmakers on both
sides of the aisle frequently attempted to remind the public that
Muslims in America were intrinsically different to "ordinary" Americans. Republican presidential nominees called for the wholesale
policing of Muslim American neighborhoods, advocated for a ban on
Muslims entering the country, proposed a national Muslim database,
and espoused the surveillance of mosques. This rhetoric was echoed
by local legislators, with Republican Oklahoma state representative
John Bennett publicly stating, "Muslims are a cancer that must be cut
out of the American society."[2] Meanwhile, the Democratic mayor of
Roanoke, Virginia, sparked an outcry when he cited the internment
of Japanese Americans as a basis for denying Syrian refugees entry to
the United States.[3]

Hillary Clinton, the presidential contender who appeared the
likeliest ally to the American Muslim community, failed to prove
herself to fully be one. Despite shining the national spotlight on
Khzir Khan, father of a fallen American Muslim soldier, she also
reminded the American public of their differences. In a presidential
debate on October 19, 2017 Clinton stated that American Muslims

were America's "eyes and ears" on the front lines, characterizing their utility as being rooted in their ability to help prevent terrorist attacks.[4] Rather than treating the community like any other group, by highlighting their differences and seeming knowledge about threats to the public, she merely reinforced their visibility.

At the time of writing, almost two decades after the September 11 attacks, it is perhaps unsurprising then that the public views American Muslims unfavorably. Polls conducted over the course of the 2016 presidential campaign demonstrated a rising tide of resentment against Muslim Americans. For example, a YouGov survey found that only 19% of Americans had very favorable or somewhat favorable attitudes toward Islam, contrasted with 61% of Americans who had very unfavorable or somewhat unfavorable attitudes.[5] Additionally, Americans were not blind to the implications of this, with the same YouGov poll finding that approximately half of all respondents agreed that Muslim Americans were facing increasing discrimination. This is not to say, however, that Americans who believed Muslims faced high levels of discrimination agreed that such discrimination should be reduced. Rather, a majority of Republican supporters and nearly half of all Americans endorsed policies that negatively targeted U.S. Muslims.

Within two weeks of Donald Trump's election, the Southern Poverty Law Center (SPLC) detailed a rise in the instances of harassment and intimidation faced by stigmatized groups, with many perpetrators invoking the name of the incoming president (SPLC, 2016). The SPLC (2016) identified hate incidents involving Muslims – or those perceived to be Muslim – as composing 6% of the total recorded. The SPLC (2016) report detailed some of these incidents, including, for example, a man at a Chicago hospital reportedly telling a Muslim woman: "Fuckin' sand-nigger. Thank God Trump is now president. He's gonna deport your terrorist ass" (SPLC, 2016). Muslim women wearing the hijab became particularly vulnerable to assault (Dana et al., 2018; SPLC, 2016),[6] while many Muslim Americans reported being questioned about their patriotism, purportedly due to an assumed incompatibility between their Muslim and American identities.[7] Furthermore, the report found that the incidences of hate crimes had risen drastically, with those targeting Muslims doubling between 2015 and 2016.[8]

When Trump assumed his presidency in 2017, the climate of fear and intimidation only worsened. On January 27, in one of his first acts in office, Trump signed Executive Order 13769, barring citizens of seven predominantly Muslim countries from entering the United States. Nicknamed the "Muslim Ban," two more versions of the order were issued on March 16, 2017 and September 24, 2017.

There is a great deal of evidence demonstrating that American Muslims are aware of and distressed by their negative representation within mainstream American society. A Pew (2017) report found that three-quarters of U.S. Muslims agreed that "there was a lot of discrimination against Muslims." In the wake of the 2016 presidential campaign, Arab and Muslim Americans reduced their online visibility and retreated from public life (Hobbs and Lajevardi, 2019). They also reported heightened levels of anxiety and increased experiences of discrimination (Kalin and Lajevardi, 2017). And, with the War on Terror and more recent incidents of terrorism in the U.S. and abroad ushered in by ISIS, conditions appear to have worsened further for the American Muslim community (Calfano, Lajevardi, and Michelson, 2019).

As the 2016 campaign season and the first year of Trump's presidency unfolded, American Muslims found they were no longer facing just micro-aggressions, but rather a heightened risk of physical harm. The Council on American–Islamic Relations (CAIR), the nation's largest Muslim civil rights and advocacy organization, received 3,358 bias reports from U.S. Muslims in 2014; 3,786 in 2015; 4,282 in 2016; and 2,599 in 2017. In July 2017, CAIR released a quarterly report demonstrating that the number of hate crimes against U.S. Muslims in the first half of 2017 had increased by 91% compared to the same period in 2016 (CAIR, 2017). This was particularly striking as civil rights organizations were in general agreement that 2016 had been the worst year thus far for anti-Muslim incidents. The CAIR (2017) report details that of the 946 reports of potential bias incidents it received between April 1, 2017 and June 30, 2017, 451 contained an identifiable element of religious discrimination – in this case, anti-Muslim bias. While at the time of writing the 2018 FBI Uniform Crime Reports for hate crimes against Muslims has yet to be released, it can nevertheless be seen that there were 273 reported incidents of anti-Muslim bias in 2017.[9] FBI statistics offered on bias incidents against Muslims should be viewed with caution, however, given there is likely a great deal of selection and underreporting underlying such figures.

As discussed in Chapter 2, the Muslim community's distrust of the FBI has been high for some time, stemming from before the 9/11 attacks, and growing markedly in the intervening years due to surveillance programs and prolonged detentions. Muslim Americans are generally unlikely to turn to the FBI given that the organization is one of the entities perceived as causing them considerable harm. This is evidenced by the fact that of the 2,599 anti-Muslim incidents reported to CAIR in 2017, 270 were perpetrated by the FBI, which is only three incidents short of the total number of anti-Muslim incidents the FBI reports for that calendar year.[10] Other organizations, such as SAALT (South Asians Leading Together) and CAIR, have released reports indicating that 2017 and 2018 saw rises in anti-Muslim incidents (CAIR, 2018; SAALT, 2017). Even more troubling for the prospects of Muslim American inclusion is evidence that the anti-Muslim rhetoric espoused by President Trump has been associated with increased anti-Muslim hate crimes across the country (Müller and Schwarz, 2019).

Across the country, anti-sharia bills are being introduced in state legislatures, with the aim of prohibiting state courts from considering foreign, international, or religious law – such as Islamic law (sharia) – in its decision-making. Between 2010 and 2017, 201 anti-sharia bills were proposed across 43 states, with 14 of them being enacted (in Arizona, Arkansas, Florida, Kansas, Louisiana,

Mississippi, North Carolina, Oklahoma, South Dakota, Tennessee, and Texas). During this period, Texas and Mississippi each introduced 20 different bills in their state legislatures. As the SPLC writes:

> [o]ne of the most successful far-right conspiracies to achieve mainstream viability, the mass hysteria surrounding a so-called threat of "Sharia law" in the United States is largely the work of anti-Muslim groups such as the American Freedom Law Center and ACT for America (ACT), an SPLC-designated hate group.[11]

June 2017 saw "anti-sharia" rallies organized by ACT for America – a nonprofit, right-wing activist organization – being held in 28 cities across the country, attracting white nationalists, armed right-wing militias, and neo-Nazis. Despite such hysteria, strong and ample safeguards against the application of foreign law in U.S. courts in fact already exist. For example, the Establishment Clause of the Constitution requires that laws be passed in a secular fashion and not by religious authorities, since no religious tradition (e.g. sharia law) can be established as the basis of laws applying to all people.[12]

There was an unexpected glimmer of hope for Muslim Americans in the aftermath of the 2016 presidential election, with public opposition high after the first Muslim ban executive order was announced. Tens of thousands of protesters descended upon airports and landmarks across the country, chanting slogans such as, "no hate, no fear, refugees are welcome here." Solidarity against the ban also manifested in 350,000 individuals donating $24 million to the American Civil Liberties Union in a 24-hour period. Leading politicians from both parties responded publicly and critically against the ban, painting it as at odds with American norms of egalitarianism and democracy, while numerous challenges to each of the orders were filed in courthouses across the country, as widespread opposition to the ban mounted. Research has even found that individual-level public opinion shifted *against* the ban, particularly among high-American identifiers (Collingwood, Lajevardi, and Oskooii, 2018), and remained so almost a year later (Oskooii, Lajevardi, and Collingwood, 2019).

Moreover, the 2018 midterm elections saw two Muslim women of color elected to the U.S. House of Representatives: Rashida Tlaib (Michigan 13) and Ilhan Omar (Minnesota 5). In the November 2018 general election, Tlaib won 84.2% and Omar 80.59% of the vote in their respective districts. Their election challenged the trope of "modest" Muslim women, and though the two were met with anger and disdain by some in the House, as well as by some members of the public, they also gave voice and descriptive representation to Muslims across the country.

This, then, is the sociopolitical context in which this book is situated. While Muslim Americans certainly appear to be confronting a rising tide of discrimination, anecdotal evidence is not enough. In response, this book attempts to unpack three overarching questions. First, to what extent do Muslim Americans face discrimination by legislators, the media, and the general public? Second, how do Muslims view themselves as a group within the U.S. sociopolitical context? Third, what would it take to reduce discrimination against American Muslims? Through addressing these questions, the book aims to provide a multidimensional account of hostility toward Muslim Americans in the post-9/11 era.

In the chapters that follow, a myriad of quantitative methods – including survey experiments, field experiments, and textual analysis of media transcripts – are employed to examine whether discrimination by elected officials, the media, and the general public inhibits Muslim inclusion in American democracy. The evidence shows that American Muslims are viewed negatively by the public, portrayed negatively by the media, and treated negatively by political elites. In investigating whether this treatment has gone unnoticed by their community, the book shows that Muslims are in fact well aware of their exclusion from the American polity. Since citizenship is not required in order to be considered part of this group, for the purposes of this book, I use the terms "Muslim Americans,"

"Muslims in America," "U.S. Muslims," and "American Muslims" interchangeably. Finally, the book assesses whether interventions could shift both the general public and Muslims toward having more favorable attitudes to the American Muslim community.

While I do not posit that any one of my empirical tests is sufficient in itself to provide concrete evidence of widespread discrimination against Muslim Americans, I do contend that combined they provide overwhelming evidence of bias in each of the domains examined. These findings have stark implications for the quality of Muslim American participation and representation in American democracy.

I.2 WHO ARE U.S. MUSLIMS AND WHY SHOULD WE CARE? DEMOGRAPHIC CONSIDERATIONS

With an estimated 1.6–2.1 billion adherents globally, Islam constitutes the second largest religion behind Christianity.[13] It is also the fastest-growing religion in the world today, with the Muslim population forecast to increase by 35% in the next 20 years.[14] Pew estimates that, as of 2017, there are 3.45 million Muslims living in America,[15] but it is difficult to determine the true size of the Muslim American population as the U.S. Census does not track religious affiliation, and some estimates go as high as 12 million people.[16]

As the U.S. Religion Census shows,[17] Muslims are concentrated in a few select states. On average, U.S. states have 54,945 Muslims, with only eight states where Muslims compose more than 100,000 residents. U.S. Muslims mirror the rest of the population in a number of socioeconomic dimensions. Regarding education, for example, 30% of the U.S. population holds either a college or postgraduate degree, compared to 32% of Muslims in America.[18] Higher education is more pronounced among Muslim immigrants, with 38% holding a college or postgraduate degree. Muslims in America also mirror the rest of the population with regards to income, being equally as likely as other Americans to report household incomes of at least $100,000 (24% of Muslims in America compared to 23% of all Americans).[19] Nevertheless, there are important variations within the Muslim group that should be taken into account. Twenty-nine percent of foreign-born Muslims make incomes of $100,000 or more, while U.S.-born Muslims are much more likely to earn lower incomes than the American population as a whole: 45% of the U.S.-born Muslim population earns less than $30,000, compared to 32% of the wider American public.

Moreover, while 42% of Muslim Americans were born in the United States, many others are recent arrivals, with Pew estimating that 32% of Muslims arrived in the country after the year 2000.[20] Among foreign-born Muslims, 56% arrived in the country after the turn of the century, with only 1% arriving prior to 1970; 3% arriving between 1970 and 1979; 6% arriving between 1980 and 1989; and 11% arriving between 1990 and 1999.[21]

There is a great deal of racial and ethnic diversity within the U.S. Muslim population (Dana and Barreto, 2019), with no single racial or ethnic group constituting a majority. Using Census categories to look at racial identification among the population, Pew finds that 41% of all U.S. Muslims identify as White,[22] 20% as Black, 28% as Asian, 8% as Latino, and 3% as other. Certain racial and ethnic groups are more likely to be born in the United States than others. For example, Muslims grouped into the white and Asian categories are more likely to be foreign born (45% and 41%, respectively) than their Black or Latino counterparts (11% and 1%, respectively).[23]

Racial, ethnic, and national origin backgrounds play important roles in shaping individuals' experiences, with many Muslim Americans occupying a number of intersecting identities, each of which attracts discrimination. For example, though African Americans constitute one-fifth of the entire U.S. Muslim population, a much larger proportion of Black Muslims born in the U.S. (two-thirds) say they have not always identified as Muslim.[24] Moreover, U.S.-born Black Muslims are more likely to agree that it has become harder in recent years to be Muslim in the United States. In fact, American-born Black Muslims interpret discrimination on the basis of religion and race at high and nearly equal levels, with 96% saying there is a lot of discrimination against Muslims in America, and 94% saying there is also a lot of discrimination against Black people in the country. By contrast, 49% of the U.S. Muslim population overall claim there is a lot of discrimination against Muslims in America.[25]

The space that Black Muslims occupy within the broader Muslim community cannot be overstated. The presence of Black Muslims within the Nation of Islam movement and behind leaders like Malcolm X and Louis Farrakhan was a critical component of the Civil Rights movement. While little systematic empirical research exists about the subgroup, it is clear anecdotally and from robust qualitative scholarship that the U.S.-born Black Muslim population experience inclusion and discrimination differently than their counterparts. It should be acknowledged that this is not something this book directly tackles and is therefore an important avenue for future research.

Another reason that U.S. Muslims are an important group in terms of research is that they constitute a significant proportion of the population in swing states. Despite discrimination, Muslims have remained a relevant group in American politics. More than one million Muslims are registered to vote, and have done so in numerous elections since 2001 despite being viewed as "election year outcasts" (Barreto and Dana, 2010; Zoll, 2008). Mosques have played an increasingly important role in ensuring that Muslims are engaged in politics, and a 2011 report by the Islamic Society of North America found strong evidence that political participation by Muslims had grown markedly: in 2000, only 18% of U.S. mosques reported that their core social service function was in the area of "community organizing, social issue advocacy" and "voter registration" (Bagby, 2012); by 2011, this had risen to 44% (Bagby, 2012).

Muslims will likely become increasingly relevant in U.S. political contests and discussion in key battleground states. Pew's population projections indicate that the number of Muslims in the U.S. will rise from 3.45 million in 2017 to 6.2 million in 2030.[26] During this time, Pew forecasts that the Muslim share of the U.S.

population will grow at such a rate that Muslims will be roughly as numerous as Jews or Episcopalians are today.[27]

1.3 RELIGION OR ETHNICITY? MUSLIM AMERICAN RACIALIZATION AND PANETHNICITY

An important consequence of the shifting sociopolitical position of Muslim Americans is the development of a panethnic Muslim American identity. This has presented a challenge to scholars. After 9/11, not all scholars agreed on which panethnic label to attach to this now-ostracized and amorphous group, with some studying Arab Americans (e.g. Salaita, 2005) and others Middle Eastern Americans (e.g. Tehranian, 2007; Wald, 2008); some evaluating national origin groups (e.g. Maghbouleh, 2017) and others Muslim Americans (e.g. Barreto, Masuoka, and Sanchez, 2008; Jamal, 2005, 2009).

This lack of scholarly focus on a single group is understandable. Prior to 9/11, these groups differentiated themselves by language (e.g. Arabic, Turkish, Farsi); religion (e.g. Muslim, Christian, Baha'i, Jewish); ethnicity (e.g. Arab, Turkish, and Persian); and immigration histories. Today, Muslim Americans are a demographically diverse religious group, but are often perceived as monolithic (Khan and Ecklund, 2013; McCarus, 1994; Nyang, 1999). Understanding, theorizing, and measuring discrimination against Muslim Americans is complex and imperfect, and it is important to consider if the root of discrimination is about race, national origin, region, or religion.

Though the "Muslim" label does not refer to a racial category, the distinction between racism and religious discrimination is often conflated (Allen and Nielsen, 2002; Khan and Ecklund, 2013). Intersectionality is an important space many Muslims occupy, especially with respect to gender and religion (e.g. hijabi women), or race and religion (e.g. African American Muslims). Exploring the roots of public attitudes against Muslim Americans and how they manifest in policy support or voting choices is therefore multilayered, and must be treated and explained with caution. The diversity with this "group" highlights the inherent difficulties in assigning those within it a collective, unified, and easily definable identity. This applies to both those attempting to impose a label and those resisting such a label being imposed.

After 9/11, there was not only resistance by some to being grouped together with other Muslims under reputational assault, but also an inability on the part of the media and the public to identify exactly the group it was worried about in relation to domestic terrorism and the War on Terror. Irrespective of whichever identity a particular subgroup of Muslim Americans might wish to assert, a blanket identity has been imposed upon them. This fact, which is linked to an ever-evolving climate of racialization, has been taken for granted by scholars (see Calfano et al., 2019), meaning very little scholarship has gone into unpacking how the Muslim identity developed in the first place. While the aim of this volume is not to trace how and why U.S. Muslims became a panethnic group, I often refer to this fact throughout this book. This is important, as many elite and public attitudes are sweeping, and are not limited to any one particular subgroup. When used today, "Muslim American" is often employed as a catchall term for any individual from the Middle East, the Arab world, or South Asia, irrespective of their actual religious background or experiences.

This imprecise labeling is not without consequence, ignoring as it does Muslims from other groups, such as Black, Latino, and East Asian Muslims. It also erroneously encompasses many who hail from other faiths, such as Hinduism, Judaism, Christianity, Bahaism or Zoroastrianism, among others. This sweeping group labeling again demonstrates the amorphous nature of the Muslim American group when viewed through the lens of the general public. Moreover, Muslim Americans have become increasingly racialized since 9/11, with external markers such as dress, skin color, accent, and language functioning as heuristics for a religion constructed as a threat to American culture and national security (Dana et al., 2018; Jamal, 2009; Selod, 2015). This racialization process, however, did not develop in a vacuum. Considerable evidence demonstrates that

Muslims have historically been linked to stereotypes of violence, intolerance, and extremism (Esposito, 1999; Khan and Ecklund, 2013; Said, 1979; Shaheen, 2003), and that the attacks of September 11, 2001 and their aftermath fed into this to play an important role in shaping Americans' perceptions of Muslims (Dana et al., 2018).

Myriad institutional practices targeting Muslim Americans, abundant political discourse equating Islam with radicalization, negative media coverage, and anti-Muslim rhetoric espoused by public figures together entrench negative stereotypes through a process of racialization (Dana et al., 2018). Omi and Winant (2004) define this process as "the extension of racial meaning to a previously racially unclassified relationship, social practice, or group," whereby the "group" in question is coded as inherently dangerous, disloyal, or inferior (Fleras, 2011; Lajevardi, 2017; Lajevardi and Oskooii, 2018; Selod, 2015). Thus, Muslim Americans have been racialized due to their cultural and religious values being perpetually communicated as anti-American, foreign, misogynistic, and violent (Barreto, Dana, and Oskooii, 2013; Jamal, 2009; Said, 2003; Selod, 2015; Sides and Gross, 2013).

1.4 CHALLENGES FOR BOTH APPROACHES

Given there is ample evidence that Muslims are facing a heightened episode of discrimination that does not appear to be diminishing, it is imperative that scholars develop creative techniques of measuring not only how public attitudes toward them have shifted, but also how Muslims have responded in light of their situational positioning in America.

Several impediments limit scholarly research. Scholarly interest in attitudes toward Muslims (as a foreign group), Islam (the religion), and Muslim Americans (the domestic group) only peaked after 2001. As available Roper polls demonstrate at the time of this writing, only three public surveys are available to scholars measuring attitudes toward the group prior to 2001, complicating attempts at identifying how Muslim Americans were viewed prior to 9/11.

While a nascent political science scholarship exploring mass attitudes toward American Muslims has begun to emerge, this literature is based on formulating an all-encompassing theory evaluating how the group fares in the face of all facets of American democracy. Moreover, the questions posed about U.S. Muslims in surveys are often either uninformative – for example favorability scores – or based on stereotypes typically attributed to other groups.

Studying the behaviors of U.S. Muslims is complex and difficult, while tracking how Muslims have responded to the heightened climate of discrimination introduces its own challenges. The Census does not track religious identification information, and the "white" racial category obfuscates any variation in national origin Muslims may want to highlight.

Studies on the attitudes and behaviors of other marginalized groups in American politics are less inhibited by data concerns. Studying their micro (individual) and macro (aggregate) level behaviors and attitudes is aided by the fact that data has been collected over a longer period of time. Studies of racial, ethnic, and religious groups are typically aided by the fact that we know where they are located, who they are, and how their populations may have changed. With this base level of information, scholars can trace the aggregate behaviors of these individuals in order to evaluate how groups are responding to sociopolitical changes. Studies of Muslim Americans lack such advantages, as there simply is no information available to do this. As a result, there is very little objective information on how the group is adapting to this climate of increased fear.

* * * * * * * * * * * *

The guiding question of this book is: "What is the status of Muslim Americans in American democracy?" This question is explored from the perspectives of the general public, legislators, and the media, which taken together provide ample evidence of rampant discrimination. The book is organized as follows:

Chapter 2 provides background on the history of membership rights within subgroups among the Muslim American population. The chapter examines this history before and after the attacks on September 11, 2001. It also introduces the book's theoretical framework.

Chapter 3 provides further information on the measure of hostility toward Muslim Americans it introduces, and assesses how it matters for political preferences, attitudes, and behavior. Evidence is presented that negative attitudes toward Muslim Americans are pervasive and that these attitudes matter for vote choice and policy preferences.

Chapter 4 evaluates the prospects for the political incorporation of Muslims into one survey and two candidate evaluation experiments. The results reveal that not only does the public hold hostile attitudes toward Muslim Americans, but also that they are unwilling to vote for Muslim American candidates, irrespective of the candidate's racial background.

Chapter 5 addresses an empirical concern: assessing how Muslim Americans were portrayed to and perceived by the public prior to 9/11 is difficult to measure, and is complicated by the fact that little information on aggregate attitudes toward Muslims and Muslim Americans is available for scholarly examination. The book instead turns to the news media as a vital lens in assessing how Muslims and Muslim Americans have been portrayed to the mass public over a period of 25 years, specifically in the decade prior to 9/11 and the decade and a half following it. I assess the sentiment of news coverage involving Muslim Americans, and analyze how it compares when set alongside coverage of other groups scholars have regularly demonstrated are framed negatively.

Chapter 6 examines the effect on mass attitudes of negative and positive news media coverage about Muslims and Muslim Americans. Three survey experiments are utilized to explore whether attitudes toward U.S. Muslims and policies targeting them can be improved after exposure to news media. As a robustness check, the book compares how exposure to a control, negative, and positive coverage about immigrants, and negative and positive coverage about Latinos affects hostility toward Muslim Americans.

Chapter 7, in an effort to evaluate the status of Muslim Americans in the U.S. sociopolitical context, focuses on how they are treated and valued by legislators. Two audit studies are conducted, testing responsiveness to constituent requests. The first study tests whether Muslim Americans can integrate and find work in America's political system, with the second exploring whether Muslim leaders have more success than individual members in garnering access to politics for their communities.

Chapter 8 shifts the focus to Muslim Americans themselves. A marginalized group's understanding of and response to discrimination is important for analyzing how it reacts in the face of exclusion. Given increasing national security concerns about Muslims and their behaviors, tracking Muslim Americans' reactions empirically seems a better method than imposing existing stereotypes.

The Conclusion offers avenues for future research.

2 Theoretical Framework: The Sociopolitical Positioning of Muslim Americans

For the purposes of theory building, some background on the history of membership rights to subgroups within the Muslim American population is necessary. Exploring the granting and revocation of whiteness from non-Western groups, as well as understanding how whiteness can be mismatched in the law and on the ground, reveals a great deal about how thin and fleeting privileges of whiteness are for those non-Western groups "fortunate" enough to be granted such de jure rights (Maghbouleh, 2017).

The current climate of negativity toward Muslim Americans raises an interesting puzzle. Scholars contend that minority groups enter a cycle of racialization the moment they arrive in the United States. Many groups – for example Chinese and Japanese immigrants – have faced de jure discrimination in the form of laws based on express racial and national origin classifications that have expressly excluded them from opportunities. Meanwhile, one can look to the discrimination endured by Jewish, Italian, Polish, Catholic, and Irish immigrants for evidence of de facto exclusion. Over time, many of these groups – and especially those whose racial characteristics did not prevent them from appearing "white" – eventually "whitened" under the law.

The Muslim American population is racially and ethnically diverse. According to the Pew Research Center, which provides the most reliable and up-to-date figures, no single racial, ethnic, or national origin group makes up the majority of the U.S. Muslim population.[1] Rather, a plurality (41%) is categorized under the "white" category, consisting of Arabs, Middle Easterners, and Persians/Iranians. Almost one-third (28%) are grouped under "Asian," primarily those from South Asia. Blacks constitute 20% of the U.S.

Muslim population, and Hispanics 8%. Importantly, most converts to Islam hail from these latter two backgrounds (49% of Black Muslims and more than half of Hispanic Muslims).[2]

It is this diversity that makes a homogeneous racial history of the group impossible. Struggles for assimilation and group histories have differed greatly based on racial, ethnic, and national origins. As such, when unpacking the history of attaining "whiteness" for naturalization purposes, particular attention must be paid to the experiences of "white" Muslims, who hail primarily from the Middle East and constitute the largest grouping within the U.S. Muslim population today.

Unlike other groups, many of those who emigrated from the Middle East to the United States of their own volition, beginning in the late 1800s to early 1900s especially (that is, not enslaved Africans), were not immediately inserted into the racial hierarchy. Instead, they were mostly granted a cloak of (legal) white privilege (and protections), with little attention placed upon them. These Middle Eastern immigrants therefore experienced a rather different legal history of "whiteness," being legally classified as white before the great wave of Muslim immigrants began in the 1950s. Also, while some of these individuals were Muslim, most were Christian (Read, 2008). Historically, this legal victory enabled Middle Easterners to vote, own land, and escape formal segregation. However, this racial formation would later prove complex (Lajevardi, Marrar, and Michelson, 2014).

Today, Muslim Americans – particularly those of Middle Eastern descent – are in a comparatively disadvantaged position, having lost this status. Despite their legal Whiteness, U.S. Muslims of Middle Eastern background have been targets of both public and private discrimination (Lajevardi, Marrar, and Michelson, 2014). As Tehranian (2008, p. 38) notes:

> The assumption that Americans of Middle Eastern descent have not suffered systemic racial prejudice in American society is disingenuous. Indeed, quotidian realities quickly reveal the

problematic governmental categorization of Middle Easterners as white. As any Arab, Turkish, or Iranian American will tell you, Middle Easterners are infrequently treated as white people in their daily lives.

The Muslim American question lies at the heart of some of the most pressing issues of our time. The 9/11 attacks, the subsequent War on Terror, the declaration of the "Axis of Evil" countries, the implementation of numerous surveillance programs targeting Muslim communities, the rise of ISIS, the prolonged detention of Middle Eastern citizens in the U.S., the pervasive anti-Muslim rhetoric of candidates in the 2016 campaign season, and Trump's travel ban are just a few examples of how Muslims are situated at the forefront of the national debate.

The rest of this chapter sets out a theory that can be broken down into three parts. First, in the decades prior to 9/11, Muslim Americans faced far less de jure discrimination than other marginalized groups. Many Muslims, and particularly those originating from the Middle East, were protected under the law and given the privileges of "whiteness," a rare feat given that many other groups were immediately racialized upon their arrival. Moreover, when they did face discrimination, it was often on the basis of national origin. Second, 9/11 and its aftermath have led to a massive shift in attitudes toward Muslim Americans. As the frequency of negative Muslim portrayals increased, stereotypes linking the domestic group to tropes connected to violence, danger, and terror became commonplace. This shift is reflective of the limitations of the privileges bestowed by official and legal "Whiteness." Third, this discrimination is so acute that both Whites and Muslims perceive its existence. The culmination of each of these points leads to actual deep-seated discrimination being the predicted outcome.

2.1   BEFORE 9/11

Muslims have been in the United States since the country's founding, the earliest of which likely arrived as slaves in the early 16th century from the Senegambian region of Africa.[3] Though the Islam brought to America by enslaved Africans did not endure for very long, with many forcibly converted to Christianity,[4] traces endure to the present day, as efforts to practice Islam persisted and were conducted in secret.[5] For example, an enclave of African Americans on the Georgia coast maintained their faith until the early part of the twentieth century, evidenced in the practice of the "Ring Shout." The Ring Shout, originally inherited from enslaved Muslims, is a form of religious dance mimicking the ritual circling by Muslim pilgrims of the Kaaba in Mecca, and involves men and women rotating counterclockwise while singing, clapping their hands, and shuffling their feet.[6]

A second wave of Muslim immigrants arrived in the United States between 1878 and 1923. This saw immigrants coming in large numbers from the Middle East, particularly Syria and Lebanon, settling mostly in Midwestern states such as Ohio, Michigan, Iowa, and the Dakotas.[7] These migrants arrived mostly in pursuit of economic opportunity, with many working as manual laborers alongside African Americans in factories.[8]

During this period, the Great Migration of African Americans to the north saw a revival of the Islamic practice and culture destroyed during slavery, and a consequent growth of the African American Muslim Nationalist movement. Their migration also saw the establishment of Muslim communities, and by 1952 North America had over 1,000 mosques built by Arab immigrants and African Americans.

The Immigration and Nationality Act of 1952 saw a fresh wave of Muslim migrants arriving from Arab countries such as Palestine, Iraq, and Egypt,[9] followed a decade later by waves of Southeast Asian Muslims.[10] Then, in the 1970s, a further wave of migrants arrived from Iran, many of them arriving in pursuit of educational opportunities.

2.1.1   *"Faustian" Pact and Protection with Whiteness*

When examining the history of Muslims in America, it is almost impossible not to conflate religion, ethnicity, and national origin.

In large part this is due to courts and decision-makers having focused on markers other than religion in order to determine who could legally be recognized as "white" under the law. These markers included nationality, originating from areas near the Caucasus, being of Aryan origin, perceived skin color, and perceived group membership. As such, the experiences of Muslims in the United States have been inextricably intertwined with race, region, and national background, requiring an analysis of other group classifications, such as region (e.g. Middle Easterners) and national origin (e.g. Syria, Lebanon).

From 1790 until 1952, Congress restricted naturalizations to "white persons." Thus, the struggle for "whiteness," exemplified by the social and legal construction of the concept, arises in part from who was permitted to become a naturalized citizen (Lopez, 1997). Whether a person was "white," however, was often no easy question, and was left to the courts, which then had to wrestle in their decisions with the nature of race in general, and of white racial identity in particular.

The courts heard 52 racial prerequisite cases between 1878 and 1942 including two by the U.S. Supreme Court: *Ozawa* v. *United States* (1922) and *United States* v. *Thind* (1923). In deciding these racial prerequisite cases, the lower courts were divided almost evenly between applying a "common knowledge" test or a "scientific evidence" test. The "common knowledge" rationale relied on widely held conceptions of race and racial divisions expressed by the general public. The "scientific evidence" test relied on supposedly "objective, technical, and specialized" knowledge, with experts analyzing, for instance, variations in name, and differences in complexion, hair, and skull shape (Lopez, 1997). The problem, over time, was that the common knowledge and scientific evidence tests would often contradict one another. In the 1923 *United States* v. *Thind* case, the Supreme Court held that the common knowledge test applied, reinforcing the social construction of race and whiteness. As immigration increased, countless individuals found themselves arguing their racial identity in order to naturalize. From 1907 to 1920, over one million people gained citizenship under the racially restrictive naturalization laws. As Lopez (1997, p. 1) writes, "[t]hese cases produced illuminating published decisions that document the efforts of would-be citizens from around the world to establish their Whiteness at law."

Historically, whiteness came with many legal, economic, and sociopolitical privileges. By limiting naturalization and voting rights to "free white persons," the 1790 Naturalization Act thereby restricted voting rights and other political power to European immigrants. Many states only allowed white citizens to own or lease land. These restrictions remained in place, with only minor adjustments to allow for African Americans and former slaves to become citizens, until the McCarran–Walter Act of 1952. The aforementioned privileges were limited only to a specific group of Whites, with the definition of whiteness changing over time to benefit or further marginalize particular groups of people. For example, the borders of whiteness were originally drawn to include those originating from Europe, but geopolitical influences eventually led to drawing borders that encompassed those originating from outside of Europe (Omi and Winant, 2004). Unsurprisingly, the social construction of whiteness became a vehicle for the perpetuation or alleviation of oppression. Thus, during this time, many individuals, including those hailing from the Muslim world and the Middle East, fought to be recognized as white by the U.S. legal system (Tehranian, 2007).

For many groups this recognition was elusive; applicants from Hawaii, China, Japan, Burma, and the Philippines failed in their arguments. Conversely, courts ruled decisively that applicants from Mexico and Armenia were white (Lopez, 1997). However, courts were mixed regarding the whiteness of petitioners from Syria, India, and the Arab world. For Middle Easterners, the attainment of whiteness was eventually successful, and they were directed to check the "white" box on the U.S. Census and other government forms. Checking the "other" category automatically reassigned them to white.

While this victory first enabled Muslims of Middle Eastern descent to own land (Lajevardi, Marrar, and Michelson, 2014), currently they are not eligible for affirmative action programs that have hiring preferences, nor government contracts or funding to individuals, businesses, or organizations from historically disenfranchised groups. Furthermore, it does not enable special consideration for acceptance to colleges and universities (Lajevardi, Marrar, and Michelson, 2014).

The historical and institutionalized discrimination against Muslims, dating back to events such as the Palestinian–Israeli conflict, the Iran–Iraq War, Iran Contra affair, the Persian Gulf War, the wars in Iraq and Afghanistan, and systemic racial profiling post-9/11, led to an almost socially acceptable discrimination justified by patriotism and national security. While society has increasingly condemned discrimination against Black, Latino, and Asian people, racism against Muslims of Middle Eastern descent is tolerated and sometimes even encouraged. This was particularly so after the 1979 Iranian hostage crisis, and continues today after having been rekindled by the 9/11 attacks (McCarus, 1994). As Tehranian (2007, p. 70) notes: "Middle Easterners have come to represent enemy aliens, and even an enemy race, in the popular imagination."

In the wake of the mass waves of migration, many Muslims of Middle Eastern descent have found themselves caught in racial loopholes whereby they are sufficiently white to escape racially motivated discrimination and hate crimes, but are too white to reliably secure race-based protection and legal redress for any violent and discriminatory acts committed against them (Maghbouleh, 2017).

2.1.2   *Legal Battles for Naturalization and Subsequent Discrimination*

The early 1900s saw a number of cases make their way up the courts, establishing the legal ground for the naturalization of individuals originating from the Middle East.[11] To attain naturalization, claimants had to go through "racial prerequisite" cases, whereby claimants could argue to local naturalization and federal courts that they were on the white side of the racial cutoff point (Maghbouleh, 2017). On some occasions, courts would rely on cartographic and continental borders; on others, they would measure social closeness and distance from the Middle East to assess who could be white (Maghbouleh, 2017).

In the landmark 1915 *Dow* v. *United States* case, the court recognized a Syrian man to be white, thereby granting de jure privileges of whiteness.[12] The judge, however, acknowledged the limits of whiteness when he wrote that it would only affect the "inhabitants of a portion of Asia, including Syria, [who are] to be classed as white persons." The judge also clarified which groups were not to be extended the privileges of whiteness, including other Asian claimants from China or Japan. Instead, "include[d] within the term 'white persons' [are] Syrians, Armenians, and Parsees."[13]

As outlined above, a great number of Muslim immigrants from the Middle East came to the United States after the *Dow* v. *United States* decision. The second wave of Muslim migration ended in 1923 with the Johnson–Reed Immigration Act, which enacted immigration quotas and restricted all arrivals from Asia. Then, with the Immigration and Nationality Act of 1952, migration to the United States from the Middle East began once again as part of a quota system, and saw the arrival of highly educated elites from countries such as Egypt, Iraq, and Syria. Finally, and with the 1965 Immigration Act, which removed the national origin quota system, another wave of immigration from the Middle East, including Iran, began. During these mass waves of migration, Muslim immigrants from the Middle East were de jure considered white under the law, meaning they were permitted to enjoy "white privilege" long before other groups were granted similar rights. However, de jure classifications of "whiteness" did not translate into de facto treatment as white persons, with discrimination against Muslims of Middle Eastern descent persisting during this time.

Such discrimination, though, was tailored to a person's country of origin, rather than their religious background, with, for example, the 1979 Iranian hostage crisis and the 1985 TWA hijacking in Lebanon resulting in widespread racial slurs and ethnic epithets (such as "camel jockey") being used against individuals of Middle Eastern origin (Aziz, 2009; Elver, 2012). During this time, Muslim Americans were generally perceived as model immigrants, with high education levels (the second highest level of education among the major religious groups) and low crime rates,[14] and were rarely discussed in the media. Thus, a pre-9/11 empirical measure is needed as a baseline to assess when portrayals of Muslim Americans began and the extent to which they have worsened.

A number of studies have explored the political experiences of Muslim Americans prior to 2001 (for examples, see: Austin, 1984; Esposito, 1999; Esposito and Haddad, 1998; Haddad and Lummis, 1987; Haddad and Smith, 1993; Khan, 1998; McCloud, 1995; Naff, 1993; Smith, 1993; Suleiman, 1999; Wormser, 1994). This scholarship documents that many of the challenges faced by Muslims today – for example government scrutiny and outgroup-based discrimination – were present prior to the 9/11 attacks (though to a lesser extent). Beydoun (2018, p. 78) writes that post–Cold War relations with the Middle East and Islam saw the United States not only find "a suitable replacement [for the Soviet Union as the next geopolitical embodiment of evil], but a more visually foreign and religiously inspired archrival."

A significant drawback of these volumes, however, is that they are primarily qualitative, which makes research replication difficult (Calfano et al., 2019). Some of the literature of this period, moreover, focuses on groups other than Muslim Americans, often conflating Muslim Americans, Arab Americans, Middle Easterners, and various national origin groups. Despite this, their explorations of the stereotypes of violence, danger, and foreignness promulgated in the pre-9/11 period are very useful. Other pre-2001 scholarship provides analyses of Muslim history, racial and ethnic diversity, immigration trends, the effects of slavery and civil rights struggles, and attempts at assimilation (for an overview, see Calfano et al., 2019). These works communicate a common narrative of U.S. Muslims facing some discrimination prior to 9/11.

Not all the scholarship on U.S. Muslims during this era high-lights the discrimination they faced. Perhaps one of the most scathing and well-cited published works about Muslims is Huntington's *The Clash of Civilizations* (1997), which argues that democratic societies must be wary of Islamic teachings and those that follow them. It has since been dismissed by many as a reductionist theory insulting to Islam's over 1 billion adherents (see for example, Esposito, 1999), but regardless of such attempts at adding nuance to the Muslim experience, scholarship suggests that Muslims were widely linked to stereotypes of violence, intolerance, and extremism long before 9/11 (Esposito, 1999; Said, 1979). As Lee (2008) writes, "[w]hile the image of the Arab-as-Terrorist is not a new stereotype, it has become increasingly entrenched in the public imagination since 9/11 because of the increased frequency of news coverage of actual Islamic terrorism."

What is also noteworthy about U.S. Muslims prior to 9/11 is their attempts at political mobilization. The 2000 presidential elec-tion was the first to see the emergence of a Muslim American political identity, with Muslim Americans closing ranks behind President Bush and the Republican Party (Barreto and Bozonelos, 2009; Dana, Barreto, and Oskooii, 2011; Findley, 2001).[15] This was due to a num-ber of reasons. As Findley (2001) and Barreto and Bozonelos (2009) explain, the foreign policy issue of Jerusalem as the "undivided and undisputed" capital of Israel, and dissatisfaction with Joseph Lieber-man, an Orthodox Jew, as the Democratic running mate, nudged the Muslim American vote within the Republican Party's reach.

2.1.3   *September 11, 2001*

The attacks of September 11, 2001, as well as subsequent events, played a substantial role in shaping American perceptions of

Muslims, ushering in a new tide of even more pronounced anti-Muslim sentiment. The attacks placed Muslims front and center of the national discourse, with the negative attention only increasing in the years since. Muslim Americans – and, by extension, their cultural and religious values – have long been viewed as anti-American, foreign, misogynistic, and violent. It should therefore come as no surprise that such stereotypes met little resistance in the wake of 9/11.

There is no doubt that the September 11 attacks had a devastating impact on American lives, foreign policy, and global power. Thousands were killed, families were destroyed, and New York City – a symbol of America's global might – was shattered. The attacks received perpetual news coverage, with Americans reportedly viewing 8.1 hours of news coverage the day of the attacks. Viewers responded emotionally to the coverage, which arguably served as a heuristic device in forming opinions and attitudes (Finnegan, 2006). The media, political leaders, journalists, and the American leaders all lined up behind their president and country (Finnegan, 2006). The attacks were followed by the equally terrifying threat of anthrax. Meanwhile, the Justice Department repeatedly claimed that al-Qaeda operatives were still in the country and that another attack was imminent. Perpetual reminders of the attacks, including media coverage of official warnings and the nation's threat level,[16] arguably helped to shape public opinion and to create a national witch hunt to identify those responsible.

For months, no group or person took responsibility for the attacks; the only firm information disseminated to the public being the nationalities of the 19 hijackers: 15 were from Saudi Arabia, 2 from the United Arab Emirates, 1 from Egypt, and 1 from Lebanon. It is not unlikely that repeated media images of young Middle Eastern men with beards, olive skin, and foreign dress served as markers identifying similar-looking individuals as a threat. This process is substantiated by a rich comparative literature on the construction of Muslim men as violence-prone, which argues that similar imagery has led to European publics identifying such Muslim men as a threat (Dwyer, Shah, and Sanghera, 2008; Ewing, 2008b; Hopkins, 2004).

Within months, blame was attributed to al-Qaeda, the Patriot Act was passed, and the U.S. launched a war in Afghanistan. As a result, the national spotlight was collectively cast on U.S. Muslims, Middle Easterners, and Arab Americans. Even at the time, it was clear political elites were cognizant of the reaction of the general public to Muslim Americans, and the linkages being made. On September 20, 2001, George W. Bush spoke directly to Muslims and assuaged their concerns of being targeted:[17]

> I also want to speak tonight directly to Muslims throughout the world. We respect your faith. It's practiced freely by many millions of Americans and by millions more in countries that America counts as friends. Its teachings are good and peaceful, and those who commit evil in the name of Allah blaspheme the name of Allah. The terrorists are traitors to their own faith, trying, in effect, to hijack Islam itself. The enemy of America is not our many Muslim friends. It is not our many Arab friends. Our enemy is a radical network of terrorists and every government that supports them.

This remark from the then-president came only nine days after the attacks, and while it can be read as reaching out to the Muslim community, as well as warning the American public not to jump to conclusions, an important and unaddressed question is: Why did the administration find it necessary, in the immediate aftermath of one of the most devastating attacks on U.S. soil in history, to make a statement highlighting the potential of Muslim American discrimination? It could be suggested that this statement all but proves the administration was aware that both the attacks and the subsequent U.S. response would result in a backlash against the Muslim community. The quote also reveals that the administration moved quickly in an attempt to mitigate whatever future backlash might occur.

Legislators also acknowledged the pervasive nature of Muslim American discrimination within the very text of the USA Patriot Act (U.S. H.R. 3162 Title I, Sec. 102), which was signed into law on October 26, 2001, barely a month after the attacks:

(a) Congress makes the following findings:

   (1) Arab Americans, Muslim Americans, and Americans from South Asia play a vital role in our Nation and are entitled to nothing less than the full rights of every American.
   (2) The acts of violence that have been taken against Arab and Muslim Americans since the September 11, 2001, attacks against the United States should be and are condemned by all Americans who value freedom....
   (3) Muslim Americans have become so fearful of harassment that many Muslim women are changing the way they dress to avoid becoming targets.

A couple of points are worth highlighting. First, the legislation references three groups – Arab Americans, Muslim Americans, and Americans from South Asia – suggesting that the "outgroup" has yet to be identified. This conflation has proven difficult for researchers, which is in part why scholars have at various times studied the experiences of Arab Americans, Middle Easterners, and Muslim Americans. Figure 5.1 presents evidence on why Muslim Americans have been determined as the group most relevant for study in the context of this book. Second, the very fact that the legislation begins by discussing the rights and fears of Muslim Americans is telling regarding the reality, scope, and magnitude of the discrimination to come.

2.2   AFTER 9/11

In the wake of the 9/11 attacks, there was a curious dearth of scholarship examining the treatment of Muslim Americans in America in mainstream political science (but see Abdo, 2005; Bakalian and Bozorgmehr, 2009; Barreto and Bozonelos, 2009; Barreto, Masuoka, and Sanchez, 2008; Jamal, 2005, 2009; Kalkan, Layman, and Uslaner,

2009; Nacos and Torres-Reyna, 2002, 2007; Panagopoulos, 2006), and it is only more recently that the literature has finally begun to empirically trace their sociopolitical treatment (see, e.g., Barreto and Dana, 2010; Calfano, 2018; Calfano and Lajevardi, 2019; Chouhoud, Dana, and Barreto, 2019; Dana, Barreto, and Oskooii, 2011; Dana, Wilcox-Archuleta, and Barreto, 2017; Lajevardi, 2017; Oskooii, 2016). In the meantime, ever since September 11, 2001, U.S. domestic counterintelligence efforts have been largely framed as targeting the transnational Muslim American terrorist, while Muslim Americans have become the victims of hate crimes, racial profiling, and discrimination by the American public, the mass media, and politicians (Bakalian and Bozorgmehr, 2009).

During the post-9/11 era, the U.S. has endorsed or overseen legislation, policies, and interventions that have affected the lives of Muslims both foreign and domestic. These include the Patriot Act, the establishment of the Guantanamo Bay Prison, the Iraq War, the Abu Ghraib Prison abuse scandal, and the creation of the Controlled Application Review and Resolution program. Abdo (2005) argues that these policies were racial in nature and implemented with Muslims in mind, despite widespread obedience by Muslim Americans to law enforcement, due to fear of punishment for noncompliance (Tyler, Schulhofer, and Huq, 2010). Abdo (2005) contends that some of these policies stemmed from the American public's fear that a lack of integration into the American mainstream would eventually lead to the radicalization of Muslims on U.S. soil. In reality, however, these policies have marginalized the Muslim American population. Abdo (2005) further notes that Muslims are no strangers to unlawful detentions, deliberate security checks, and raids on their homes, offices, and mosques in the name of the War on Terror, and that it is this unwelcome attention that continues to foment a cycle of alienation.

There is evidence that Americans view Muslims unfavorably. For example, despite Muslims being one of the most socioeconomically integrated groups in the country, a 2010 Gallup study found that Americans have sharply negative attitudes toward Muslims.[18] Even among those Americans who claim not to have any personal prejudice toward Muslim individuals, one-third report holding an unfavorable opinion on Islam (36%). Moreover, those with prejudice against Muslims do not hold negative beliefs about religious minority groups in general.

This book anticipates that three factors have substantially shaped and impacted public views: (1) events, including 9/11 and subsequent incidents; (2) the media; and (3) legislators. It is contended that these factors combined have led to an increase in discrimination against Muslim Americans. The 9/11 attacks and their aftermath thrust Muslim Americans into the national spotlight, prompting many Americans who had never previously given Islam a second thought to try to make sense of these incidents and the faith that ostensibly inspired them. At the same time, legislators created narratives that were transmitted to the public both directly and indirectly. Through correspondences, speeches, newsletters, and media appearances, legislators provided the wider public with information on Muslims, and much of their discussion of Muslims was overwhelmingly negative. Moreover, the media played a dual role in shaping discrimination against Muslims. First, it was a conduit for the political communications of others. Second, based on these messages, it generated negative frames it then disseminated to the public. As a result, the attitudes of the wider public have been influenced by the messages received from the media and policymakers.

2.2.1   Muslim Americans' Responses to a Climate of Hostility

There is some evidence that Muslims themselves are aware of these attitudes and their current positioning in the American sociopolitical context. A 2011 Pew survey reveals that Muslim Americans believe it has become more difficult to be a Muslim after 9/11 (Pew, 2011). Additionally, a majority (52.02%) of respondents felt the government singled them out in its antiterrorism policies.

It also appears that U.S. Muslims have reacted negatively to this climate of discrimination and are retreating from public spaces. Racialized minorities have been known to respond to rampant political discrimination either by retreating from public life or increasing their visibility. Research has indicated that such minorities are negatively affected psychologically when they perceive greater discrimination, or when members of their group are devalued in popular culture (Branscombe, Schmitt, and Harvey, 1999; Crocker and Major, 1989). Those minorities who see prejudice as indicating rejection by the dominant group are at risk of internalizing negative evaluations, and therefore exhibiting lower levels of self-esteem and participating in fewer civic activities (Branscombe, Schmitt, and Harvey, 1999; Oskooii, 2016, 2018). Conversely, minorities can also react to negative assessments by the dominant group by cultivating positive self-esteem and increasing their involvement in activities that enhance their group status (Branscombe, Schmitt, and Harvey, 1999; Crocker and Major, 1989; Oskooii, 2016). For example, in some cases discrimination has been shown to act as a motivator for groups such as Blacks, Asian Americans, and Latinos to become more engaged in the public sphere and politics (Barreto and Woods, 2005; Pantoja, Ramirez, and Segura, 2001; Parker, 2009; Ramakrishnan, 2005; Ramírez, 2007).

The 2016 election season saw presidential frontrunners deliver considerable doses of anti-Muslim rhetoric, with Donald Trump proposing a ban on Muslims entering the country, a national database of all Muslims in the United States, and the wholesale surveillance of mosques; Ben Carson arguing that a Muslim should never be president; and Ted Cruz running on a platform of empowering law enforcement to patrol and secure Muslim neighborhoods. Muslim Americans, in turn, experienced unprecedented amounts of discrimination. In response, some imams in the country recommended invisibility, instructing their congregations to take extraordinary measures to protect their physical safety, and even to conceal their Muslim identities by taking off the hijab (Calfano et al., 2019).

It would be reasonable to assume that many Muslim Americans actually followed these recommendations, seeking invisibility as a means to avoid future discrimination. Scholarship has indeed shown that Muslims have retreated from public spaces, with Hobbs and Lajevardi (2019), for example, examining whether Muslim Americans have decreased their participation in public life by presenting findings from three data sources: (1) television news coverage of Muslims; (2) social media activity of individuals with Arabic names (both Americans and U.S. residents); and (3) a survey of Muslim Americans. Their results provide macro- and individual-level evidence that Arab and Muslim Americans have been reducing their visibility in public spaces, both online and offline. Furthermore, Hobbs and Lajevardi (2019) suggest that Muslim Americans' retreat from public spaces can occur in a matter of days to weeks after a major political event, and can be sustained for many months, perhaps even years, after the event. This retreat is alarming, with the decreased visibility of Muslim Americans indicating they have become even further removed from the national discourse than scholars previously imagined.

3 Introducing the "Muslim American Resentment" Scale

3.1 BACKGROUND ON ATTITUDES TOWARD MUSLIM AMERICANS

How does the wider American public view Muslim Americans? Do these attitudes matter in terms of shaping public preferences toward policies such as increasing the surveillance of mosques and targeting Muslims at airport screenings? Furthermore, do these attitudes matter in terms of the political representatives we elect? These are some of the guiding questions this book aims to address. As Oskooii, Dana, and Barreto (2019, p. 1) write, "Delving deeper into predictors of mass attitudes toward Muslim Americans is necessary given the tremendous hostility that this group has experienced." If the public holds negative attitudes toward Muslim Americans, this can very well translate into the election of candidates and the passage of policies that can potentially harm the community.

In what follows, the extant literature on attitudes toward African Americans and Latinos is reviewed, which provides an important foundation in considering how to capture attitudes toward Muslim Americans. Next, the "Muslim American Resentment" (MAR) scale used throughout the book to measure attitudes toward the U.S. Muslim population is previewed. As will be unpacked, the scale consists of nine statements, with survey respondents guided to indicate their level of agreement. The MAR scale captures particularized attitudes toward Muslim Americans, moving beyond generalized ethnocentrism, racial resentment measures, and stereotypes employed with other marginalized groups in mind.

Like other scholars who posit that group attitudes have specific content (see, e.g., Oskooii, Dana, and Barreto, 2019), I contend that public attitudes toward Muslim Americans are nuanced, specific, and deeply rooted. As many survey instruments do not contain items about Muslims – let alone Muslim Americans – current scholarship on attitudes toward Muslim Americans is greatly limited. With the exception of Oskooii, Dana, and Barreto's recent work (2019), scholars have yet to examine how group-specific beliefs explain negative attitudes toward U.S. Muslims and support for policies that harm them. The MAR measure, in response to this, recognizes the distinct experiences of Muslims in the country. As Lajevardi and Abrajano (2019, p. 38) write: "MAR both captures racialized attitudes on a variety of dimensions and asks respondents for their attitudes about Muslims in the US specifically."

This chapter demonstrates the utility of the MAR scale across numerous surveys during the period 2016–2019. Furthermore, it posits that MAR is a form of modern resentment, rooted in old-fashioned racist beliefs (also see Lajevardi and Oskooii, 2018). The analyses that follow demonstrate the scale's strength in predicting voter preferences and policy support.

This book is organized around capturing the treatment of Muslim Americans through several distinct lenses, all of which involve measuring resentment, hostility, and bias in different ways. The MAR scale is therefore a tool that will be used in subsequent chapters to measure public attitudes toward Muslims in the U.S., as well as the relationship these group attitudes have with candidate support and support for policies directly targeting the Muslim population.

3.2   PREVIOUS LITERATURE ON ATTITUDES TOWARD AFRICAN AMERICANS AND LATINOS

There is no doubt that race is central to shaping political attitudes and behaviors (Hutchings and Valentino, 2004), as well as to understanding why the public supports particular policies or presidential candidates. Moreover, understanding how racialized beliefs inform public opinion and attitudes is important as these are often related to preferences toward policies, votes, sociopolitical discrimination, and even hate crimes.

That the public harbors explicit negative attitudes toward racial and ethnic groups and that this acts as a predictor of their support for policies harming outgroups is nothing new. From the very founding of the United States, numerous religious, racial, and ethnic groups have been stigmatized and faced alienation (Bruyneel, 2007; Kim, 1999; Ngai, 2014; Omi and Winant, 2014; Smith, 1993), with a substantial segment of the white population long believing that African Americans, in particular, were intellectually and biologically inferior (Baker, 1998; Plous and Williams, 1995).

Such beliefs were not only restricted to Blacks, however, with similar prejudices applied to numerous other groups. As Kteily et al. (2015) and Goff et al. (2008) argue, history is replete with dominant groups casting specific outgroups as subhuman and associating them with animals, with, for example, Nazi propaganda portraying Jews as pests, advocates of American slavery depicting African Americans as apes, and Romani people being described as "vermin." As Goff et al. (2008) demonstrate, dehumanization can also facilitate discrimination, though it remains an open question in political science as to the extent to which it affects support for policies and vote choice. Lajevardi and Oskooii (2018) also point to examples of explicit discrimination toward Chinese and Japanese people, who were characterized as "subhuman apes," "untrustworthy," "morally corrupt," and possessing superhuman endurance and strength (Dower, 1986); Native Americans, who were often referred to as "savages" and "uncivilized" (Bruyneel, 2007); and Mexican Americans, who have been described as "greasers," "dirty," "cowardly," "unintelligent collies," and "criminals" (Lopez, 2009). As late as the 1940s, many public opinion surveys in the U.S. showed that a majority of Whites nationwide openly subscribed to the ideology of white supremacy (Kinder and Sanders, 1996; Mendelberg, 2001), and supported policies that entailed de jure and de facto racial discrimination (Bobo and

Kluegel, 1997; Bobo, Kluegel, and Smith, 1997; Hyman and Sheatsley, 1956; Lajevardi and Oskooii, 2018; Pettigrew, 1982).

Over time, and with the onset of the Civil Rights era, the overt manifestation of racial attitudes – or what has come to be known as "old-fashioned racism" – and support for policies further marginalizing non-Whites appeared to diminish (Bobo, Kluegel, and Smith, 1997; Mendelberg, 2001; Tesler, 2012). By the mid-twentieth century, most Whites expressed a willingness to reject racist arguments that Blacks were intellectually and biologically inferior (Bobo, Kluegel, and Smith, 1997; Mendelberg, 2001). Publicly espousing beliefs rooted in old-fashioned racism eventually became "taboo," and the once-familiar appeals to white supremacy began to abate (Bobo, 2001; Kinder and Sanders, 1996; Mendelberg, 2001).

In its place, however, scholars found that implicit discrimination continued to thrive (Mendelberg, 2001). While most Whites appeared more egalitarian, at least when directly asked about their racial attitudes (Firebaugh and Davis, 1988; Schuman, Steeh, and Bobo, 1985; Taylor, Sheatsley, and Greeley, 1978), a new and subtle form of racism was emerging to justify existing racial hierarchies and privileges (for an overview, see Lajevardi and Oskooii, 2018; Tesler, 2012). This was evident in the fact that though white opposition toward school and residential segregation was purportedly high (Sears, Henry, and Kosterman, 2000), support for policies cultivating greater integration and equality was low (Kluegel and Smith, 1986; Schuman et al., 1985; Steeh and Schuman, 1992). The paradox between endorsing racially egalitarian principles while opposing policies that would engender such principles is referenced by a myriad of terms, including symbolic racism (Kinder and Sears, 1981; McConahay and Hough, 1976; Sears, 1988; Sears and Henry, 2003; Sears et al., 2000; Sears and Kinder, 1971), modern racism (McConahay, 1986), laissez-faire racism (Bobo et al., 1997), racial resentment (Kinder and Sanders, 1996), subtle prejudice (Pettigrew, 1982), racial ambivalence (Katz, 1981), and aversive racism (Gaertner and Dovidio, 1986).

A good deal of scholarship has focused on unpacking racial resentment toward Blacks (e.g. Kalmoe and Piston, 2013; Yadon and Piston, 2019), which is understandable given that the relationship between Whites and Blacks is one of America's greatest historical horrors. The legacy of slavery, segregation, and discrimination cannot simply be erased, and white attitudes continue to be shaped by a history that placed them at the top of the racial hierarchy and Blacks at the bottom.

Over time, and as other groups became racialized (e.g., Latinos and Asian Americans), surveys such as the ANES (American National Election Study) began to ask questions on favorability toward these groups, in order to assess: (1) public attitudes toward them; and (2) how attitudes toward these groups varied relative to one another. Public opinion toward these groups has largely predicted support for exclusionary immigration policies (Citrin, Reingold, and Green, 1990; Hainmueller and Hopkins, 2014).

3.3   PARTICULARIZED ATTITUDES TOWARD MUSLIM AMERICANS

Studying mass attitudes toward Muslim Americans means distinguishing between "Islam," "Muslims," and "Muslim Americans." "Islam" refers to the religion, which has 1.6 billion adherents (approximately one-quarter of the world's population); "Muslims" refers to Islam's adherents around the world (both foreign and domestic); while "Muslim Americans" refers specifically to the Muslim population residing in the United States. The objective of this book in evaluating mass attitudes and preferences is to unpack attitudes toward "Muslim Americans" – a domestic group – and not "Islam" (a religion) or "Muslims" (a generic term encompassing overseas members of the group).

Since 9/11, scholarly work has demonstrated that Muslim Americans are viewed unfavorably and evaluated negatively along a series of stereotypes that are largely negative and that overall opinion on many questions about Muslims foreign and domestic remains divided and particularly fractured along partisan lines (see, e.g., Kalkan et al., 2009; Khan and Ecklund, 2013; Panagopoulos, 2006; Sides and Gross, 2013).[1] Furthermore, substantial parts of the American public, especially Republicans and those who lean toward the GOP, rate Muslims far less positively than members of most other major religious groups.[2] Even the mean thermometer score for Muslims in the 2016 ANES survey was 56 on a 0–100 scale.[3]

There are also strong reasons to expect long-standing and well-developed group-specific attitudes toward U.S. Muslims. The discourse on Orientalism, in particular, reveals a distorted lens through which Western societies have understood and processed Muslims, Islam, and the Arab world (Said, 1979, 2003). As Oskooii, Dana, and Barreto (2019, p. 3) write, "This distorted lens has led to inaccurate depictions of how Muslims, Arabs or Middle East-erners think, behave, and interact, creating serious misconceptions regarding the belief structure of Muslims world-wide." These misrepresentations are so overwhelming that they have resulted in "subtle and persistent Eurocentric prejudice against Arabo-Islamic peoples and their cultures" in spaces such as the arts, literature, news media, political discourse, and scholarly research (Oskooii, Dana, and Barreto, 2019; Said, 1979). As a result, these tropes have now become mainstream, such that the general public and political elites view Muslims as "culturally inferior, uncivilized, and out of touch with modern social and democratic norms" (Oskooii, Dana, and Barreto, 2019, p. 3).

Prior studies and polls measuring racial attitudes are helpful places to begin in assessing group-specific attitudes toward U.S. Muslims. There are rich literatures and compelling tests of racial resentment in the case of African Americans (Bobo, 1983; Entman, 1990; Kinder and Sanders, 1996), Latinos (Abrajano and Hajnal, 2015; Garcia-Rios and Ocampo, 2018), and even Asian Americans (Lee, 2000; Masuoka and Junn, 2013). However, aside from questions on stereotypes that were originally developed with other racialized groups in mind and simple favorability scales that seemingly conflate

Muslims (a foreign group), Islam (a religion), and Muslim Americans (the domestic group), no attitudinal measures of Muslim Americans exist in the American politics literature.

One important contribution of this book, therefore, is to introduce a measure of attitudes toward Muslim Americans, while another is to demonstrate the utility of the Muslim American Resentment (MAR) scale for predicting vote choice and support for a myriad of policy positions. The MAR scale was developed in the hope it would help unpack how attitudes toward Muslim Americans have affected political outcomes in the U.S. As Lajevardi and Abrajano (2019, p. 298) write: "Existing measures of Muslim American resentment (e.g favorability ratings, feeling thermometers, group stereotypes) lack enough contextual specificity to capture the unique experiences of Muslims in the United States, particularly in light of the specific group stereotypes that have arisen in the aftermath of 9/11 and the War on Terror."

Research on European attitudes toward Muslims is a helpful place to start (see, e.g., Agirdag, van Houtte, and Loobuyck, 2012; Juchtmans and Nicaise, 2013; Modood and Kastoryano, 2006; Savelkoul et al., 2010; Simpson and Yinger, 2013; Strabac and Listhaug, 2008). What this research shows, of course, is that European scholars are well aware that in order to understand European anti-Muslim attitudes, more specific items referring to group stereotypes are needed. Strabac and Listhaug (2008), for example, evaluate whether the aggregate level of prejudice against Muslims is higher than the level of prejudice against other non-Western immigrants in the 1999–2000 wave of the European Values Study. They measure anti-Muslim prejudice by employing a dichotomous empirical measure of prejudice based on a question asking respondents if they would oppose having Muslims as neighbors.

Savelkoul et al. (2010) construct a more detailed measurement by building on Sniderman, Hagendoorn, and Prior (2003) and Sniderman and Hagendoorn (2007). Their scale measures attitudes ranging from "do not agree at all" to "agree entirely" with respect to the following statements: (1) "Muslim women who wear a scarf do not adapt to our society"; (2) "Muslims are dangerously fanatic"; (3) "Muslims use religion for political aims"; (4) "Muslims easily resort to violence"; (5) "Muslim husbands dominate their wives"; (6) "Muslims raise their children in an authoritarian way"; (7) "Muslims lock themselves out of Dutch society"; (8) "Muslim parents have no authority over their children outdoors"; and (9) "Most Muslims have no respect for homosexuals" (Savelkoul et al., 2010).

Agirdag, van Houtte, and Loobuyck (2012) move away from cultural stereotypes and instead focus on Muslim integration into ordinary Flemish society, measuring teacher attitudes toward Muslim students on a scale ranging from "absolutely disagree" to "totally agree." The statements used are: (1) "Muslim students reject jihad and violence"; (2) "The Flemish Muslim students will integrate successfully into Flemish society"; (3) "Besides lessons in Catholicism, Catholic schools with Muslim students should also organize lessons in Islam"; (4) "Flanders should increase Muslim immigrant community to satisfy the labor shortage"; (5) "The majority of Muslim students have behavioral problems"; (6)"Muslim immigrant students lack basic Dutch language"; (7) "Many Muslim students look favorably on jihad"; and (8) "Wearing headscarves should be banned in all schools."

The MAR scale relies heavily on items adapted from the European literature cited above, including Agirdag, van Houtte, and Loobuyck (2012), Bevelander and Otterbeck (2010), and Heitmeyer and Zick (2004). Nine items are employed to characterize the extent to which respondents hold resentful attitudes toward Muslim Americans, specifically: (1) "Most Muslim Americans integrate successfully into American culture"; (2) "Muslim Americans sometimes do not have the best interests of Americans at heart"; (3) "Muslims living in the US should be subject to more surveillance than others"; (4) "Muslim Americans, in general, tend to be more violent than other people"; (5) "Most Muslim Americans reject jihad and violence"; (6) "Most Muslim Americans lack basic English language skills";

(7) "Most Muslim Americans are not terrorists"; (8) "Wearing head-scarves should be banned in all public places"; and (9) "Muslim Americans do a good job of speaking out against Islamic terrorism."

I chose these items because they are closely related to scales that have already proven successful in measuring attitudes toward Muslims in the Western world, are reflective of contemporary stereo-types of Muslim Americans, and are specifically tailored toward Muslims in America, rather than conflating Islam or overseas Mus-lims. Furthermore, the MAR scale takes into account the myriad ways in which the public perceives and has critiqued U.S. Muslims (Lajevardi and Oskooii, 2018). One critique of scales of this sort is that they give rise to acquiescence bias, whereby survey respondents develop a tendency to agree with all the questions. In order to address this, items 1, 5, 7, and 9 present positive stereotypes of Muslim Americans, and should be reverse coded to indicate greater resentment. Another critique of the scale is that it includes two policy items (3 and 8). Group attitudes are often not combined with policy attitudes, and, as such, scholars should feel free to use items 3 and 8 as independent variables in vote choice models, while excluding them when using the full set of items to predict policy attitudes.[4] Even so, as noted in Lajevardi and Abrajano (2019, p. 297):

> MAR is a comprehensive measure and is meant to capture a
> combination of (a) how the public perceives the group and
> (b) what the public thinks the government should do about them.
> We conceive of MAR in political terms; similar if not analogous to
> group consciousness, which is nominally about group attitudes,
> but in fact incorporates a political orientation insofar as it
> includes the belief that members of one's group should work
> together in politics to achieve their ends.

Other published research has already begun to assess the explanatory power of the MAR scale. Lajevardi and Oskooii (2018) demonstrate the effectiveness of the MAR scale in channeling the impact of old-fashioned racism and dehumanizing attitudes

(Kteily et al., 2015) on support for a number of restrictive policies affecting Muslim Americans. MAR was found to mediate old-fashioned racism and dehumanizing attitudes on patrolling Muslim neighborhoods by 80.1%; on limiting immigration from Muslim countries of origin by 82.2%; on limiting Muslim American reentry into the country by 80.1%; and on limiting the political influence of Muslims by 79.9% (Lajevardi and Oskooii, 2018). The MAR scale also mediated the effect of old-fashioned racist and dehumanizing beliefs on Trump support by 86.1% in the 2016 presidential election.

The usefulness of the MAR scale is further demonstrated in Lajevardi and Abrajano (2019), which shows that MAR was a strong and significant predictor of supporting Trump in the 2016 election, even when controlling for a whole host of other factors. The results also demonstrate the significant predictive power that negative attitudes toward Muslim Americans played in explaining presidential vote choice in 2016, vis-à-vis other standard predictors of the vote (Abramson, Aldrich, and Rohde, 2002; Alvarez and Nagler, 1995; Carmines and Stimson, 1980; Lajevardi and Abrajano, 2019). The analyses also evaluate how MAR fares compared to alternative measures employed by other research, and find that the MAR scale is the only measure of Muslim American sentiment that consistently explains the likelihood of voting for and supporting Trump. Without MAR, the extent to which anti-Muslim public attitudes influenced the 2016 presidential vote can arguably not be fully understood. In fact, it is potentially left grossly misunderstood.

3.4   PUBLIC ATTITUDES TOWARD MUSLIM AMERICANS

The global Muslim population is on the rise: the Pew Research Center estimates that by 2050, 10% of all Europeans will be Muslim, while in the U.S. the Muslim population will double in proportion, making up 2.1% of the country's population.[5] Part of this rise in the U.S. Muslim population is due to how immigration visas are being delineated, with a 2013 Pew report estimating that the proportion of Muslims granted permanent residency status (green cards) had increased from 5% in 1992 to 10% in 2012.[6] Just how pervasive, then, are negative attitudes toward this growing population? As mentioned previously, empirical scholarly work – especially since 9/11 – has demonstrated the existence of negative attitudes among the U.S. public toward Muslims (see Kalkan et al., 2009; Khan and Ecklund, 2013; Panagopoulos, 2006; Sides and Gross, 2013). In addition, Pew has reported on public attitudes toward Muslims, both around the world and in the United States.[7]

A 2017 Pew survey asked American respondents to rate members of nine religious groups on a feeling thermometer, and found that Muslims received an average rating of 48, similar to atheists (50).[8] When asked to rate seven other religious groups (Jews, Catholics, mainline Protestants, evangelical Christians, Buddhists, Hindus, and Mormons), Pew found that respondents viewed these groups more warmly.

These attitudes, moreover, appear to have a partisan bent. Respondents who identified as Republican or leaned toward the Republican Party gave Muslims an average rating of 39, which was much lower than the average rating given by Democrats (56). This partisan difference extended into other questions relating to Muslims and Islam. Republicans were more likely than their Democratic counterparts to indicate that they were very concerned about extremism in the name of Islam, both around the world (67% v. 40%) and in the U.S. (64% v. 30%). Democrats and Republicans were also split on whether Islam is part of mainstream society (68% v. 37%) and whether a natural conflict exists between Islam and democracy (65% v. 30%).

Pew found much more variation in how Europeans viewed Muslims. In a 2016 survey addressing residents of ten European countries, Pew found that in most cases respondents believed that "just some" or "a few" Muslims in their country supported extremist groups such as ISIS. However, in Italy, 46% of respondents said that "many" or "most" Muslims do.[9] When asked to rate Muslims favorably or unfavorably, more variation was apparent, with Pew finding negative attitudes less common in France, Germany, the United Kingdom, and elsewhere in northern and western Europe, but pervasive in Hungary, Italy, Poland, and Greece. These attitudes were also split ideologically, with those individuals placing themselves on the right more likely than those on the left to perceive Muslims negatively.

Thus, the findings of prior empirical scholarship and the Pew surveys both indicate that negative attitudes toward Muslims are pervasive, and are more pronounced along partisan lines. As such, it is important to assess how hostility toward Muslim Americans shapes political preferences and decision-making.

3.5   MAR AND MASS ATTITUDES: PROSPECTS FOR MUSLIM AMERICANS' SUBSTANTIVE REPRESENTATION

How does MAR predict vote choice, presidential approval, attitudes toward Islam and Muslims, and support for policies potentially harmful to Muslims both foreign and domestic? In this section, results from ten public opinion surveys conducted from 2016 to 2019 are presented, each of which contains the MAR measure and a support, approve, or vote for Trump variable.[10] The sample size and representativeness of the datasets vary greatly, but each is useful for examining the relationship between MAR and support for Trump – a politician, later elected president, who is openly hostile toward Muslim Americans. Summary statistics for each of the variables used in the datasets can be found in Tables A1–A10.

Table A11 displays the mean MAR measures across each of the ten datasets. In each dataset, the MAR scale was rescaled to range from 0 to 1 for ease of interpretation, as the scale items were not asked as a continuous variable across datasets. While the mean varies between the surveys, it can be seen that it never dips below 0.33 and never rises above 0.43. Moreover, while these are cross-sectional surveys, there appears to be a trend toward increased MAR levels among respondents in late 2018 and early 2019, with the mean averaging above 0.4.

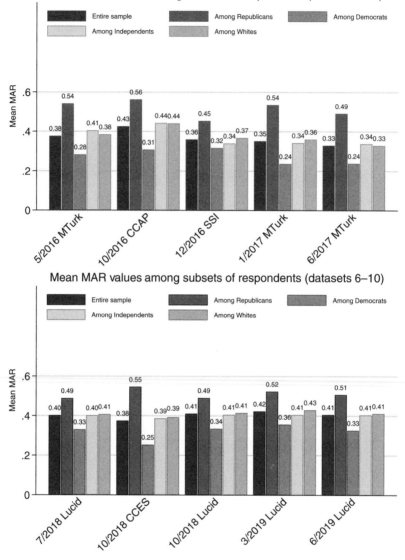

FIGURE 3.1 Mean MAR across each dataset

To unpack some of the heterogeneity behind the MAR measure, Figure 3.1 displays mean MAR values among specific groups, including: the entire sample; Republicans; Democrats; Independents; and Whites. In each dataset, the mean MAR value among Republicans is higher than that of the rest of the sample, echoing the 2017 Pew survey discussed above. In the ten datasets, Republicans' mean MAR hovers around 0.5 and never falls below 0.45. Conversely, Democrats' mean MAR never rises above 0.36 in any of the datasets. MAR levels for Independents fall between those of Democrats and Republicans, and mean MAR for Whites mirrors that of the survey population as a whole.

3.5.1   Exploring the Relationship between MAR and Support for Trump

Public support for particular policies and the election of particular candidates can both result in outcomes harmful to the Muslim American community. Table A13 demonstrates the association between respondents' MAR and their support for Trump. Given Trump was one of several presidential contenders who targeted the Muslim population at home and abroad, it is important to evaluate how MAR is related to his level of support. The results from Table A13 come from ten online surveys, with the CCAP, SSI, CCES, and Lucid surveys conducted on national samples, and the rest (MTurk) conducted on convenience samples of Americans.[11] Each dataset asked the "support for Trump" variable slightly differently (as can be seen in Table A12).[12] For ease of interpretation, the key independent variable – MAR – is rescaled to range from 0 to 1 across each survey. Because the dependent variable does not assess policy positions, the full MAR scale is used.

Across the board, the effect of respondents' MAR on their support for Trump is found to be positive and significant: an increase in MAR results in more support for Trump and a greater likelihood of voting for him. In other words, MAR played and continues to play an important role in shaping Trump support and vote choice.

Next, it is necessary to evaluate the strength of the MAR scale compared to other commonly used measures of attitudes toward Muslims, as well as compared to racial resentment. Whenever available in a given dataset, in Table A14 I control for (1) MAR, (2) Racial resentment,[13] (3) Favorability of Muslims, (4) Favorability of Muslim Americans (MAM), and stereotype items about Muslims including (5) Muslims: Patriotic, (6) Muslims: Intelligent, (7) Muslims: Foreign, (8) Muslims: Lazy, (9) Muslims: Violent, (10) Muslims: Trustworthy, and (11) Muslims: Hardworking. Each of these additional attitudinal measures has also been rescaled to range from 0 to 1 for ease of interpretation.

Several noteworthy points should be highlighted. First, MAR is a powerful measure across the board. While racial resentment only appears in Models 1, 2, 5, 6, 7, 8, 9, and 10, it is the only indicator to rival MAR's explanatory power in Models 1, 6, and 10. Other indicators of attitudes toward Muslims are not as substantively large – if at all significant – in explaining this relationship. On the flip side, the coefficient on MAR is consistently substantively large and significant.

Table A15 examines whether this relationship persists after including controls also known to influence vote choice. Lajevardi and Abrajano (2019) evaluate how controlling for other measures of attitudes toward Muslim Americans affects vote choice, and find that even with their inclusion, MAR continues to be the strongest predictor of vote choice and Trump support. This finding holds even with the inclusion of racial resentment items. For ease of interpretation, Figure 3.2 displays coefficient plots from bivariate and multivariate regressions exploring the relationship between MAR and Trump support. The difference between the models presented in Lajevardi and Abrajano (2019), and the models presented in this book is that five additional datasets have been introduced to demonstrate the repeated strength of the measure post the 2016 election season.[14]

As can be seen, the positive and significant relationship between MAR and candidate support/vote choice has persisted. Even more telling about the importance of MAR in shaping candidate support during the 2016 election is while the size of the coefficients decreases, it is not by much, even when controlling for covariates. The models also demonstrate that, aside from partisanship, MAR

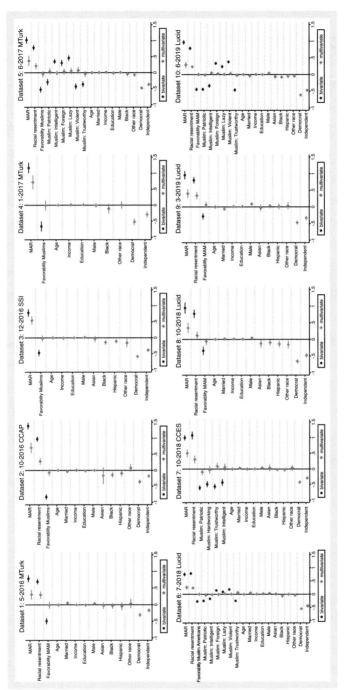

FIGURE 3.2 Relationship between MAR and Trump support (Datasets 1–10)

plays an important role in shaping vote choice and candidate preference. While racial resentment also continues to shape support for Trump, the MAR coefficient is substantively larger in all the models where racial resentment is available. Moreover, the favorability items and stereotype measures fail to approach significance except in a couple of cases, specifically Muslims: Trustworthy in the 7/2018 (Lucid) survey and Muslims: Patriotic in the 10/2018 (CCES) survey. Given that the patriotism and trustworthiness of Muslim Americans have regularly been called into question, it makes sense that these two stereotype measures might be relevant to evaluations of them. The other stereotypes of Muslims employed by some surveys do not significantly or substantively explain Trump support, and thus if surveys continue to employ them, scholars might miss out on understanding how negative attitudes toward U.S. Muslims shape political preferences.

The results shown in Figure 3.2 demonstrate that hostility toward Muslim Americans had important consequences regarding who the general public supported and voted for in the 2016 election. Furthermore, halfway into Donald Trump's presidential term, MAR continues to strongly shape approval toward him. MAR is a strong, positive, and significant predictor of voting for Trump in 2016, and remains so even when racial resentment and ethnocentrism measures are included. While racial resentment also has a substantive impact on voting for Trump, the ethnocentrism measure largely fails to predict the Trump vote. The findings indicate that MAR shaped Trump support during the primary season, vote choice during the presidential election, and continued presidential approval more than two years after he assumed office in 2017.

3.5.2   *Exploring the Relationship between MAR and Policy Support*

The "Muslim" Ban
The 2016 election season saw numerous candidates for office espousing policy positions directly targeting the Muslim population. Trump

proposed several policies targeting Muslims both foreign and domestic, including a Muslim registry (which at the time of writing he has yet to follow through on). One campaign promise he delivered on within a week of assuming office, however, was the "Muslim Ban." From January 2017 to September 2017, President Trump issued three executive orders restricting entry into the U.S. by citizens of several Muslim-majority countries. While public opinion quickly shifted against the ban (Collingwood et al., 2018), and remained steadfastly opposed up to one year later (Oskooii, Lajevardi, and Collingwood, 2019), many in the public continued to support the policy position. The Supreme Court upheld the third and final version of the ban in *Trump* v. *Hawaii* (2018), banning citizens from North Korea, Syria, Iran, Yemen, Libya, Somalia, and Venezuela from coming to the United States. Five of the seven countries are Muslim majority.

The Muslim ban had many consequences for Muslims in the United States. The majority of U.S. Muslim adults (58%) hail from other parts of the globe, particularly the Muslim world, and arrived in the country mostly after the 1965 Immigration and Nationality Act, which served to lower barriers to immigration. This meant many Muslim immigrants were afraid to visit family in their home countries for fear their visas may not be reissued. As the ACLU (American Civil Liberties Union) notes: "on Dec. 4, 2017, America began to ban millions of Muslims from the United States, even if they have family members, jobs, academic spots, or other compelling connections here, and even if they would otherwise be fully entitled to receive a visa to come here."[15]

Limiting Muslim Americans from Reentering the Country
Given that many Muslims living both abroad and in the U.S. were affected by the policy, it is important to examine how attitudes toward Muslim Americans shaped public support for it. Below, MAR is evaluated to show how it shaped support for the strictest form of the Muslim ban – that is, restricting the rights of American citizens to return to their country. Six of the ten datasets asked about banning

Muslim Americans from reentering their country,[16] though the question was framed (very) slightly differently across datasets.[17] In terms of mean ban support, the six datasets ranged as follows: 0.367 in 5/2016 (MTurk); 0.398 in 12/2016 (SSI); 0.403 in 7/2018 (Lucid); 0.5098 in 10/2018 (Lucid); 0.476 in 3/2019 (Lucid); and 0.423 in 6/2019 (Lucid).

Table A16 presents the bivariate relationship between an individual's MAR and support for the ban. Across each of the ten datasets, MAR has a positive, strong, substantive, and significant effect on support for the policy. Next, in Table A17, MAR is once again evaluated to assess how it fares in comparison to other attitudinal measures, such as racial resentment, favorability items, and stereotype measures. In these models, the strength of the MAR coefficient diminishes, though it still remains strong, substantive, and significant. Once again, the coefficient for racial resentment is significant, though nowhere near as powerful as the MAR measure. Turning to the other attitudinal measures more specific to Muslims, there are instances in which favorability and the stereotype measures stand out as significant. However, the relationship between these items and support for the ban is not systematic across datasets, nor is it very substantive. The coefficients are generally considerably smaller than that of the MAR (alt) measure, suggesting that in many cases these attitudinal measures may simply be failing to pick up on how particularized attitudes toward Muslim Americans are shaping policy support.

To test the true strength of the relationship between MAR and policy support for the Muslim ban, indicators for education, age, gender, income, race, and partisanship are included, as well as the MAR scale and any other resentment or attitudinal questions available. For ease of interpretation, Figure 3.3 displays coefficient plots from bivariate and multivariate regressions exploring the relationship between MAR and support for the Muslim ban (see Table A18 for the full models). The inclusion of these controls reveals a few things. First, the relationship between MAR and the policy persists, with

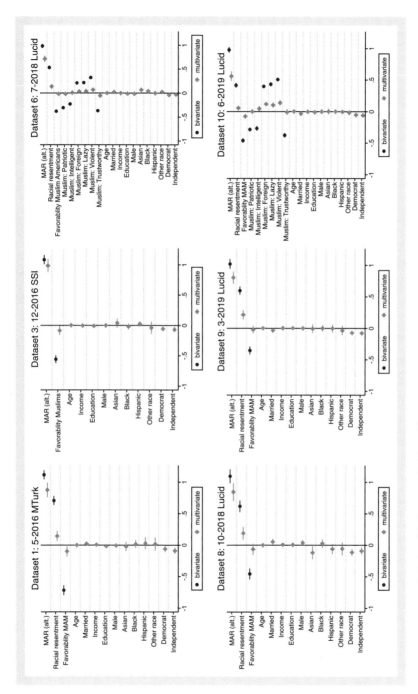

FIGURE 3.3 Relationship between MAR and ban support

no significant change to the coefficients on MAR (as in Table A17). Second, while partisanship has a significant and consistent effect on this relationship, the coefficient is rather small. Third, factors such as income, race, and education, which it might be thought would play an important role in shaping policy positions, do not appear to have a consistently significant relationship with support for the ban.

These results indicate that public opinion in favor of banning Muslim Americans from reentering the U.S. was arguably not high, but also that it was shaped by hostility toward Muslim Americans. Understanding the determinants of support for one of the most harmful policies toward Muslim Americans implemented to date is particularly important given that candidates are increasingly running on platforms that seek to oppress, harass, and exclude members of marginalized groups.

3.5.3   Limiting Immigration from Muslim Countries of Origin

Next, another version of the Muslim ban question is examined, aimed primarily at overseas Muslims. The phrasing of this policy item varied slightly across datasets, but generally asked respondents their support for a policy stating, "We need to limit immigration from Muslim countries of origin until the nation's representatives can figure out what is going on." Ostensibly, the targeted individuals do not have inalienable rights of entry into the U.S. This policy item was asked in five surveys, with the mean values ranging as follows: 0.484 in 5/2016 (MTurk); 0.478 in 7/2018 (Lucid); 0.629 in 10/2018 (Lucid); 0.561 in 3/2019 (Lucid); and 0.521 in 6/2019 (Lucid). While this is not a panel dataset, and so it cannot be known for certain, it appears support for the policy increased after the 2016 election season, peaked around the 2018 midterm election, then remained high in the half year that followed.

As with the previous policy statement on the ban, MAR has a positive, strong, and significant effect on shaping policy support (see Table A19). When additional attitudinal controls are included (see Table A20), it can be seen that racial resentment plays a much larger role than is the case with the policy item banning Muslim Americans from reentering the U.S., though the substantive size of the racial resentment coefficient is still less than that of the MAR scale. Other attitudinal measures appear to be more consistently significant, especially the "Muslims: Patriotic" and the "Muslims: Foreign" variables, which are perhaps more tailored to stereotypes about Muslims than other minority communities.

Finally, additional demographic and partisanship controls are added to these models, as can be seen in Table A21 and Figure 3.4. With these controls added, MAR continues to be the most significant predictor of policy position. While the racial resentment and stereotype measures do have a substantive and significant impact on shaping policy support, their coefficients are not as powerful as that of the MAR measure.

Patrolling Muslim Neighborhoods

Next, we turn to a policy proposal targeting Muslims espoused by another Republican on the 2016 presidential campaign trail. Ted Cruz called for law enforcement to increase their policing of Muslim neighborhoods, repeatedly comparing this to an increased police presence in areas with known gang activity.[18]   Cruz said in a statement, "[o]ur European allies are now seeing what comes of a toxic mix of migrants who have been infiltrated by terrorists and isolated, radical Muslim neighborhoods." The same week, Trump offered support for this policy, saying it was "a good idea."

As will be discussed in Chapter 8, the relationship between law enforcement and U.S. Muslims has been, at best, strained since 9/11, though arguably this extends to eras considerably prior to September 11, 2001. In August 2016, the NYPD issued a report entitled "An Investigation of NYPD's Compliance with Rules Governing

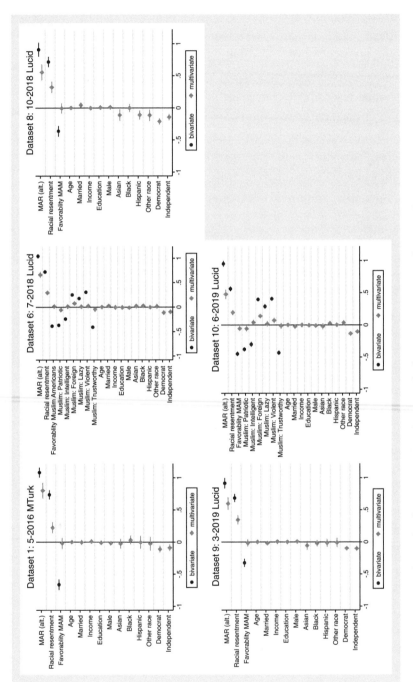

FIGURE 3.4 Relationship between MAR and support for limiting immigration from Muslim countries

Investigations of Political Activity,"[19] which revealed in its first footnote that:

> [b]ased on its review, OIG-NYPD determined that the individuals under investigation were predominantly associated with Muslims and/or engaged in political activity that those individuals – associated with Islam more than 95% of all files reviewed for this investigation – although NYPD does not use such categorizations in its approval documents. However, in the past, investigations have focused on others, including Black and Latino activists, student groups, socialists, and political protesters.

Thus, while U.S. Muslims constitute just 3% of the population in New York City, they were the subjects of more than 95% of the NYPD's surveillance efforts.[20] As CAIR notes, the surveillance of Muslim communities is a policy that has already begun, but is subject to little oversight or public debate.[21]

In five of the ten datasets, I asked respondents about their support for the following policy: "We need to empower law enforcement to patrol and secure Muslim neighborhoods before they become radicalized." Mean support for the policy ranged as follows across each of the surveys: 0.495 in 5/2016 (MTurk); 0.441 in 7/2018 (Lucid); 0.528 in 10/2018 (Lucid); 0.497 in 3/2019 (Lucid); and 0.444 in 6/2019 (Lucid). While mean support rises above 0.5 in only one of the surveys, it hovers around 0.45 elsewhere, indicating fairly broad support for this policy among members of the American electorate.

How, then, does MAR shape support for a policy targeting Muslim communities and neighborhoods? Table A22 reveals MAR has a positive, substantive, and significant effect on policy support for patrolling Muslim neighborhoods. When other attitudinal measures are included (see Table A23 and Figure 3.5), two important points emerge. First, while the substantive size of the MAR coefficient diminishes somewhat, it continues to explain policy support for patrolling neighborhoods. Second, while the stereotype item on patriotism is not significant in this case, "Muslims: Foreign" and "Muslims: Violent" are significant across the two datasets where

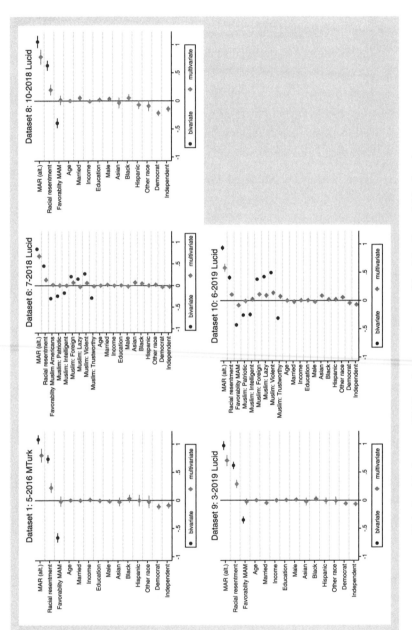

FIGURE 3.5 Relationship between MAR and support for patrolling Muslim neighborhoods

they are present (in Models 2 and 5). Once again, different stereotype items stand out based on the specific policy at hand, rather than being consistent across various policy items, as is the case with the MAR scale. In Model 5, "Muslims: Trustworthy" is also significant, but as it did not reach significance in Model 2, the overall explanatory power of this variable is questionable.

Finally, additional demographic and partisanship controls are introduced as a final check to test whether the relationship between MAR and policy support persists, and indeed they show that the inclusion of such additional controls does not diminish the relationship. While racial resentment does play a substantive role in shaping this relationship, its coefficient does not rival that of MAR. Even partisanship tells a mixed story insofar as the coefficients on Democrat and Independent are typically small, failing even to reach significance in Model 1 in Table A24.

Birthright Citizenship

Has this relationship between MAR and the public's support of policies targeting Muslims continued through to 2018, when new policies were announced? In the days leading up to the 2018 midterm election, the president once again brought themes of race, immigration, and terrorism into the national discourse, writing: "Sadly, it looks like Mexicos Police and Military are unable to stop the Caravan heading to the Southern Border of the United States. Criminals and unknown Middle Easterners are mixed in. I have alerted Border Patrol and Military that this is a National Emergency. Must change laws!"[22]

While his rhetoric was not primarily directed at Muslims, he nevertheless managed to intertwine this question of immigration with Middle Easterners bringing with them a threat of terrorism. Nonetheless, the president's son, Donald Trump Jr., posted a link to an article entitled, "100 ISIS Terrorists Caught in Guatemala as

Central American Caravan Heads to U.S."[23] after having Tweeted: "The caravan thing is an obvious political stunt, but what better way to get terrorists into the country than imbed them in the flood? Leftist policies just endanger our kids."[24]

Amid this climate of hysteria, President Trump proposed a policy ending birthright citizenship. Here, results are presented from a Lucid Academia survey conducted on 709 U.S. adults. The survey was fielded on October 31, 2018 – one day after President Trump announced his plan to end birthright citizenship and one week before the 2018 midterm election. Respondents in the 10/2018 Lucid survey were directed to answer the following question:

> As you may or may not know, President Trump has recently indicated he will enact an executive order to end birthright citizenship for children born in the United States to non citizens (e.g. "anchor babies"). Please indicate if you agree or disagree with the following places that could be affected by this executive order: (a) all countries, (b) Latin America, (c) Asia, (d) Middle East, (e) Africa, and (f) Europe.

Respondents rated their support for these policies on a Likert scale from 1 to 5, with higher values indicating greater support. For the purposes of the analyses here, these variables have been rescaled to range from 0 to 1. Column 2 in Table 3.1 displays the mean responses.

To assess low, medium, and high levels of MAR, the sample was subsetted into those with low levels of resentment (those falling in the 25th percentile or below) (Column 5); middle levels of resentment (those falling between the 25th and 75th percentile) (Column 4); and high levels of resentment (those falling in the 75th percentile or above) (Column 3).

Table 3.1 shows broad support for the birthright citizenship policy, with greater preference among respondents that it apply to

Table 3.1. *Support for Revocation of Birthright Citizenship by MAR*

Region	Mean Entire Sample	Mean High MAR	Mean Med. MAR	Mean Low MAR
All countries	0.506	0.751	0.508	0.192
Latin America	0.504	0.746	0.506	0.188
Asia	0.497	0.731	0.506	0.182
Middle East	0.513	0.758	0.521	0.185
Africa	0.513	0.758	0.521	0.185
Europe	0.498	0.721	0.521	0.192
	n = 713	n = 196	n = 363	n = 154

those from the Middle East and Africa over those from Europe and Asia. When subsetting by individuals' resentment levels, it can be seen that those with the highest levels of MAR oppose birthright citizenship most for those immigrants from the Middle East and Africa, then those from Latin America, then Asia, then finally Europe.

These results provide a first step in evaluating whether MAR continued to shape support for policy positions affecting Muslims, both foreign and domestic, proposed in another election cycle – in this case the 2018 election. While MAR appears correlated with the birthright citizenship policy proposal, without further datasets exploring the same variables, it is wise to be cautious about the strength of this relationship.

3.6   IMPLICATIONS

This chapter has introduced the MAR measure and demonstrated its strength in predicting vote choice, candidate support, and policy support, particularly in cases where candidates engage in discourse about Muslims, and where policies target Muslims, both foreign and domestic. Across several policies, it has been demonstrated that MAR is stronger in its predictive power than other previously proposed means (e.g. favorability items and stereotype items) to measure group attitudes about Muslim Americans. Moreover, it surpasses the standard racial resentment measure across the board.

MAR powerfully shaped vote choice for Trump as a candidate, as well as support for a number of policies that he and other Republican presidential contenders proposed during the 2016 campaign. Even at the time of writing, in 2019, MAR also continues to shape support for these policy items and for Trump.

Such results are worrisome. If those bearing hostility toward Muslim Americans are voting for candidates that ostracize and target the community, then Muslim Americans are arguably being marginalized by a sizable segment of the American public. Furthermore, if MAR is indeed an important predictor of vote choice and there is considerable support among the general public for policies negatively impacting Muslim Americans, this calls into question the prospects for the community's substantive representation.

4   Muslim American Prospects for Political Incorporation

> But let us remember that we form a government for millions not yet in existence. I have not the art of divination. In the course of four or five hundred years, I do not know how it will work. This is most certain, that [Catholics] may occupy that chair, and [Muslims] may take it. I see nothing against it.
>
> William Lancaster, Delegate to the North Carolina Convention, July 20, 1788

Does MAR matter for the election of Muslim American officials, and the enhancing of Muslim American descriptive representation? This chapter addresses this question by evaluating the prospects for Muslim American political incorporation. One way to measure public attitudes toward minorities is to evaluate the public's willingness to vote into political office racial, ethnic, and religious minorities. Minority candidates have continued to face discrimination from Whites who – up until the late 1980s – still rated them below white candidates. The disinclination of Whites to vote for minority candidates not only reveals a great deal about their racial biases, but impacts the ability of such groups to gain representation.

Whites are the largest ethnic group in America today, and constitute an even greater proportion of the voting-eligible population. According to the U.S. Census, non-Hispanic Whites constitute 60.7% of the total population, followed by Latinos (18.1%), African Americans (13.4%), and Asian Americans (5.8%).[1] Of the voting-eligible population, Whites constitute 65.72%, Latinos 14.34%, Blacks 12.75%, and Asian Americans 4.04%.[2] The voting-eligible population is skewed toward Whites and away from Latinos and Asians due to the large immigrant populations represented in the latter groups. Considering the size of the white population, and discounting for the time being how districts are drawn, assessing white support for minority candidates is an important normative and empirical question. In order to answer it, two candidate evaluation survey experiments were conducted on Amazon Mechanical Turk and through Survey Sampling International, in which the party, race, and religion of fictional candidates were varied in a hypothetical primary election for congressional office.

In aggregate, the results demonstrate that the American public discriminates against Muslim American candidates compared to Whites, all else being equal. Importantly, the Muslim candidate's race plays no role in mediating this discrimination in Democratic primaries. White Muslim, Arab Muslim, and Black Muslim candidates all suffer a penalty in vote choice and likelihood of winning in Democratic elections. With respect to party, the results indicate that Muslim candidates fare better in Republican primaries, with no significant difference in votes and likelihood of winning between the white candidate and the white Muslim, Arab Muslim, and Black Muslim candidates. These results test an important finding in the race and ethnic politics literature: that minority Republican candidates for office fare better than their Democratic counterparts (Barreto, 2007).

Finally, to tease out the effect of a candidate's Muslim identity (communicated through their name) and their racial identity (communicated through their picture), a replication experiment is run on a national sample of Americans. Importantly, the results demonstrate that it is religion – and not race – that leads to discrimination against Muslim candidates. In other words, Muslims, regardless of race, are significantly less likely to be viewed as likely to win. When the religion signal is removed, this significance is eliminated across the board.

These results provide evidence of the disadvantaged position that Muslims occupy in American democracy. Muslim American candidates for political office experience actual deep-seated discrimination by publics who are unwilling to vote for them and/or regard them as unlikely to win elections. The only mediating effect for Muslim American candidates is their partisanship. The totality of these results suggests that variations in public preferences for Muslim American candidates are largely driven by party and religion, and not by racial background.

4.1   LITERATURE ON MUSLIM AMERICAN DESCRIPTIVE REPRESENTATION

Empirical research on Muslim American representatives is limited. On the face of it, we know such legislators make a difference through symbolic representation, frequently discussing and defending the rights of Muslim Americans on their websites, social media pages, and in interviews. Even so, scholars still do not know whether having a Muslim American in office yields better representation for Muslims as a marginalized group. Martin's 2009 study is the only article to date examining Muslim American substantive representation. In it, the author compares roll-call votes in the 109th Congress (2005–2006) to Muslim policy preferences regarding three issues particularly relevant to them, and finds that the percentage of Muslims in a congressional district has a positive and significant effect on the probability of the district's representative voting in line with their preferences on surveillance and domestic counterterrorism votes.

Two published candidate evaluation studies have explored whether Muslim American candidates can successfully receive electoral support from the public and win elections. Braman and Sinno (2009) conducted an experiment on 54 undergraduate students, who evaluated one of two newspaper articles. One described an election for attorney general in New Jersey, the other an election for U.S. senator. In each fictional election, the race was between a Republican incumbent and a Muslim challenger named "A. J. Lami." Kalkan, Layman, and Green (2018) conducted candidate evaluation experiments in 2007 and 2010 on the CCES, testing differences in respondents' ratings of candidates bearing what they argue is a Muslim surname. In their 2007 experiment, they use the surname

"Choudhary," signaling a South Asian and Muslim background. Their conditions are worth discussion. While the control candidate signals a Muslim identity through their name, the other treatments all have a "foreigner" dimension, explicitly stating that the individual emigrated from the U.A.E. and is a naturalized citizen. The control may not therefore be a true control, as it varies nativism, name, and the inclusion/exclusion of a religious signal. Importantly, however, the 2010 experiment assesses the intersectionality of U.S. Muslims, examining how the religion (Islam) and the race (Black) interact to affect a candidate's electoral support. Braman and Sinno (2009) and Kalkan, Layman, and Green (2018) are foundational for the two studies testing similar questions conducted in this chapter.

4.2   THEORY AND EXPECTATIONS

As previewed in the introductory chapter, statements made by Democratic elites during the course of the 2016 presidential election campaign raise concerns about whether even Democrats continue to be a source of representation for Muslim Americans. Legislators discussed foreign and domestic Muslims frequently throughout the course of the campaign, with, for example, the Democratic mayor of Roanoke, Virginia, calling for the incarceration of Syrian refugees – many of whom are Muslim – in internment camps. Even Hillary Clinton, the Democratic presidential nominee, framed U.S. Muslims in terms of national security by stating that American Muslims needed to be "our eyes and ears on our front lines." The conflation of overseas Muslims with Muslim Americans can threaten the latter, especially if legislators, the media, and the masses do not distinguish between them. Given that Muslim Americans appear not to be receiving unwavering support from elected officials, and that they are currently a target for racialized policies, it could be that becoming political representatives themselves is the only available means for shaping the policies affecting them. However, it is to be anticipated that Muslim American candidates face discrimination on a number of levels, some of them on the candidate-side of the equation and others will be on the voter-side.

4.2.1   Candidate-Level Characteristics

Beginning with candidate characteristics, it is anticipated that a candidate's Muslim identity will likely affect voters' evaluations of them. The electoral importance of political candidates' racial and social characteristics is particularly striking in contemporary American politics. Like their racial background and partisanship, a candidate's religion may also matter to voters who rely on information shortcuts to make political decisions (Brady and Sniderman, 1985; Popkin, 1994). Thus, voters may use a candidate's ties to Islam as a shortcut in their evaluations, with the expectation of this book being that a candidate's Muslim background will act as a powerful and negative electoral cue. This can be summed up in the following hypothesis:

Hypothesis 1: Muslim American candidates will perform worse than their white and non-Muslim counterparts in terms of vote choice and likelihood of winning, all else being equal.

It is also to be expected that the partisanship of a Muslim American candidate is likely to have a mediating effect on their electoral success, with scholars documenting bleak outcomes for minorities who run as Democrats in majority-white districts (Bowler and Segura, 2011; Canon, Schousen, and Sellers, 1996; Epstein and O'Halloran, 1999; Lublin, 1999). Despite modest dissent among scholars (Highton, 2004; Swain, 1995; Thernstrom and Thernstrom, 2009), the evidence demonstrates overwhelmingly that Black and Latino candidates often struggle to win white support (Lublin, 1999; Segura and Fraga, 2008). However, evidence of successful minority candidates can point to important lessons. Minority Republicans appear uniquely advantaged, in that they can count on substantial support from Whites in a nearly all-white party that welcomes crossover voting from traditionally Democratic communities of color (Barreto, 2007, 2010). For example, the two Black Republican members of Congress – Mia Love and Will Hurd – were elected in overwhelmingly white districts and without meaningful Black support. This leads to the following two hypotheses:

Hypothesis 2: Muslim American Republican candidates will fare equally well as their white Republican counterparts.

Hypothesis 3: Muslim American Republican candidates will fare better than their Muslim American Democratic counterparts.

Crucially, the candidate's race is also likely to affect and complicate voters' evaluations of Muslim American candidates. The chapter therefore explores how voters evaluate Arab/Middle Eastern candidates, given that this is the group that most readily comes to mind when many Americans think of Muslims. However, Americans are much more likely to encounter a Black candidate at the ballot box – of the four Muslim members of Congress elected thus far, three have been Black. Moreover, Black Muslims constitute 20% of the U.S. Muslim population, with research indicating they are more politically engaged than other Muslims (Djupe and Green, 2007). It is therefore important to explore how the intersectionality between being Muslim and being Black affects voter evaluations of Black Muslim candidates. Finally, and as a baseline, the chapter explores how voters evaluate white Muslim candidates for political office. Many Muslims identify as "white" (Tehranian, 2007) and are plentiful across southeastern Europe, in countries such as Bosnia and Albania. Given these differences in Muslim racial identity, the following two hypotheses are put forward:

Hypothesis 4: Black Muslim candidates will fare better than their white Muslim and Arab Muslim counterparts.

Hypothesis 5: All Muslim candidates, regardless of race, will fare worse than the white non-Muslim control treatment.

4.2.2   Voter-Level Characteristics

Voters' decision-making processes at the ballot box take place within a particular social context, meaning variations in that context may affect voting patterns in important ways. The literature has demonstrated that party identification is one such context to be explored when evaluating voters' decision-making processes (Campbell et al., 1960). In this vein, this book anticipates that a voter's Republican partisanship will result in opposition to Muslim candidates, especially when the candidate is a Democrat. This is for several reasons. First, since 9/11 and particularly throughout the 2016 campaign season, many Republican opinion leaders have disseminated negative information about Muslims, both foreign and domestic. It is therefore to be expected that many Republican voters have internalized this rhetoric, particularly if they do not share a similar partisan background. Second, it is anticipated that Republican voters oppose President Obama's and presidential nominee Clinton's perceived alignment with Muslim Americans, and that given existing linkages between Obama and birtherism (Layman, Kalkan, and Green, 2014; Tesler, forthcoming), this will result in large-scale opposition to a Muslim candidate. Finally, it could be that, given the movement of Muslims into the Democratic Party's fold, voters perceive a broader alignment between Democrats and Muslim Americans (Barreto and Bozonelos, 2009). As such, they might reject a Muslim candidate based on partisan preference.

Hypothesis 6: Republican voters will discriminate against Muslim American candidates for office compared to their white non-Muslim counterparts in Democratic elections.

Hypothesis 7: Republican voters will not discriminate against Muslim American candidates compared to their white non-Muslim counterparts in Republican elections.

4.3   CANDIDATE EVALUATION EXPERIMENT: STUDY I

These experiments build on previous candidate evaluation studies (Abrajano, Elmendorf, and Quinn, 2018; Hainmueller and Hopkins, 2014; Hainmueller, Hopkins, and Yamamoto, 2013; Iyengar et al., 2010; Kalkan et al., 2018; Kam, 2007; Lerman, McCabe, and Sadin, 2015; McConnaughy et al., 2010; Philpot and Walton, 2007; Reeves, 1997; Sigelman et al., 1995; Stephens, 2013; Terkildsen, 1993; Visalvanich, 2017; Weaver, 2012) to test how Muslim American candidates fare in American democracy. Survey respondents were randomized into one of eight hypothetical elections, with the race and party identification of the second candidate (Candidate B) manipulated in order to explore their prospects for success in primary elections for congressional office. To cultivate a baseline comparison measure, respondents were randomized into two control treatments: a Democratic or Republican primary election between two white fictional candidates, namely Stephen Johnson and Eric Miller. Many other candidate evaluation experiments simply present information on a single candidate to respondents. However, to mimic the settings of a true election, information on two candidates was provided in a pamphlet that had previously served as real-life primary election campaign material. To measure voter evaluations of the race and religion of Muslim American candidates for political office, respondents were also randomized into Democratic and Republican primary elections between Stephen Johnson and Dean Abdul-Qaadir (a white Muslim); Stephen Johnson and Ahmed Al-Akbar (an Arab Muslim); and Stephen Johnson and Louis Muhammad (a Black Muslim).

4.3.1   *Representing Muslim Identity: Name Labels*

Dean Abdul-Qaadir, the white Muslim candidate, was given an ambiguous first name due to the fact that some Muslims who also identify as white go by "Americanized" names. The candidate's surname, however, provides a clear signal of the candidate's Muslim background. Ahmed Al-Akbar, the Arab Muslim candidate, has both a foreign first and last name for external validity purposes. Most Muslim Americans are foreign born and more than half of those individuals hail from Iran or neighboring Arab countries. Finally, Louis Muhammad, the Black Muslim candidate, was given a name reminiscent of other Black Muslims in America. This is in line with the history of African Americans increasingly adopting Muslim names alongside the rise of the Nation of Islam movement and conversions to Islam beginning in the 1930s.

4.3.2   Representing Racial Identity: Photographs

To signal racial identity, differing photographs were used for the white Muslim, Arab Muslim, and Black Muslim treatments, photographs of actual legislators from non-U.S. countries utilized for the purposes of external validity. There are, of course, problems with using photographs; while they are useful in communicating racial information, they also inevitably convey nonracial information, such as the subject's age, attractiveness, wealth, size, friendliness, and competence (Abrajano et al., 2018; Olivola and Todorov, 2010). To address this, the same photographs were utilized in both the Democratic and Republican treatments, thereby maintaining a useful and informative comparative baseline.[3]

4.3.3   Experimental Design

The first survey experiment was conducted from November 2015 to January 2016 on Amazon Mechanical Turk. The survey instrument randomly assigned 934 respondents to one of eight fictional primary election materials. Respondents were assigned materials about a Republican or Democratic primary election, featuring information about a contest between either a white v. white candidate, white v. white Muslim candidate, white v. Arab Muslim candidate, or white v. Black Muslim candidate. As iterated above, the religious background of the candidate was signaled through their name, while their race was signaled through the picture accompanying the candidate's blurb. The experimental design is shown in Table 4.1.

Table 4.1. *Experimental Design*

Primary Race:	Democratic	Primary Race:	Republican
white v. white Candidate		white v. white Candidate	
Stephen Johnson v. Eric Miller	n = 116	Stephen Johnson v. Eric Miller	n = 114
white v. Muslim Am. Candidates		white v. Muslim Am. Candidates	
Stephen Johnson v. Dean Abdul-Qaadir	n = 115	Stephen Johnson v. Dean Abdul-Qaadir	n = 122
Stephen Johnson v. Ahmed Al-Akbar	n = 118	Stephen Johnson v. Ahmed Al-Akbar	n = 118
Stephen Johnson v. Louis Muhammad	n = 114	Stephen Johnson v. Louis Muhammad	n = 117

The hypothetical candidates were also given blurbs that remained consistent across each type of election and treatment. These blurbs were altered slightly between Democratic and Republican primaries, in order to indicate shifts in partisan leanings. These election materials were constructed out of a real primary election voter guide. Information in the candidate blurbs was generated after reading through biographies on the websites of current members of Congress. Table 4.2 presents the candidate blurbs that were randomly assigned for each election.[4]

4.3.4   Choice Task: Vote Choice

After being presented with the election materials and instructed to read them carefully, respondents answered a question on vote choice, namely: "If you had to chose between Stephen Johnson OR (Eric Miller/Dean Abdul-Qaadir/Ahmed Al-Akbar/Louis Muhammad) who would you vote for?" The variable is dichotomous, with 1 indicating a vote choice for the second and experimentally altered candidate and 0 indicating support for Stephen Johnson.

4.3.5   Choice Task: Likelihood of Winning

Next, how the respondent feels about a given candidate's likelihood of winning is assessed through the question: "After having been presented with this information, who do you think is more likely to win the election: Stephen Johnson OR (Eric Miller/Dean Abdul-Qaadir/Ahmed Al-Akbar/Louis Muhammad)?" This variable is also dichotomous, with 1 indicating that the second and experimentally altered candidate is more likely to win, and 0 indicating Stephen Johnson the more likely candidate to win.

4.3.6   Findings: Study 1

Table 4.3 depicts the aggregate findings between those respondents randomized into either the control Republican or Democratic primaries between two white candidates, and those randomized into either Republican or Democratic primaries involving a white candidate and a Muslim candidate.

Table 4.2. *Candidate Blurbs*

	Democratic Primary	Republican Primary
Candidate A's Blurb: (Stephen Johnson)	Stephen Johnson's roots in this community run deep. He attended elementary school locally and during his college days, he resided next door to the house he grew up in. As a lifelong member of his community, he supports a number of causes and organizations including the Rotary Club, the American Legion, and businesses that promote sustainability and efficiency. Johnson is a strong advocate for American families. His mission is to protect social welfare programs and expand affordable healthcare for all. In Congress, he will seek to break down barriers, work tirelessly for his constituents, and ensure that everyone will get a chance at success under the American Dream.	Stephen Johnson's roots in this community run deep. He attended elementary school locally and during his college days, he resided next door to the house he grew up in. As a lifelong member of his community, he supports a number of causes and organizations including the Rotary Club, the American Legion, and businesses that promote sustainability and efficiency. Johnson is a strong advocate for American families. His mission is to limit the expansion of social welfare programs that drain the economy and to repeal Obamacare. In Congress, he will seek to break down barriers, work tirelessly for his constituents, and ensure that everyone will get a chance at success under the American Dream.
Candidate B's Blurb: (Eric Miller / Dean Abdul-Qaadir / Ahmed Al-Akbar / Louis Muhammad)	(Eric Miller / Dean Abdul Qaadir / Ahmed Al-Akbar / Louis Muhammad) has been a leader in his local community, championing a myriad of issues including but not limited to passing legislation that protects the environment and creating a more progressive tax system that increases taxes on high earners. (Miller / Abdul-Qaadir / Al-Akbar / Muhammad)'s philosophy is one of "generosity and inclusiveness." Having won awards from his local chamber of commerce, his roots as a community activist and his message of inclusivity through democratic participation resonate with his community. His priorities in Congress include supporting traditional American values, revitalizing our economy, and promoting peace and prosperity for all Americans.	(Eric Miller / Dean Abdul Qaadir / Ahmed Al-Akbar / Louis Muhammad) has been a leader in his local community, championing a myriad of issues including but not limited to repealing tax increases implemented in the last eight years to foster economic growth and ensuring America's energy independence by tapping into its vast natural resources. (Miller / Abdul-Qaadir / Al-Akbar / Muhammad)'s philosophy is one of "generosity and inclusiveness." Having won awards from his local chamber of commerce, his roots as a community activist and his message of commerce limiting democratic fraud and protecting the vote resonate with his community. His priorities in Congress include supporting traditional American values, revitalizing our economy, and promoting peace and prosperity for all Americans.

Table 4.3. *Aggregate Experimental Findings*

Aggregated Treatments	Vote Choice Candidate B	Diff. with White Treatment	Candidate B Likely to Win	Diff. with White Treatment
white v. white	54.78%		50.43%	
white v. Muslim Am.	44.60%	10.18%**	17.47%	32.96%***

Note: * p < 0.05, ** p < 0.01, *** p < 0.001

In the aggregate, it can be seen that Muslim American candidates faced discrimination in voting and in likelihood of winning, confirming Hypothesis 1. In the control treatments, respondents voted for Candidate B – Eric Miller – over Stephen Johnson 54.78% of the time. By contrast, respondents voted for the Muslim candidate – Dean Abdul-Qaadir, Ahmed Al-Akbar or Louis Muhammad – 44.60% percent of the time, a 10.18% difference that is statistically significant.

With respect to the likelihood of winning, Muslim candidates suffer an even greater penalty in terms of voter evaluation. While 50.43% of voters indicated that they thought Eric Miller was more likely to win relative to Stephen Johnson in the control treatments, only 17.47% thought the Muslim candidate in the treatment conditions could win, a significant 32.96% difference.

If party identification of the candidate is taken into account, important differences begin to emerge, with the partisanship of the Muslim American candidate having a far-reaching and mediating effect on the individuals' electoral success. Table 4.4 displays the aggregate findings for Democratic and Republican primaries, and shows that Muslim Democrats suffer an electoral penalty when they run for office compared to their white counterparts. In the fictional elections, white Democrats received 50% of the vote and Muslim Democrats 37.18% of the vote compared to Stephen Johnson, a significant difference. The white Democrat treatment was also considered likely to win 47.41% of the time, compared to the Muslim treatments, which were considered likely to win only

Table 4.4. *Aggregate Findings for Study 1 by Party*

Aggregated Treatments	Vote Choice Candidate B	Diff. with White Treatment	Candidate B Likely to Win	Diff. with White Treatment
white v. white (Democrat)	50.00%		47.41%	
white v. Muslim Am. (Democrat)	37.18%	12.82%*	16.43%	30.98%***
white v. white (Republican)	59.64%		53.51%	
white v. Muslim Am. (Republican)	51.82%	7.82%	18.49%	35.02%***

Note: * p < 0.05, ** p < 0.01, *** p < 0.001

16.43% of the time, a significant difference. Republican Muslim candidates, however, were uniquely advantaged, being able to count on substantial support from respondents, confirming Hypothesis 2. Muslim candidates were no less significantly likely to beat Stephen Johnson in Republican primaries than their white counterparts. These results hold even when the findings are disaggregated by treatment (see Table 4.5).

Muslim candidates in Republican primaries were no less significantly likely than their white counterparts to beat Stephen Johnson in this hypothetical election. As Table 4.5 demonstrates, the white candidate, Eric Miller, won 59.65% of elections in the control treatment, while Dean Abdul-Qaadir, Ahmed Al-Akbar, and Louis Muhammad beat Stephen Johnson respectively 50%, 51.70%, and 53.85% of the time. None of these differences was statistically significant. Republican Muslim candidates did suffer a penalty, however, when voters gauged whether they were likely to win, with voters in each treatment deeming Muslim candidates less likely to beat Stephen Johnson than their white counterparts.

We can see from the disaggregated results for vote choice in Table 4.5 that the results in the combined analyses are seemingly being driven to a large extent by the Arab Muslim condition (whereby

Table 4.5. *Disaggregated Treatments in Study 1*

Disaggregated Treatments	Vote Choice Candidate B	Diff. between Parties' White Treatments	Candidate B Likely to Win	Diff. with White Treatment
white v. white (Democrat)	50.00%		47.41%	
white v. white Muslim (Democrat)	39.13%	10.87%+	9.56%	37.85%***
white v. Arab Muslim (Democrat)	38.14%	11.86%**	22.88%	24.53%***
white v. Black Muslim (Democrat)	34.21%	15.79%+	16.67%	32.17%***
white v. white (Republican)	59.65%		53.51%	
white v. white Muslim (Republican)	50.00%	9.65%	18.03%	35.48%***
white v. Arab Muslim (Republican)	51.70%	7.95%	13.56%	39.95%***
white v. Black Muslim (Republican)	53.85%	5.8%	23.93%	29.58%***

Note: + $p < 0.1$, * $p < 0.05$, ** $p < 0.01$, *** $p < 0.001$

race and religion are conflated). In the Democratic conditions, the white Muslim condition does produce significant effects, although the results appear to be larger in the cases of the Arab and Black (Democratic) conditions. This is an impressive finding and so because the first name of the white Muslim condition is already quite Americanized.

Next, Hypothesis 3 can be evaluated by assessing how the Muslim American candidates in Republican and Democratic candidates performed relative to each other. This is an important exercise as it gets around the problems discussed above regarding photographs communicating nonracial information. Given the same photographs are utilized for the white Muslim, Arab Muslim, and Black Muslim

Table 4.6. *Disaggregated Comparisons of Treatment Types in Democratic and Republican Primaries*

Disaggregated Treatments	Vote Choice Candidate B	Diff. with White Treatment	Candidate B Likely to Win	Diff. with White Treatment
white v. white (Democrat)	50.00%		47.41%	
white v. white (Republican)	59.65%	−9.64%	53.51%	−6.09%
white v. white Muslim (Democrat)	39.13%		9.56%	
white v. white Muslim (Republican)	50.00%	−10.87%[+]	18.03%	−8.47%
white v. Arab Muslim (Democrat)	38.14%		22.88%	
white v. Arab Muslim (Republican)	51.69%	−13.56%**	13.56%	9.322%
white v. Black Muslim (Democrat)	34.21%		16.67%	
white v. Black Muslim (Republican)	53.85%	−19.63%*	23.93%	−7.26%

Note: [+] $p < 0.1$, * $p < 0.05$, ** $p < 0.01$, *** $p < 0.001$

treatments in both Democratic and Republican primaries, it can be assessed whether the party effect observed previously is a function of party cue or of attractiveness.

Table 4.6 displays these comparisons and indicates no significant differences for the Eric Miller baseline treatment between Democratic and Republican primaries. Nonetheless, in each Republican election, white Muslim, Arab Muslim, and Black Muslim candidates fared significantly better compared to their Democratic counterparts. Thus, Hypothesis 3 that Muslim American Republican candidates will fare better than their Muslim American Democratic counterparts is confirmed.

Given Muslims in America hail from a multitude of races, the survey explored how white, Arab, and Black Muslims each fared, in order to assess whether certain racial groups were rated more favorably than others. As is evident in Tables 4.5 and 4.6, there is no support for Hypothesis 4 that Black Muslim candidates will fare better than their white Muslim and Arab Muslim counterparts. In fact, the race of the Muslim candidate appears to have no effect on respondents' evaluations of Muslim candidates. There is, however, support for Hypothesis 5 that all Muslim candidates, regardless of race, will fare worse than the white control treatment.

Table B1 displays the bivariate relations between vote choice and the Muslim candidate treatments. As Model 1 in Table B1 denotes, Republican respondents significantly discriminated against Candidate B when the candidate was Muslim compared to the white control treatment, confirming Hypothesis 6. Importantly, Democrats (Model 2) and Independents (Model 3) did not discriminate against the Muslim candidate treatments. This potentially suggests that Muslim candidates running for office can look to coalitions with Democrats and Independents in pursuit of electoral victories. Finally, model 1 in Table B2 confirms Hypothesis 7, because Republicans did not discriminate against Muslim Candidates in fictional Republican elections.

4.3.7   Lingering Concerns

The results from Study 1 point to some important conclusions. First, when Muslim candidates run as Republicans, they are able to defeat Stephen Johnson almost as easily as they beat the Eric Miller control. Also, when evaluating voters' characteristics by party identification, it is noteworthy that it is solely Republicans who discriminate by being significantly less likely to vote for Muslim candidates compared to their Democratic and Independent counterparts. Finally, the aggregate results suggest that Muslims running for office fare worse than their white counterparts, regardless of their race.

However, this finding raises lingering concerns. Given the race of the Muslim American candidate (signaled through the picture) did not significantly impact their success in any election, it remains unclear whether, without the signal of religion, race would have mattered for voters' evaluation of the candidates. In other words, religion (signaled through the candidate's surname) may have overpowered respondents' evaluations of the candidates. One critique, then, is that the controls (one Republican and one Democratic) appear to contain two non-Muslim White candidates. Moreover, without conditions for a non-Muslim Arab candidate and a non-Muslim Black candidate, it is impossible to isolate the effect of race relative to religion. As such, Study 1 has only revealed information about the effect of the Muslim label, not that of the Arab (or Black) label. While Study 1 provides some evidence that the racial identities of different Muslim candidates affect respondents' perceptions of the candidates' likelihood of winning and vote choice, it does not sufficiently disentangle whether the discriminatory effects observed are a result of the religious signal or the picture (race) of Candidate B.

4.4   CANDIDATE EVALUATION EXPERIMENT: STUDY 2

Study 2 was conducted in December 2016 on a sample of Americans through Survey Sampling International. Respondents were randomly assigned to one of the same four Democratic primary election treatments as were used in Study 1, but to disentangle the effect of race and religion, an additional three treatments were added, resulting in a total of seven hypothetical Democratic primaries.

4.4.1   Experimental Design

The three additional treatments were situated in Democratic primaries where the race (picture) of the candidate was signaled, but their religious background was not. In other words, the same pictures were employed for Candidate B as were used in the white Muslim, Arab Muslim, and Black Muslim treatments, but the candidates were given "Americanized" names. The now solely Black treatment was named "Joe Buckner," while the now solely Arab treatment was

Table 4.7. *Study 2 Experimental Design*

Primary Race:	Democratic
white v.	
white candidate	
Stephen Johnson v. Eric Miller	n = 99
white v.	
Muslim Am. candidates	
Stephen Johnson v. Dean Abdul-Qaadir	n = 101
Stephen Johnson v. Ahmed Al-Akbar	n = 101
Stephen Johnson v. Louis Muhammad	n = 102
white v.	
American candidates	
(race signal only)	
Stephen Johnson v. Richard Porter	n = 99
Stephen Johnson v. Neil Richardson	n = 102
Stephen Johnson v. Joe Buckner	n = 102

named "Neil Richardson." Additionally, the former white Muslim and now solely white treatment was named "Richard Porter." By adding these three additional treatments, it was possible to assess whether discrimination was a result of racial or religious signals. Study 2's experimental design is displayed in Table 4.7.

4.4.2   MAR and Candidate Evaluation

Study 2 also explores how respondents' resentment toward Muslim Americans affects how they rate a Muslim American candidate for office, irrespective of partisanship. A 2015 Gallup poll found that 60% of Americans would vote for a Muslim candidate for office.[5] While on the face of it this may seem a relatively high number, it in fact only surpassed support for an atheist (58%) or socialist (47%) candidate, and fell substantially below support for Catholic (93%), female (92%),

Black (92%), Hispanic (91%), Jewish (91%), Mormon (81%), gay or lesbian (74%), and evangelical Christian (73%) candidates.

Evidence from a June 2017 survey conducted on a sample of 1,056 respondents from Amazon Mechanical Turk also suggests that the election prospect for Muslim Americans is low and is related to MAR levels.[6] Only 46.81% of respondents said that they would vote for a Muslim candidate for president. When broken down by individual's level of MAR, the hostility toward Muslim Americans accounts for a great deal of variation: 76.19% of respondents with low levels of MAR would vote for a Muslim president; compared to 45.53% of respondents with medium levels of MAR; and 18.17% with high levels of MAR. A similar pattern emerges when examining support for a Muslim candidate for Congress. Overall, 49.04% of the sample said that they would vote for a Muslim candidate for Congress, but once again there was great variation by MAR levels: 77.77% of respondents with low levels of MAR would vote for a Muslim congressional candidate; compared to 49.03% of respondents with medium levels of MAR; and 18.65% with high levels of MAR.

Thus, Study 2 explores how respondents' attitudes and potential hostility toward Muslim Americans account for their candidate preferences. It is anticipated that a voter's resentment toward Muslim Americans will have profound effects in determining how they rate a Muslim candidate for office, irrespective of partisanship. While research on Muslim American resentment is limited, Layman, Kalkan, and Green (2014) have found that ethnocentrism should be a strong predictor of attitudes toward Muslims in America and therefore individuals' willingness to support Muslim candidates. Given the current sociopolitical landscape, it is to be expected that such negative attitudes translate into significantly less electoral support for Muslim American candidates. Taken together, this leads to the following hypothesis:

Hypothesis 8: Respondents with high levels of resentment will be significantly less likely to vote for Muslim candidates compared to respondents with medium and low levels of resentment.

4.4.3 Findings: Study 2

Table B3 displays the experimental effects on vote choice and likelihood of winning. While the finding that respondents discriminate in vote choice between white and Muslim candidates is not replicated, the results show that it is the signal of religion and not race that affects respondents' perceptions of a candidate's likelihood of winning. In treatments where the candidate's name – and therefore the signal of their religious identity – is changed from a "Muslim"-sounding name to an "American"-sounding name, the discriminatory effects are eliminated across the board.[7]

Turning to how resentment predicts support for Muslim candidates, I subset respondents in this study into those with low, medium, and high levels of MAR. The MAR items were asked pre-treatment and those who fell into the low MAR category were between the 0th and 25th percentile on the MAR scale (measured from 0 to 100). Those who fell into the medium MAR category fell between the 25th percentile and 75th percentile on the MAR scale, and those in the high MAR category scored in the 75th percentile or above on the MAR scale. I explore whether individuals voted for the Muslim candidate in Table B3. Models 1, 2, and 3 subset these results across respondents with low, medium, and high levels of MAR, respectively. Across these three models, I find that only those with low levels of MAR are significantly more likely to vote for a Muslim candidate.

The results from Studies 1 and 2 provide evidence that Muslim American candidates for political office – irrespective of race – experience discrimination by the general public, many of whom are unwilling to vote for them and perceive them as being unlikely to win elections. The only mediating effect for Muslim American candidates is their partisanship. The totality of these results suggests that variations in public preferences for Muslim American candidates are largely driven more by their party and religion than their racial background.

4.5   IMPLICATIONS

This chapter has demonstrated how hostility toward Muslim Americans matters for both policy preferences and vote choice, and that irrespective of race Muslim Democrats consistently lose to white candidates, with the candidate's religion and the respondent's level of MAR operating as strong factors governing vote choice. It can be seen that even those with medium levels of MAR are unwilling to vote for Muslim candidates. As such, studying the general public's candidate and policy preferences is critical to understanding how Muslim Americans fare in American democracy. Given the public has the voting power to elect candidates who will be responsive to their policy preferences, if the public largely views Muslim Americans negatively, then this will be reflected in the policy positions they support and candidates they vote for.

Taken together, the results from this chapter raise critical questions regarding the prospects for Muslim American representation. Large segments of the public support candidates and policies that directly threaten Muslims, both foreign and domestic, and, moreover, there is now evidence that the public is generally unwilling to vote for Muslim candidates, irrespective of race. Once elected, however, American Muslims may fare better in American democracy, and there is reason to be hopeful that they are now more descriptively represented than previously.

The 2016 election saw a number of Muslims getting involved in politics, while on November 7, 2017, Mazahir Salih became the first Muslim Sudanese woman elected outside of Sudan to public office (Iowa City Council at-large).[8] Elsewhere, Abdul El-Sayed – a Rhodes scholar, medical professional, and professor of a public health –

ran as a Democratic candidate for governor in the August 2018 Michigan primary. This was an important race, with Muslim, Black, Indian, and female Democrat candidates running. The 2018 midterm election also saw the rise of two Muslim women – Rashida Tlaib and Ilhan Omar – to national political office. How these candidates offer more meaningful representation to their Muslim constituents is an important avenue of future research.

5   The News Media's Portrayals of Muslim Americans

The preceding chapters have demonstrated that the public largely holds negative attitudes toward Muslim Americans and that those attitudes matter for vote choice and policy preferences. Despite these results, one critical limitation remains. Thus far, the evidence has been rooted in surveys and experiments that began in 2016 and ran through to late 2018. However, this limited time frame does not provide a long enough baseline to assess how Muslim Americans have been communicated to the general public over time. Such an assessment is further complicated by the fact that little information is available for scholarly examination on aggregate attitudes toward Muslims and Muslim Americans prior to the 9/11 attacks. As noted previously, a search on the Roper Center's iPoll database at the time of this writing yielded just three publicly available surveys assessing attitudes toward "Muslim Americans" before September 11, 2001.

Most of the scholarship that exists on Muslims pre-9/11 is qualitative, and therefore not amenable to replication testing, despite being theoretically rich. Moreover, few empirical studies or surveys have measured attitudes toward this critical group, especially before the turn of the century. Prior studies are helpful but fail to provide the broader picture, and none provide a landscape of how U.S. Muslims were presented to the public over an extensive period of time. Thus, a pre-9/11 picture of U.S. Muslims is difficult to paint.

This book therefore turns to the news media as a vital lens in assessing how Muslims and Muslim Americans have been portrayed to the general public. This is due to two primary reasons. First, evaluating how groups have been treated in the news media provides a unique and broad perspective on their situation in the American sociopolitical context over time. As data from the news media spans

the decade before 9/11, it is useful for assessing how various groups –
and Muslims and Muslim Americans in particular – were discussed
before and after the attacks. Second, it is posited that the news media
may be mistreating Muslim Americans as well. Much, if not all, of the
information the American public receives about Muslim Americans
is disseminated by cable news media. This information frequently
conflates Muslims (the "general group" inclusive of foreign Muslims)
and Muslim Americans (the domestic group), and connects this general group with political violence and terrorism (Nacos and Torres-
Reyna, 2007; Powell, 2011; Shaheen, 2003; Terman, 2017). It would
be unsurprising, then, if audiences of the news media also conflated
the two groups. Even if there is no such conflation, it could also be
the case that negative coverage of the foreign group has consequences
for attitudes toward the domestic group.

One way to construct a more complete picture of U.S. Muslims pre- and post-9/11, therefore, is to evaluate the news media's
discussion of them. The volume of news coverage of a racialized group
signifies that group's salience at a given point in time, while the
sentiment of such coverage can signal how Muslim Americans are
being framed for – and perhaps even perceived by – the mass public.
Moreover, understanding how Muslims and Muslim Americans are
portrayed in the news media is particularly important given that the
2016 presidential election saw them consistently (and often negatively) discussed throughout the campaign season. Various presidential hopefuls discussed the group at campaign events, in interviews,
and in debates, and the frequency with which the American public
heard about Muslims, both foreign and domestic, raises questions
about how this discourse shaped attitudes toward them.

In this chapter, coverage of Muslims and Muslim Americans
in the cable news media both before and after 9/11 is investigated.
Specifically, this chapter traces the tone of Muslim American news
coverage, and compares it to coverage of other racialized groups that
scholars have regularly demonstrated are framed negatively. The data
covers an extensive time period, from 1992 to 2016, providing a

comprehensive overview of Muslim and Muslim American coverage pre- and post-9/11.

Overall, the results demonstrate that media coverage of Muslims and Muslim Americans is broadly negative and has worsened over time. Whereas the coverage of Muslim Americans prior to 2001 closely mirrors that of Asian Americans, Blacks, and Latinos, after 9/11 the sentiment of such coverage shifts to being more negative relative to the other groups. The big picture is clear: coverage of Muslim Americans has changed over time and become decisively and significantly more negative than that of other marginalized groups in America.

5.1   THE NEWS MEDIA'S ROLE IN PORTRAYING GROUPS

Studies have argued that the news media is an important conduit for conveying messages to the public (Chomsky, 1997; Markham and Maslog, 1971), shaping attitudes, influencing the national discourse, and generating stereotypes (Brummett, 2014). The news media, however, is neither neutral nor value-free, and scholars examining how media sources frame minority racial groups to the general public have found that they tend to portray such minorities as troublesome constituents (Abrajano and Singh, 2009; Baum, 2003; Branton and Dunaway, 2008; Entman, 1990; Gilliam Jr. and Iyengar, 2000; Gilliam Jr. et al., 1996; Iyengar, Peters, and Kinder, 1982; Kellstedt, 2003, 2005; Prior, 2005; Wortley, Hagan, and Macmillan, 1997). Moreover, media coverage of marginalized groups has embraced a set of binary oppositions, situated in "us" versus "them" terms, that have subsequently compromised these groups' status in society (Gilliam Jr. and Iyengar, 2000; Kellstedt, 2000, 2003, 2005; van Dijk et al., 1995).

The media sustains particular frames, such as associating welfare with "undeserving blacks" (Gilens, 1999) and social security with Whites (Winter, 2006, 2008), and has an enormous impact on the development of racial attitudes (Entman and Rojecki, 2001; Kellstedt, 2000). Past research suggests the ways in which outgroups are represented in the media impacts the public's perceptions, attitudes, and behaviors toward them (Harwood et al., 2013; Haynes, Merolla, and Ramakrishnan, 2016; Mastro, 2009; Merolla, Ramakrishnan, and Haynes, 2013; Saleem, Yang, and Ramasubramanian, 2016), as well as shaping support for policies that harm members of these outgroups (Mastro and Kopacz, 2006; Ramasubramanian, 2011; Tan, Fujioka, and Tan, 2000).

It is anticipated that these findings extend to Muslim Americans, especially given that those associated with this group (e.g. Arabs, Middle Easterners, and foreign Muslims) are frequently linked with violence, terrorism, and aggression by American media outlets (Alsultany, 2012; Nacos, 2016; Nacos and Torres-Reyna, 2002, 2007). Indeed, research has found that a reliance on the media for information about Muslims, rather than having direct contact with them, is associated with negative emotions, stereotypic beliefs, and support for harmful policies (Alsultany, 2012; Saleem et al., 2016).

This body of work sets the foundation for theory building. Media portrayals of Middle Easterners, for instance, have long been related to narratives of terrorism, violence, threat, and fear (see Behm-Morawitz and Ortiz, 2013; Esposito, 1999; Gadarian, 2010; GhaneaBassiri, 2013; Said, 1979; Selod, 2015; Shaheen, 2003; Steet, 2000; Wilkins, 1995). Scholarship has also found that news media coverage of Muslim Americans increased in the immediate aftermath of 9/11 (Nacos and Torres-Reyna, 2002, 2007), and that the media discourse was controlled by powerful and negative fringe organizations (Bail, 2012). Furthermore, since 9/11, the news media has increasingly used the practice of "threatening information and evocative imagery" to cover foreign policy relating to Middle Easterners (Behm-Morawitz and Ortiz, 2013; Gadarian, 2010; Merolla and Zechmeister, 2009). Finally, an extensive examination of newspaper coverage over 35 years reveals that stereotypes of Muslims as a cultural threat have been consistently perpetuated by tying together themes of Muslim women and gender inequality (Terman, 2017).

Variations in the news media's framing of different racial groups make it possible to systematically assess how various groups are processed by the general public. Media information about groups is not, however, necessarily static, and can shift over time, affecting how a particular group is portrayed to and understood by the public.

The analyses in this chapter take advantage of a standardized dictionary approach to sentiment analysis, comparing the coverage of Muslims and Muslim Americans to that of Blacks, Latinos, and Asian Americans, and testing how negative and positive coverage is shaping public attitudes.

5.2   METHODOLOGY

To assess the news media coverage of Muslims and Muslim Americans, the volume and sentiment of the discourse need to be considered. To achieve this, available broadcast news transcripts from CNN, Fox, and MSNBC for the period 1992–2016 were collected using the Lexis Nexis Academic platform. The study period begins in 1992 for several reasons. First, at the time data collection began, the Lexis Nexis Academic portal did not have a comprehensive set of pre-1992 broadcast transcripts. Second, 1992 allowed for a long-term pre-9/11 measure to evaluate how Muslims have been treated by the news media. Analysis was focused on CNN, Fox, and MSNBC, as these are the three cable TV networks that significant portions of the American public reported watching during this time period. It should be noted, however, that only CNN broadcasts are available from 1992–1997. Fox News broadcasts are available from 1998, and MSNBC broadcasts from 1999. Thus, a complete dataset of all coverage only truly begins in 1999.

Lexis Nexis search results originally yielded 731,106 broadcast transcripts from CNN, 104,114 transcripts from Fox from 1998 to 2016, and 24,749 from MSNBC from 1999 to 2016. Next, I removed online news broadcasts and those transcripts with over 30,000 words because the average length of the remaining broadcast transcripts was 2,658.55 words (~15 minutes) and because those transcripts over 30,000 words (~176 minutes) typically consisted of programming that spanned more than three hours, unlike typical news broadcasts. This yielded a final total of 459,036 CNN transcripts, 104,110 transcripts from Fox, and 24,734 from MSNBC. The unit of analysis, then, is an individual broadcast, as determined by CNN, Fox, and MSNBC, which can contain multiple segments from a given evening broadcast, for example.

As Gallup notes, the 1990s and early 2000s marked the emergence of cable news networks as popular daily news sources. In 2002, for example, a Gallup poll found that 41% of Americans claimed to get their news from "cable news networks such as CNN, Fox News Channel, and MSNBC" every day, putting it on par with the nightly network news shows. Fast forwarding to 2017, Americans continued to watch these three cable TV news networks, with MSNBC, CNN, and Fox each posting double-digit viewership growth in the year's second quarter.[1]

Once an initial dataset of downloaded articles was compiled and categorized by year, sentiment analysis was conducted on all transcripts using the Hu and Liu dictionary (2004).[2] Sentiment analysis empirically determines the tone of a text by examining incidences of positive and negative words in a corpus of documents (Bhonde et al., 2015), so in this case a sentiment score for each broadcast transcript was computed based on the number of positive words less the number of negative words it contained (Hu and Liu dictionary; Barberá, 2014). The raw Hu and Liu sentiment score for each broadcast transcript was standardized for ease of interpretation.

The dictionary approach is a relatively basic technique aimed at understanding how positive, negative, or neutral a given text observation is relative to other text observations in the corpus. Despite the simplicity of the method, the dictionary approach is considered to achieve a high degree of accuracy (see Barberá, 2014, Figure 2; González-Bailón and Paltoglou, 2015).[3]

Since the focus of the research was on (1) the volume of coverage of Muslims and Muslim Americans; and (2) the sentiment of coverage of Muslims and Muslim Americans compared to other marginalized groups, the data was subsetted into separate corpuses for each group: Muslims, Muslim Americans, Blacks, Latinos, and Asian Americans. Corpuses for Arab American, Middle Eastern American, and national origin American groups were also looked at. Table C1 presents a definitional list of the search terms used to subset and create each corpus.

In sum, the final CNN dataset has 89,116 broadcasts: 32,928 about Muslims, 2,172 about Muslim Americans, 29,415 about Blacks, 21,343 about Latinos, and 3,258 about Asian Americans. The final Fox dataset consists of 25,027 broadcasts, 10,212 of which are about Muslims, 822 about Muslim Americans, 7,124 about Blacks, 6,269 about Latinos, and 600 about Asian Americans. The final MSNBC dataset has 15,877 broadcasts, 4,394 of which mention Muslims, 406 mention Muslim Americans, 5,851 mention Blacks, 4,712 mention Latinos, and 514 mention Asian Americans. The analyses that follow compare these five groups – or corpuses – to one another.

I rely on the "Muslim" corpus to capture stories pertaining to followers of Islam generally, which encompasses mostly foreign Muslims, and the "Muslim American" corpus to include coverage related to domestic Muslims. Given each corpus is based on the group in question being mentioned in a particular broadcast, and because more than one group can be mentioned in a single broadcast, these corpuses do feature some spillover. For example, transcripts in the Black corpus sometimes overlap with the Latino corpus. Finally, the Muslim (foreign group), Muslim American (domestic group), Black, Latino, and Asian American corpuses were appended to one another.

Tables C2–C4 display the frequency of each group's mentions by year by outlet, and Table C5 displays the frequency of group mentions across all outlets. The rest of the analysis compares these five corpuses – or groups – with one another.

5.3   WHY MUSLIM AMERICANS?

An important question to be asked in relation to any study of Muslim Americans is why the scholar is studying this group in particular.

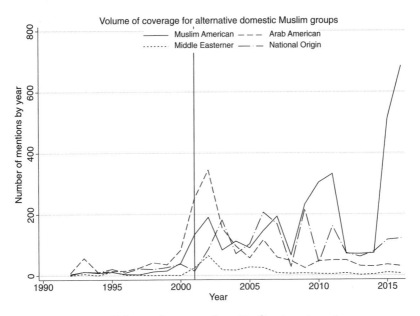

FIGURE 5.1 Volume of coverage about Muslim Americans increases more than that about National Origin Americans, Middle Easterners and Middle Eastern Americans, and Arab Americans

In terms of this book and chapter, the focus is on media portrayals of Muslim Americans, rather than, say, Middle Easterners or Arab Americans. This is because Muslim Americans are the group most commonly referred to in the U.S. news media today. The volume of coverage has increased more than for any other comparable group since 9/11.

Figure 5.1 compares the volume of coverage of Muslim Americans, Middle Eastern Americans, Arab Americans, and national origin American groups (e.g. Iranian American, Lebanese American, etc.) across the CNN, MSNBC, and Fox platforms by year. The vertical line appears at year 2001 as a proxy for the 9/11 attacks. It shows that after the 9/11 attacks the volume of coverage for each of these groups increases, indicating that perhaps the media did not know which group to settle on, with Arab Americans in fact significantly more likely than other groups to be mentioned in news media coverage in the two years after the September 11, 2001 attacks. Over time,

Table 5.1. *Volume of mentions of Muslims, Muslim Americans, Arab Americans, Middle Easterners, and National Origin Americans across All Three Platforms by Year (in transcripts < 30,000 words)*

Year	Muslims	Muslim Americans	Arab Americans	Middle Easterners	National Origin
1992	503	2	8	0	4
1993	1,354	12	57	5	12
1994	853	8	10	0	10
1995	741	11	14	12	21
1996	449	4	15	2	9
1997	423	3	25	2	22
1998	439	12	42	0	20
1999	814	15	35	1	26
2000	1,034	40	83	0	37
2001	2,147	133	252	25	14
2002	2,469	190	345	65	86
2003	2,555	83	155	18	181
2004	2,626	112	96	17	71
2005	2,513	90	57	27	103
2006	3,307	146	116	25	206
2007	2,141	193	59	8	168
2008	1,357	66	48	6	28
2009	1,997	232	24	7	217
2010	2,072	304	47	5	42
2011	2,595	332	50	4	161
2012	2,160	71	50	7	73
2013	2,009	70	31	1	61
2014	2,262	73	29	3	78
2015	3,929	514	35	9	116
2016	4,785	684	30	6	120

though, the news media decreased its coverage of Arab Americans and increasingly began discussing Muslim Americans.

Table 5.1 displays the number of mentions of Muslims, Muslim Americans, Arab Americans, Middle Easterners, and National Origin Americans across CNN, Fox, and MSNBC by year. As can be seen, Muslim Americans entered the news media, and perhaps even the public consciousness, only slowly and over time. In the pre-9/11 years, there was little coverage, perhaps indicating they were not perceived as a coherent or even relevant group. Instead, their salience gradually increased. In 2016, there were 684 news broadcast mentions of Muslim Americans, a substantially large increase compared to 20 years previously. The same year, Arab Americans were mentioned in 30 segments, and Muslims in 4,785 segments. Media coverage of other groups that could perhaps also be interpreted as referring to Muslim Americans declined markedly as the years moved on, supporting the empirical argument made by this book that the most relevant group to study is Muslim Americans.

It makes logical sense that the group the news media – and ultimately political elites and the general public – settled on was Muslim Americans. During the period under examination, a drastic increase in the volume of coverage of Muslims – an all-encompassing term referring to Muslims abroad – can be seen. During 1992–2016, the coverage of Muslims increased even more drastically than the other groups examined. Prior to 2001 (in the dataset), the coverage of Muslims never exceeded 1,500 in any given year, which is negligible compared to their appearance in 4,785 transcripts in 2016. One anomaly in the dataset is 1993, in which Muslims were mentioned in 1,354 transcripts; this coincides with the bombing of the World Trade Center.

5.4 SENTIMENT AND VOLUME OF MUSLIM AND MUSLIM AMERICAN NEWS COVERAGE

Table C5 also presents the yearly mean standardized sentiment scores for each group across all examined media outlets. However, because Fox and MSNBC did not enter the dataset until 1998 and 1999 respectively, the mean sentiment score for each group by year by network is provided in Tables C2 (CNN), C3 (Fox), and C4 (MSNBC).

For ease of interpretation, Figure 5.2 displays line plots demonstrating the trends in these tables. The panels demonstrate two important points. First, each group's yearly mean coverage tended

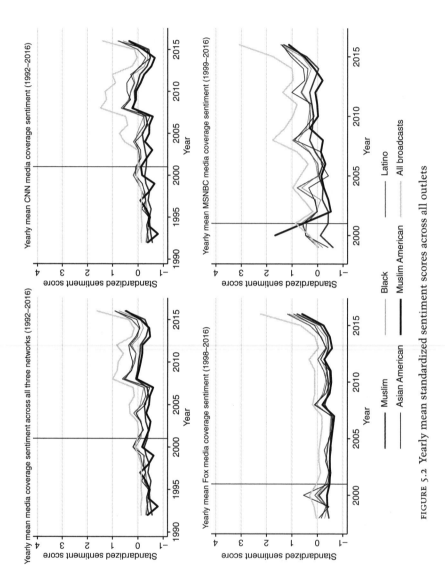

FIGURE 5.2 Yearly mean standardized sentiment scores across all outlets

to fall below the average sentiment for *all* broadcasts in the aggregate (top left-hand panel) and on CNN (top right-hand panel), Fox (bottom left-hand panel), and MSNBC (bottom right-hand panel). This result provides face validity for the standardized sentiment measure because it serves as empirical support for prior studies that argued that Black and Latino coverage was more negative than other coverage airing on the news.

Second, across platforms, and in the aggregate, news coverage sentiment of Muslim Americans appears to be mixed over time. Prior to 9/11, the coverage sentiment of Muslim Americans is similar to that of other groups, and is even positive when looking at the CNN and MSNBC panels. However, after 2001, there seems to be a gradual downward movement of the Muslim American line in all four panels.

It is also important to note how often each of these groups appeared in news media coverage. The top right-hand panel in Figure 5.3 displays the proportion of coverage which mentioned Muslims, Muslim Americans, Blacks, Latinos, and Asian Americans in CNN coverage by year. I present this metric, as opposed to raw counts, for two reasons. First, it is unlikely that each of these networks has turned over every single one of its broadcasts to Lexis Nexis. As such, if we see an increase in volume of group mentions by year, we cannot draw any inferences without also taking into account increases in the overall number of broadcasts over time as well. Second, it provides descriptive statistics on how likely viewers are to see broadcasts mentioning stigmatized groups.

I find that prior to 2001, Blacks, Latinos, Muslims, Asian Americans, and Muslim Americans did not receive much coverage. From 1992 to 2000, these groups were not mentioned in even 10% of news broadcasts on CNN. However, after 2001, there was a dramatic increase in the proportion of coverage each group received by year.[4] In 2004, CNN coverage began to more frequently mention Muslims (17.54%), Blacks (8.81%), and Latinos (6.43%) in its coverage. At that time, President Bush was running for reelection, and the country was well in the throes of two wars in the Middle East. By 2006,

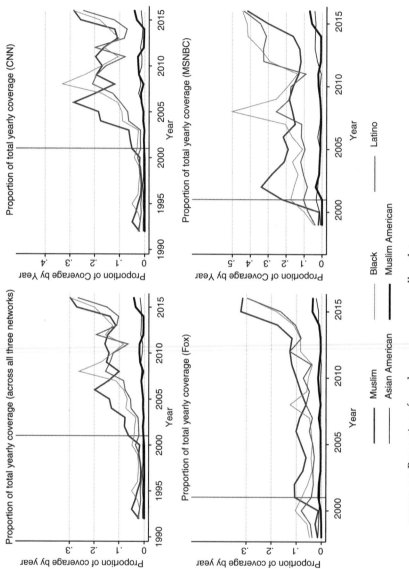

FIGURE 5.3 Proportion of yearly coverage across all outlets

this figure had increased dramatically with Muslims, Blacks, and Latinos each being mentioned in 28.41%, 10.73%, and 9.59% of CNN coverage, respectively. That year, the country was recovering from Hurricane Katrina, nationwide protests about the DREAM act were ongoing, Saddam Hussein was executed and the Iraq War was proving deadly, prompting the president to declare a surge in troops in January 2007.

By 2008 and with the election of President Obama, the tables had turned somewhat; Blacks appeared in 33.03% of CNN broadcasts, compared to Latinos in 20.89% and Muslims in 11.98% of CNN coverage. This reduction in the proportion of Muslim coverage was short-lived, however. Toward the end of the Obama administration and by 2015, which served as the start of the 2016 presidential campaign, Muslims appeared in 25.67% of CNN coverage, followed by Blacks (17.93%), and Latinos (12.13%). By 2016, each of these three groups was being communicated at high rates to the American public, with Muslims appearing in 28.46% of CNN coverage, and Blacks and Latinos in 28.70% and 24.55%, respectively. Clearly, then, by 2016, the American public was being exposed to a large amount of information about stigmatized groups – including Muslims – through news coverage, a marked increase from two decades prior.

After 2001, we see that Fox and MSNBC also began to discuss each of these stigmatized groups at high rates. Fox did not mention Muslims in more than 10% of its coverage from 2001 to 2010.[5] The rise in discussion of Muslims occurred from 2014 to 2016, when Muslims appeared in 17.66% (2014), 32.27% (2015), and 31.53% (2016) of available broadcasts. Blacks and Latinos also were not very present on the platform until this era as well. Prior to 2014, Blacks appeared, on average, in 3.65% to 12.54% of broadcasts per year. Latinos likewise appeared in 2.84% to 8.21% of broadcasts per year, on average. However, between 2014 and 2016, Blacks and Latinos were mentioned in 11.19% and 10.49% of Fox broadcasts in 2014, 17.95% and 16.34% in 2015, and in 29.41% and 29.67% in 2016, respectively.

MSNBC, on the other hand, mentioned Muslims more in its broadcasts than Blacks and Latinos from 2001 to 2007.[6] For example, in 2001, MSNBC mentioned Muslims in 22.15% of available broadcasts, and Blacks and Latinos in 17.39% and 10.35% of broadcasts, respectively. From 2007 to 2016, MSNBC mentioned Blacks more than any other group in its coverage, though the network did mention Blacks, Latinos, and Muslims at very high rates in its coverage. For instance, in 2016, Blacks appeared in 44.46% of broadcasts, followed by Muslims (41.65%) and Latinos (43.74%).

Having established that the proportion of coverage about stigmatized groups increased substantially from 1992 to 2016, another important question remains: Did the sentiment of Muslim American coverage significantly differ from that of Muslims, Blacks, Latinos, and Asian Americans in the pre-September 11, 2001 period and in the post-September 11, 2001 period?

Specifically, I explore whether CNN depicted each group differently in the pre-September 11, 2001 period and whether the three networks depicted each group differently in the post-September 11, 2001 period. Prior work suggests that networks are likely portraying groups differently based on their ideological tilt. For example, Martin and Yurukoglu (2017) find that Fox grew increasingly conservative from 2000 to 2008.[7] Given Fox's conservative stance, I expect the network to discuss each of the groups more negatively than MSNBC and CNN. CNN, on the other hand, is frequently perceived to be more middle of the road, while MSNBC is commonly deemed to be a liberal network sympathetic to racial and ethnic minorities and the policies they espouse. As such, I expect CNN portrayals of Muslims and Muslim Americans to be more positive than their portrayals on Fox, but more negative than on MSNBC. In the aggregate, moreover, I would expect all networks to portray Muslims and Muslim Americans more negatively than Blacks, Latinos, and Asian American because they are frequently linked to narratives of terror and violence.

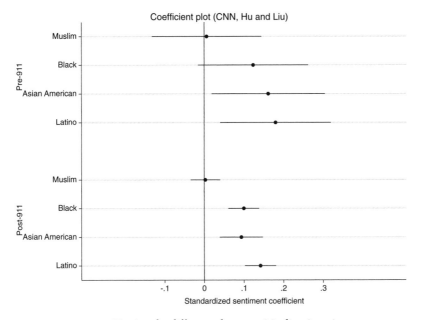

FIGURE 5.4 Testing the difference between Muslim American coverage sentiment and that of other groups in CNN broadcasts

To answer this question, I conducted fixed effect regressions, absorbed at the day level.[8] In each regression, the dependent variable is the standardized Hu and Liu sentiment score, and the key independent variables are binary indicators for the Black corpus, the Latino corpus, the Asian American corpus, and the Muslim corpus. The outgroup is a dummy variable for the Muslim American corpus.

The top panel in Figure 5.4 presents the coefficient plot for the pre-September 11, 2001 regression. This plot is based on Model 1 in Table C6. I find that the sentiment of Black and Muslim coverage does not significantly differ from that of Muslim Americans, though the coefficients are larger than in the post-9/11 period. Moreover, the sentiment of Latino and Asian American broadcasts is only slightly more positive than that of Muslim Americans.

To test whether news coverage sentiment of Muslim Americans differed from that of other examined groups in the post-September 11, 2001 period, an OLS regression was conducted,

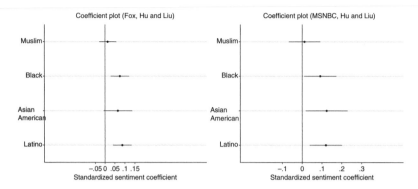

FIGURE 5.5 Testing the difference between Muslim American coverage sentiment and that of other groups in Fox and MSNBC broadcasts

examining whether the standardized news coverage sentiment score for Muslim Americans differed significantly from that of Muslims, Latinos, Blacks, and Asian Americans on CNN, Fox, and MSNBC.[9]

As the bottom panel in Figure 5.4 (Model 2 in Table C6) shows, the post-September 11, 2001 period presents a different story on the CNN platform. While the coefficients are smaller than in the pre-9/11 period, there are large and significant differences between the sentiment in Muslim American coverage and that of Blacks, Latinos, and Asian Americans. Each of these stigmatized domestic groups received relatively more positive coverage in this time period than Muslim Americans. The coverage of Muslims – the foreign group – did not significantly differ from that of Muslim Americans.

This finding is echoed on Fox and MSNBC as well. As Figure 5.5 displays, coverage sentiment for Muslim Americans was significantly below that of Blacks and Latinos, two stigmatized groups known to be portrayed negatively by the media. The same goes for the coverage of Asian Americans, except for on the Fox platform.

Thus, in the post-September 11, 2001 period, Muslim Americans received less coverage than Blacks, Latinos, and Asian Americans, and this coverage appears to not significantly differ very much. It is important to underline this point. In this era, when comparing the news media coverage of Muslim Americans to those of Blacks, Latinos, and Asian Americans – three grossly marginalized groups that we know are portrayed negatively by the media – Muslim Americans come out below them.

5.4.1   Asian American News Media Coverage

One concern regarding analyzing news coverage of Asian Americans is that the group does not receive much coverage in this dataset. This might be because of how the group was labeled as a subset – it could be, for instance, that the media refers to members of this community using specific country labels, such as Chinese Americans. This possibility is supported in the literature, with Larson (2006, p. 130), for example, writing that "in addition to the infrequency of coverage Asian Americans receive generally, certain national subgroups receive most of the attention," such as Chinese Americans and Japanese Americans.

Another concern regarding Asian American news broadcasts relates to the finding that the group receives similar or sometimes more negative coverage than Blacks and Latinos. This finding, however, is not novel, and is substantiated by previous research on Asian Americans which, to date, has focused predominantly on how they are portrayed in the entertainment industry, rather than in the news (Larson, 2006). While they are rarely included on television and in film (Larson, 2006, p. 68), when they are depicted, their national origins are often untraceable and their characters often exhibit "unfavorable stereotypes," such as the inscrutable and dangerous foreigner (Hamamoto, 1994), who is either oversexualized (in the case of Asian women) or undersexualized (in the case of Asian men) (Larson, 2006, pp. 68–69).

The above scholarship suggests two facts that are in line with the findings of this chapter's research: (1) Asian Americans receive little coverage relative to other groups; and (2) when they do appear in news media, their coverage "has stigmatized them even at times when they are treated as the stereotypically 'model minority'" (Larson, 2006, p. 130). Moreover, as Larson (2006, p. 131) notes "the image found in entertainment of Asian Americans as evil and manipulative is also evident in news coverage." At other times, Asian Americans are depicted as resented outsiders, posing an economic – rather than physical – threat. Even when they are mentioned in news stories, the literature finds that they most commonly appear in entertainment or human interest stories (Larson, 2006, p. 131).

To address some of these potential concerns, further investigation was conducted into why the Asian American sample was so small. This revealed that when Asians are reported on in the U.S. context, they are often lumped together with other races. In other words, when they are mentioned in a news broadcast, it is not uncommon to find them listed primarily as a statistic among many others groups.

Next, the search terms used to subset and create the Asian American corpus were reexamined, to check if they were problematic. In order to do this, a new "alternative Asian American" corpus was created, subsetting alternative terms capturing variations for national origin groups, specifically "Japanese American," "Chinese American," and "Indian American."

As Table 5.2 demonstrates, these searches did not increase the amount of stories extracted from the broadcast transcripts. As such, the results reiterate that Asian Americans received little news media coverage during the time period studied.

5.4.2 Black and Latino News Media Coverage

A similar potential limitation with respect to the comparison between group positions concerns the extent to which the media uses coded language to refer to particular groups. To address this, further analysis was employed to examine whether references to other keywords may help broaden and perhaps capture true coverage sentiment of Blacks and Latinos, in particular. An alternative Black and an alternative Latino corpus were therefore created, based on alternative terms and coded language that might refer to either of these groups. For the alternative Black sample, the following terms were searched for: urban, inner city, and welfare queen. For the

Table 5.2. *Frequency Table of Asian American and Alternative Asian American Mentions by Year*

Year	Asian American	Alternative Asian American
1992	137	7
1993	168	4
1994	91	6
1995	182	15
1996	144	5
1997	253	14
1998	148	10
1999	203	12
2000	321	6
2001	173	29
2002	121	30
2003	115	23
2004	97	12
2005	102	10
2006	159	22
2007	215	40
2008	147	19
2009	195	17
2010	134	26
2011	118	24
2012	223	21
2013	233	17
2014	208	14
2015	198	34
2016	289	27
Total	4,374	444

alternative Latino sample, the following terms were searched for: undocumented, DACA, dreamer/s, and Mexican immigrant/s. As displayed in Table C7, for the most part, the Black and Latino corpuses used in the main analysis and their respective alternative corpuses do not differ greatly. Yet, for the Latino corpus, some differences can be seen in 2004 and in 2008, suggesting that the terms selected for the alternative sample received much lower sentiment ratings than the Latino corpus. Overall, however, the results provide additional evidence that the original Black and Latino search terms corpuses do in fact largely function appropriately in capturing coverage of the groups in the examined broadcasts.

5.5   IMPLICATIONS

September 11, 2001 and other more recent events have raised concerns about how Muslim Americans are portrayed in the media. Anecdotal accounts demonstrate that media coverage embraces a set of binary oppositions in the context of "us" versus "them" categories, compromising the status of Muslim Americans in wider society. Many conclude, without much systematic empirical evidence, that the little coverage there is of Muslim Americans rarely depicts them in a positive light.

The evidence from this chapter points to several important conclusions. The results show that coverage of groups – including that of Muslims and Muslim Americans – has changed over time. Muslim Americans did not always hold a salient outgroup status. However, after 9/11, not only did the proportion of discourse about Muslims in the news increase sharply, it also was negative. Furthermore, the movement of different groups relative to each other over time suggests that context matters when evaluating how groups are communicated to the public.

Muslim Americans arguably hold a low position in the present American sociopolitical context. This is at odds, however, with what many American Muslims experienced prior to 9/11. Back then, they were a nonsalient religious group, with the news media, elites, and the public unable to differentiate between Muslim Americans, Arab Americans, Middle Eastern Americans, and their national origin groups. Today, however, they are a salient and racialized outgroup (Elver, 2012; Ewing, 2008a; Gotanda, 2011; Jamal, 2009; Selod, 2015).

The news media matters because it has the power to identify how groups are being processed by the mass public. Through variation in its framing of different racial groups, it is possible to systematically assess how groups fare compared to one another. How often and in what manner groups are discussed, moreover, is not necessarily fixed. The news media's treatment of a particular group can shift how often and in what manner the group is being portrayed to the public, writ large. Moreover, given that the news media portrays some groups more positively and more often than others, it potentially has the ability to shape where groups are situated in the public's mind.

6 Improving Mass Attitudes: The Media's Role in Shaping Group Attitudes and Policy Preferences

The evidence presented in this book thus far supports the existence of pervasive and negative attitudes toward U.S. Muslims among the wider public. It has also demonstrated that media coverage of Muslims and Muslim Americans increased after 9/11, with coverage proportions of Muslims rivaling that of African Americans and Latinos by 2016. Moreover, news coverage of Muslims and Muslim Americans in the post-9/11 period was more negative in sentiment than that of other examined marginalized groups, which are typically known to be negative as well.

Having established these trends, further questions arise. How are public attitudes toward Muslim Americans swayed to become more positive or more negative? Can the media play a role in shaping public opinion toward them? And does it matter if coverage is about Muslims (the foreign group) or Muslim Americans (the domestic group)? This chapter addresses these questions, employing experiments to assess how negative and positive media portrayals of Muslims and Muslim Americans affect public attitudes toward, as well as policy preferences affecting, U.S. Muslims.

These experiments causally demonstrate that the tone of media coverage matters for shaping public attitudes toward Muslim Americans. Exposure to negative media coverage increases resentment toward Muslim Americans, resulting in greater support for discriminatory policies against them. These effects are most pronounced among medium- and high-resentment respondents. Positive coverage of Muslims and Muslim Americans does not, however, always work in the same way. In two out of the three studies, positive media coverage did not reduce resentment against Muslim Americans, nor did it markedly affect levels of support for policy positions targeting their rights. In fact, the studies found that individuals with low levels of MAR prior to the study treatment became significantly more resentful, regardless of whether the treatment's coverage was positive or negative.

These results provide evidence for some of the causes of anti-Muslim American sentiment among the general public, suggesting that variations in attitudes and policy preferences are at least in part driven by negative media coverage. Furthermore, negative news coverage about the foreign Muslim group is likely shaping public attitudes toward Muslims in America. Taken together, the studies confirm that the news media matters for shaping public opinion, and is actively processing information about Muslim Americans along racialized lines, thereby perpetuating their framing as troublesome constituents.

6.1   MEDIA COVERAGE SHOULD MATTER FOR SHAPING MASS ATTITUDES

Scholarship has long shown that the mass media matter for shaping public attitudes. For example, when assessing African American media depictions, Gilens (1999) contends that media portrayals stereotype, as well as overrepresent, the number and images of African Americans in poverty, creating "racialized" attitudes toward welfare policy.

Having established the topics, tone, and volume of media coverage of Muslims and Muslim Americans in Chapter 5, it is anticipated that these portrayals are similarly consequential for public attitudes. Media coverage has the power to frame and prime public attitudes toward Muslim Americans for two primary reasons: First, ordinary Americans are likely to have only limited personal experiences interacting with Muslim Americans, given they compose just 1% of the population. According to a Pew 2014 survey, only 38% of Americans report knowing a Muslim personally;[1] as a result, the media serves as the public's principal source of information. The same survey found that when asked to rate Muslim Americans on a feeling thermometer from 0 to 100, the average rating among people who knew a Muslim personally was 49, whereas the average score for those who did not was 35. Moreover, Muslims in America are concentrated in a select few states, with, as of 2010, only eight states having Muslim populations higher than 100,000.[2] Thus, due to the limited firsthand information most Americans have about Muslim Americans, there is ample room for the media to fill the void. The increasing number of negative images the public observe in the news media could thus serve an essentializing function (Powell, 2011; Shah and Thornton, 1994).

Second, media portrayals connected with events such as 9/11, the wars in Iraq and Afghanistan, the civil conflict in Syria, and an increase in terror-related activities across Europe have produced compelling images and narratives that paint Muslims – and by extension Muslim Americans – as violent. As a consequence of Islam, Muslims, and Muslim Americans being linked in the contemporary U.S. news cycle to Iraq, Iran, Afghanistan, Syria, and ISIS, much of what American audiences know about Muslim Americans is connected to issues such as war, terrorism, and oil. Given the media's preference for sensationalist coverage, these portraits potentially give rise to moral panics.

6.1.1 How Exposure to Negative versus Positive Coverage May Shape Mass Attitudes

It is anticipated that exposure to negative and to positive media coverage will function differently in shaping public attitudes toward Muslim Americans. Specifically, it is expected that exposure to negative news media coverage will be more impactful in shaping attitudes toward and policy preferences affecting Muslim Americans. This is due to two primary reasons.

First, scholarship has shown that negative information is more likely than positive information to draw an individual's attention; it stands out as extreme, and is therefore more effective in shaping attention, attitudes, and decision-making (Helson, 1964;

Lau, 1982, 1985; Merolla and Zechmeister, 2018). Furthermore, negative information and cues are reasoned to be more effective in eliciting opinions for a number of reasons, including (1) being more informative and/or novel (Lau, 1982, 1985); and (2) giving rise to anxiety and thereby activating an individual's surveillance (or threat-detecting) system (MacLeod and Mathews, 1988; Marcus and MacKuen, 1993; Merolla and Zechmeister, 2018).

Second, Muslims in the United States already constitute an outgroup, with existing attitudes toward them mostly negative. As such, the general public is likely already exposed to high volumes of coverage painting the Muslim Americans, Muslims (as a foreign group), and Islam in a negative light. Negative coverage, then, likely only increases fear of U.S. Muslims, and, by extension, resentment, thereby making individuals more likely to support policy positions targeting them. Even if they do not already hold resentful attitudes toward Muslims, many Americans – most of whom, as already noted, do not know any Muslims personally – may only have vague ideas about them. Thus, if the media fills this void with negative information, such individuals are more likely to be moved in a negative direction.

Increasing positive coverage of Muslim Americans, however, would likely not work in the same way or to the same magnitude. While the attitudes of some people might improve slightly, the attitudes of the majority of people are likely to remain the same. This is because the small amount of positive information they are getting is unlikely to: (a) offset the negative information they are used to receiving; and (b) accord with the information they generally receive about U.S. Muslims. It is therefore not anticipated that individuals' MAR levels will move much, if at all, after exposure to positive information.

6.2   EXPERIMENTAL DESIGN

A series of survey experiments were conducted to assess whether the sentiment of news media coverage about Muslims and Muslim

Americans impacts public attitudes toward them. The first two survey experiments were fielded by SSI in June 2016, while a third was fielded by Lucid in July 2018. All three employed a within-subject and between-subject design.

In Experiment 1, respondents were randomly assigned one of four real-life broadcast news media transcripts. These transcripts included the most positive and most negative broadcasts aired on television about Muslims and Muslim Americans in 2015. Real-life broadcasts were used in order to attain a high degree of construct validity. However, the drawback of this approach is that due to the content of transcripts differing in a number of ways beyond the group discussed, it is difficult to know exactly which factors drove shifts in attitudes. To supplement this work, Experiment 2 randomly assigned another set of respondents one of four manipulated transcripts, providing improvements on internal validity due to the variation of just two dimensions: sentiment of the transcript (positive and negative) and the group being discussed (Muslims versus Muslim Americans). Experiment 2 is a useful way of investigating whether the findings from Experiment 1 are replicated in a more controlled design. Experiment 3 replicated Experiment 2, but included additional treatments for robustness.

6.3   JUNE 2016 STUDY: EXPERIMENTS I AND 2

The June 2016 survey asked respondents nine questions regarding their race, age, gender, levels of American identity, relative fears about events that might take place in the following 12 months, attitudes toward immigration policy positions, income, education, and group attitudes toward Muslims (pre-MAR). Next, respondents were told that they would be shown a broadcast transcript from a major news organization channel and that they should read this carefully, as they would be asked questions about it at a later time. Respondents were then randomized to the real-life frames experiment (Experiment 1) or manipulated frames experiment (Experiment 2). The experimental designs for these two experiments

Table 6.1. *Experimental Design: Experiments 1 and 2*

Experiment 1: Real Frames		Experiment 2: Manipulated Frames	
Treatments	Observations	Treatments	Observations
Positive Treatments		**Positive Treatments**	
T1. Muslim American positive	n = 91	T1. Muslim American positive	n = 94
T2. Muslim positive	n = 87 Total = 178	T2. Muslim positive	n = 91 Total = 185
Negative Treatments		**Negative Treatments**	
T3. Muslim American negative	n = 91	T3. Muslim American negative	n = 87
T4. Muslim negative	n = 94 Total = 185	T4. Muslim negative	n = 92 Total = 179

are displayed in Table 6.1, while Tables D18 and D19 present the balance tables.

The four experimental templates for Experiment 1 can be found in Tables D1–D4. Respondents were randomized to view either: (1) a positive transcript about Muslim Americans; (2) a negative transcript about Muslim Americans; (3) a positive transcript about Muslims; or (4) a negative transcript about Muslims. The experiment was based on selecting the most positive and most negative real-life news media broadcasts among transcripts containing 10,000 words or less.[3]

The four experimental conditions for Experiment 2 can be found in Tables D5 and D6. However, in Experiment 2 all transcripts were identical, apart from manipulations to ensure they differed in the following two ways: (a) the group being discussed (Muslim or Muslim American); and (b) the sentiment of the coverage (positive or negative).

Lastly, respondents were asked a series of post-test questions about Muslim representation in the media, policy positions regarding Muslim immigration, policy positions regarding policing Muslim communities, partisanship, voter registration, past voting behavior, ideology, and attitudes toward Muslim Americans (post-MAR), as well as favorability questions about Muslims and other racial and religious groups in America.

6.4 JULY 2018 STUDY: EXPERIMENT 3

The treatments in Experiments 1 and 2 are limited insofar as they do not reveal whether the effects recorded are specific to Muslims and Muslim Americans, or if any generic (i.e. nonspecific) immigrant group would have generated comparable results. To address these limitations, an additional survey experiment was conducted two years later on a nationally representative sample of 3,841 U.S. adults. Table D20 displays the experimental design and balance table for this replication experiment, indicating how six additional frames (highlighted in bold) were added to the original four, namely: (1) alternative Muslim American positive; (2) Latino positive; (3) Immigrant positive; (4) Latino negative; (5) Immigrant negative; and (6) control. The ten experimental treatments can be found in Appendix Tables D7–D17.

As with the June 2016 survey, respondents were told they would be shown a broadcast transcript from a major news organization channel and that they should read this carefully, as questions would be asked about it at a later time. They were then randomized into one of the ten conditions and given a news transcript. Finally, respondents were asked a series of post-test questions regarding partisanship, ideology, voter registration status, prior vote history, presidential vote choice in 2016, feeling thermometer toward groups, Muslim representations in the media, attitudes toward policy positions about Muslim immigration, approval of President Trump's travel ban, attitudes toward Muslims (post-MAR), and racial resentment.

To ensure there was a positive Muslim American treatment that did not invoke terrorism, an alternative treatment was constructed altering the Muslim American's Facebook activity from denouncing terrorism to "repeatedly and actively participating in his community and serving the most marginalized, such as the homeless." Next, positive and negative broadcast transcripts specifically tailored to immigrants and to Latinos were constructed. The immigrant frames (treatments 7 and 9), discussed an immigrant man who had repeatedly and publicly either denounced (positive) or supported (negative) illegal immigration and law-breaking. The end of the transcript is also tailored to immigrants, stating, "[t]hese posts really made us think that we need to reevaluate how we perceive immigrants around the world and that we need to understand their beliefs more carefully to make sure America knows what they think and who they are." This treatment is perhaps not as drastic as supporting or denouncing ISIS and terrorism, but is arguably perceived as similarly egregious by the American public. For the Latino condition, a (perhaps imperfect) treatment invoking Mexicans was constructed, framed as support for or denouncement of the MS-13 gang.

Experiment 3 also differs from Experiment 2 in a number of other ways. First, the sample sizes in the replication study were about three times those of the original study, meaning Experiment 3 offers much more precise estimates. Second, this study was conducted two years after the heated 2016 presidential campaign, at a time when the number of terrorist attacks in the United States and western Europe by ISIS and its followers had declined. This means it is possible that the American public would not be as resistant to positive information about Muslims and Muslim Americans as they would have been in 2016. Third, a control condition was constructed discussing ordinary Americans who use Facebook as a platform to "stay in touch with their friends, write about their day to day experiences, and post pictures of their lives."[4]

6.5   WITHIN-SUBJECT SHIFTS IN MAR

One of the lingering questions from Chapter 5 is whether exposure to news media broadcasts is consequential for public opinion toward Muslim Americans. Given that the American public is routinely exposed to coverage of Muslims, and that much of this coverage is negative, it is important to assess whether being exposed to coverage about the foreign group has downstream effects regarding attitudes toward the domestic group. Therefore, a within-subject design was incorporated within Experiments 1, 2, and 3 to find out whether individual-level attitudes toward Muslim Americans shifted after exposure to a positive or negative broadcast about Muslims (foreign) or Muslim Americans (domestic), with respondents assessed according to the MAR scale before exposure to treatment and once again at the very end of the survey.

Table D21 displays the factor loadings for each of the MAR items. Table D22 includes four demographic characteristics predicting MAR that apply to all the experiments. In Experiments 1 and 2, only information on respondents' age, income, gender, and education was available, while Experiment 3 was also able to account for marital status and race. Across the three models, being male is associated with holding resentful attitudes toward Muslim Americans, while higher levels of education appear to have an ameliorating effect on such attitudes. In Experiment 3, which has a larger sample size, being older is associated with holding more resentful attitudes, as is being married and having children. When accounting for race, it can also be seen that Blacks are significantly more likely than Whites to hold less resentful attitudes toward Muslim Americans. Finally, Table D23 presents descriptive statistics for individual-scale items measuring respondents' MAR.

6.6 RESULTS: EFFECTS OF EXPOSURE TO MEDIA COVERAGE ON INDIVIDUAL-LEVEL MAR

Do negative stories affect individuals' attitudes toward Muslim Americans? Do positive stories have the opposite effect? Does media coverage even matter at all? These are the core questions addressed by examining shifts in resentment toward Muslim Americans after exposure to the treatments in Experiments 1, 2, and 3.

Table 6.2 displays mean MAR ratings before and after exposure to a negative Muslim or Muslim American treatment across all three experiments. The differences in MAR are striking, with exposure to the treatment portraying negative Muslim American coverage increasing MAR by 0.13 (1–7 scale) in Experiment 1; 0.16 (1–7 scale) in Experiment 2; and 0.068 (1–5 scale) in Experiment 3. Exposure to the treatment portraying negative Muslim coverage increased

Table 6.2. *Mean Muslim American Resentment by Negative Treatments*

Negative Treatments	Pre-Muslim American Resentment Mean	Post-Muslim American Resentment Mean	Significance
Experiment 1: Real Frames, 1–7 Likert scale			
Muslim American	3.57	3.70	$p = 0.034$
Muslim	3.62	3.76	$p = 0.012$
Experiment 2: Manipulated Frames, 1–7 Likert scale			
Muslim American	3.62	3.78	$p = 0.001$
Muslim	3.59	3.72	$p = 0.031$
Experiment 3: Robustness Check, 1–5 Likert scale			
Muslim American	2.603	2.671	$p = 0.000$
Muslim	2.636	2.70	$p = 0.000$

MAR by 0.14, 0.13, 0.064 in Experiments 1, 2, and 3, respectively. Combined, these results indicate that exposure to negative coverage does indeed increase individual-level MAR. It should also be noted that the observed increase in MAR is based on exposure to a single broadcast. Regular viewers are likely to see broadcasts of this nature multiple times over the course of a week, if not several times a day, potentially compounding and entrenching such shifts in attitude.

Similar effects are evident in both the Muslim and Muslim American treatments, indicating that the discussion of Muslims (the foreign group) affects the American public's views of Muslim Americans. This is particularly noteworthy in light of the volume and overwhelmingly negative nature of news coverage about Muslims.

It is nevertheless still important to determine if exposure to positive coverage decreases resentment against Muslim Americans. For the most part, Table 6.3 shows that exposure to positive coverage in Experiments 1 and 2 did not significantly alter respondents' MAR either way. Strikingly, exposure to positive coverage about Muslims actually increased individuals' MAR in Experiment 2 (though the effect only borders on significance). Nonetheless, this is not a sufficient justification for discounting the role that positive coverage can play in shaping individuals' MAR.

Table 6.3. *Mean Muslim American Resentment by Aggregated Positive Treatments*

Positive Treatments	Pre- Muslim American Resentment Mean	Post- Muslim American Resentment Mean	Significance
Experiment 1: Real Frames, 1–7, Likert scale			
Muslim American	3.57	3.55	p = 0.679
Muslim	3.40	3.42	p = 0.615
Experiment 2: Manipulated Frames, 1-7 Likert scale			
Muslim American	3.49	3.50	p = 0.861
Muslim	3.51	3.61	p = 0.052
Experiment 3: Robustness Check, 1–5 Likert scale			
Muslim American	2.59	2.55	p = 0.0225
Muslim American (alt.)	2.60	2.561	p = 0.0171
Muslim	2.63	2.58	p = 0.0177

Experiment 3 presents a different story, with significant changes in respondents' mean MAR ratings pre- and post-exposure to all three positive conditions. In short, individuals became less resentful toward Muslim Americans after being exposed to positive coverage about Muslims or Muslim Americans. The differences in results between Experiment 3 and Experiments 1 and 2 might be due to the fact that the former was conducted two years after the latter two experiments, in a vastly different context. In June 2016, the nation was in the middle of an election, and faced a refugee crisis, as well as terrorist attacks on U.S. soil. By July 2018, the general public's anxieties about Muslim Americans had, comparatively, abated. The differences could also be due to Experiment 3's large sample size and its ability to detect significance.

Regarding whether positive coverage shifts individual-level attitudes to the same degree as negative coverage, Table 6.4 shows whether respondents' post-MAR after exposure to the five conditions in Experiment 3 and the control treatment differ significantly from one another. The results reveal that for all three positive conditions (Muslim American, Muslim American alternative, and Muslim), respondents did not significantly differ in their post-MAR from those respondents exposed to the control condition. However,

Table 6.4. *Experimental Effects of News Coverage Sentiment on MAR and Differences with Control Condition*

Condition	Condition Post-MAR	Control Post-Mar	Diff.
T1. Muslim American positive	2.549	2.552	0.0023
			$p = 0.9684$
T2. Muslim American positive (alt.)	2.561	2.552	0.0093
			$p = 0.8772$
T3. Muslim positive	2.585	2.552	.0334
			$p = 0.5772$
T4. Muslim American negative	2.671	2.552	0.1194
			$p = 0.0442$
T5. Muslim negative	2.704	2.552	0.1521
			$p = 0.0084$

Note: MAR is measured on a 1–5 scale, and reported differences are between the control condition and each of the treatments.
Source: July 2018 Lucid survey.

Table 6.4 does reveal significant differences in mean post-MAR ratings for the Muslim American negative and Muslim negative conditions, with respondents significantly more resentful toward Muslim Americans post-treatment. These results lead to the conclusion that negative coverage has a greater impact in increasing resentment toward Muslim Americans than positive coverage has in reducing it.[5]

6.6.1   *Heterogeneous Effects: Within-Subject MAR Shifts by Party*

It can be expected that there will be effects by party identification, with Republican viewers, for example, much more likely to watch more conservative networks (e.g. Fox), which depict Muslim Americans negatively.[6] As such, decision-making by TV viewers presents an inherent selection issue potentially impeding causal analyses.

To address this, heterogeneity analyses by party identification were conducted on the June 2016 and July 2018 samples. While one benefit of the experiments is that the source of the broadcast is never revealed to respondents, the sample sizes were not large enough to block-randomize by party identification or MAR beforehand, meaning the results are only suggestive, though still greatly informative.

Tables D24 and D25 present differences in mean pre- and post-MAR of Republicans, Democrats, and Independents/Other Party in the June 2016 and July 2018 surveys. Across both surveys, as would be expected, Republicans had the highest levels of pre-MAR, followed by Independents, and then Democrats. Moreover, the overall patterns observed across the two surveys are similar, with one exception. In both surveys, Republicans were significantly more likely to become resentful after viewing the Muslim negative condition. Democrats in the June 2016 survey exposed to the Muslim positive and Muslim American negative conditions became more resentful toward Muslim Americans (almost significant), while Democrats in the July 2018 survey became significantly less resentful after exposure to the Muslim positive condition, but significantly more resentful after exposure to the Muslim American negative condition. Finally, Independents across both surveys became significantly more resentful after exposure to the Muslim American negative and Muslim negative conditions.

Next, Tables D26 and D27 examine the differences in post-MAR between Republicans, Democrats, and Independents/Other Party taking part in the June 2016 and July 2018 surveys, respectively. The story across both surveys is fairly consistent for Republicans and Democrats, less so for Independents. For Republicans, there are significant differences in post-MAR across both surveys for those exposed to the Muslim American positive condition versus the Muslim American negative condition.

In the July 2018 survey the aggregate differences are also significant. For Democrats, post-MAR is significantly higher for those exposed to the Muslim negative condition as opposed to the Muslim positive condition. Aggregate differences in both survey experiments are also significant. Finally, although no significant differences are observable for Independents in the June 2016 study, there are significant differences in post-MAR between the Muslim American alternative positive treatment and the Muslim American negative condition.

6.7   EFFECTS OF EXPOSURE TO MEDIA COVERAGE ON SUPPORT FOR RESTRICTIVE POLICIES

We might also wonder how exposure to negative and positive treatments may have shaped support for restrictive policy positions targeting Muslim Americans. The results thus far demonstrate that negative coverage sentiment of both Muslims (foreign group) and Muslim Americans (domestic group) significantly impacts respondents' resentment toward Muslim Americans. As the statements about policy items were presented to respondents only after they were randomly exposed to their treatment, a between-subject analysis was conducted, comparing the mean ratings of those exposed to the positive treatment with the mean ratings of those exposed to the negative treatment. Results from Experiments 2 and 3, which have strong internal validity, show how randomized exposure to negative versus positive coverage about Muslims and Muslim Americans affects respondents' support for policies targeting these groups.

The first dependent variable evaluated is Limit All Immigration, which measures support for the policy statement: "Limiting all immigration from all countries of origin until the nation's representatives can figure out what is going on." This statement broadly ascertains a respondent's support for limiting immigration without respect to the identity of the immigrant.

The second dependent variable subjects evaluated is Limit All Muslim Immigration, which measures support for the policy statement: "Limiting immigration from Muslim countries of origin until the nation's representatives can figure out what is going on." The statement evaluates whether respondents feel that Muslims, rather than immigrants in general, should be restricted from immigrating to the U.S.

The final dependent variable is Limit Muslim Americans from Reentering, which measures support for the policy statement: "Limiting Muslim Americans from reentering the U.S. if they have left for any reason (i.e. vacation, work, longer visits) until the nation's representatives can figure out what is going on." This statement was the most stringent immigration policy statement evaluated, as it asked respondents to consider stripping American citizens of their right to return to their country should they leave for any reason.

Table 6.5 displays the aggregated and disaggregated mean values of support for these three policy statements. Turning to Experiment 2, across the board, respondents exposed to the negative treatment were significantly more likely to support the three policy positions than those exposed to the positive treatment, with respondents exposed to the negative treatment 0.62 points more likely to support the Limit All Immigration policy statement; 0.67 points more likely to support the Limit All Muslim Immigration policy statement; and, alarmingly, 0.78 points more likely to support the Limit Muslim Americans from Reentering policy statement.

These results also hold when the treatments are disaggregated. Comparing the mean ratings of those exposed to the negative Muslim American treatments with those exposed to the positive treatments, it can be seen that respondents were significantly more likely to support all three policy statements: by 0.51 points in the case of the Limit All Immigration policy statement, 0.56 points in the case of the Limit All Muslim Immigration policy statement, and 0.82 points in the case of the Limit Muslim Americans from Reentering policy statement. Comparing negative versus positive treatments of Muslims, respondents were again significantly more likely to support the Limit All Immigration, Limit All Muslim Immigration, and Limit Muslim Americans from Reentering policy statements, in this case by 0.73 points, 0.78 points, and 0.75 points, respectively. These effects are large, with differences in movement on the measured policy dimensions between those exposed to negative and to positive Muslim treatments in the range of 7.28%–11.57%; and those exposed

Table 6.5. T-Tests for Immigration Policy Positions by Disaggregated Treatments

	Limit All Imm. (Mean)	Sig.	Limit Muslim Imm. (Mean)	Sig.	Limit Musl. Am. from Reentering (Mean)	Sig.
Experiment 2: Manipulated Frames, June 2016 (1–7 Likert scale)						
Positive Treatments						
T1. Muslim American Positive	3.75		3.97		3.49	
T2. Muslim positive	3.69		3.91		3.31	
(Aggregate)	3.72		3.94		3.40	
Negative Treatments						
T3. Muslim American negative	4.26	p = 0.069	4.53	p = 0.045	4.31	p = 0.002
T4. Muslim negative	4.42	p = 0.006	4.69	p = 0.003	4.06	p = 0.003
(Aggregate)	4.34	p = 0.001	4.61	p = 0.000	4.18	p = 0.000
Experiment 3: Robustness Check, July 2018 (1–5 Likert scale)						
Positive Treatments						
T1. Muslim American positive	2.8		2.79		2.46	
T2. Muslim American positive (alt.)	2.88		2.84		2.49	
T3. Muslim positive	2.96		2.91		2.60	
(Aggregate)	2.88		2.85		2.52	
Negative Treatments						
T4. Muslim American negative	2.84	p = 0.635	2.91	p = 0.235	2.68	p = 0.018
T4. Muslim American negative	2.84	p = 0.719	2.91	p = 0.517	2.68	p = 0.040
T5. Muslim negative	3.02	p = 0.520	3.08	p = 0.076	2.82	p = 0.023
(Aggregate)	2.93	p = 0.386	2.99	p = 0.020	2.75	p = 0.000

to positive and to negative Muslim American treatments in the range of 10.28%–10.57%. The results for Experiment 1 are displayed in Table D28.

Experiment 3, meanwhile, reveals a slightly different pattern. In the aggregate, there are no significant differences in support for the Limit All Immigration policy between those exposed to the positive and negative treatments, though there are significant differences for the other two policy statements. When the treatments are disaggregated, however, there are no significant differences for the Limit All Immigration and Limit All Muslim Immigration statements between those randomized into the three positive Muslim American and Muslim treatments and those randomized into their negative counterparts.[7] Significant differences are only observable for the Limit Muslim Americans from Reentering policy statement, which is arguably the most stringent immigration policy evaluated.

For robustness, whether positive or negative coverage about Latinos or immigrants affected respondents' support for each of the three policy positions was explored. Table 6.8 displays the differences in support for each of the examined policies after exposure to positive and negative broadcasts about Latinos and immigrants. Apart from a significant difference in mean support between those exposed to a negative versus positive immigrant treatment for the Limit All Muslim Immigration policy statement, there are no significant differences. Additionally, Table D11 displays the differences in support for the three policy statements after exposure to each of the five conditions in Experiment 3 and the control. Here, the only significant difference in mean support for the three policy positions is between those exposed to the Muslim negative condition and the control.

The results point to a couple of conclusions. First, exposure to negative coverage increases support for more restrictive policy positions. As can be seen, negative coverage significantly shifted attitudes toward supporting all three policy statements targeting Muslim and Muslim Americans in Experiment 2. Two years later, Experiment 3 demonstrates that negative coverage continues to shape support for a policy that would restrict the ability of Muslim Americans to reenter their own country. Second, coverage of the foreign group affects policy preferences toward the domestic group. This is noteworthy in light of the volume and overwhelmingly negative nature of media coverage of Muslims. While only short-term effects are demonstrated by these experiments, consistent, long-term negative coverage might lead to opinion change over time.

6.8   MORE EVIDENCE FROM EXPERIMENT 3: HOW DOES EXPOSURE TO COVERAGE OF OTHER GROUPS AFFECT INDIVIDUALS' MAR?

Finally, this chapter assesses whether it is positive and negative coverage of Muslims and Muslim Americans that is driving differences in MAR, or whether exposure to positive and negative coverage of any marginalized group can have similar effects. In addition to the Muslim, Muslim American, and control conditions used in Experiment 3, the July 2018 survey also randomized respondents into four additional treatments: positive and negative broadcasts about immigrants and Latinos.

Table 6.6 displays differences between respondents' mean pre- and post-MAR ratings for those randomized into the positive and negative treatments of Latinos and immigrants. Overall, exposure did not yield significant differences between individuals' pre-MAR and post-MAR, with the exception of the positive immigrant treatment, which saw resentment toward Muslim Americans decrease. The difference in this instance might be due to respondents linking U.S. Muslims with immigrants, which is not a stretch, as Pew places the number of Muslims born abroad as 58% of their total population in the country. This is supported by the fact that the positive immigrant frame does not specify where the immigrant has come from. Importantly, though, negative coverage about Latinos and immigrants did not significantly increase respondents' post-MAR, suggesting that it is exposure to negative coverage about Muslims and Muslim Americans specifically that is driving negative attitudes toward them.

Table 6.6. *How Exposure to Coverage on Latinos or Immigrants Affects MAR*

Condition	Obvs.	Pre-MAR	Post-MAR	Diff.
Positive Treatments				
T1. Latino	n = 387	2.560	2.544	0.0155
				p = 0.3614
T2. Immigrant	n = 395	2.607	2.573	0.0334
				p = 0.0411
Negative Treatments				
T3. Latino	n = 377	2.599	2.618	0.0188
				p = 0.2560
T4. Immigrant	n = 384	2.671	2.655	0.0164
				p = 0.3235

Note: MAR is measured on a 1–5 scale, and reported differences are between pre- and post-MAR.
Source: July 2018 Lucid survey.

Table D29 displays the within-subject differences between respondents' pre- and post-MAR ratings in the five Muslim/Muslim American treatments conducted in July 2018, as well as the control condition. There are several important takeaway points from this table. First, there are no within-subject differences in MAR for the 385 respondents exposed to the control condition, demonstrating that it is functioning as intended. Second, and similar to the findings of the June 2016 study, respondents exposed to negative treatments about Muslims and Muslim Americans had significantly increased MAR after exposure. Third, exposure to positive treatments did have an effect in significantly reducing MAR, contrary to the findings of the June 2016 study. This is perhaps due to the fact that the sociopolitical context in the United States and in western Europe had changed, with terror groups such as ISIS having reduced the number and scale of their attacks. The American public, then, may have been less resistant to positive information given the more relaxed security climate.

Table 6.7. *Experimental Effects of News Coverage Sentiment on MAR*

Positive Condition	Post-MAR	Negative Condition	Post-MAR	Diff.
T1. Muslim American	2.549	T4. Muslim American	2.671	0.1217 $p = 0.0380$
T2. Muslim American (alt.)	2.561	T4. Muslim American	2.671	0.1100 $p = 0.0697$
T3. Muslim	2.585	T5. Muslim	2.704	0.1188 $p = 0.0424$

Note: MAR is measured on a 1–5 scale, and reported differences of post-MAR are between positive and negative conditions.
Source: July 2018 Lucid survey.

Table 6.8. *T-Tests for Immigration Policy Positions by Disaggregated Latino and Immigrant Treatments*

	Limit All Imm. (Mean)	Sig.	Limit Muslim Imm. (Mean)	Sig.	Limit Musl. Am. from Reentering (Mean)	Sig.
Positive Treatments						
T1. Latino Positive	2.92		2.96		2.568	
T2. Immigrant Positive	2.92		2.84		2.53	
Negative Treatments						
T3. Latino Negative	3.02	$p = 0.3463$	2.89	$p = 0.4642$	2.67	$p = 0.2987$
T4. Immigrant Negative	3.04	$p = 0.2212$	3.03	$p = 0.0438$	2.65	$p = 0.2145$

Note: The three dependent variables are measured on a 1–5 Likert scale, with increasing values indicating more support for the resentful policy.
Source: July 2018 Lucid survey.

Moreover, respondents exposed to positive coverage of Muslim Americans or Muslims differed significantly in their post-MAR values compared to those exposed to negative coverage. As can be seen in Table 6.7, respondents exposed to negative coverage of Muslim Americans and Muslims were significantly more resentful after exposure. These results mirror the June 2016 results, demonstrating that the experiment was replicable two years later.

Table 6.8 examines whether it is negative coverage of Muslims or Muslim Americans in particular that leads to increased support for more punitive policy preferences, or if negative coverage of other marginalized groups can work in the same way. Respondents answered three questions evaluating their support for the policy positions tested in the July 2018 survey.

The results displayed in Table 6.8 reveal that exposure to positive or negative coverage about Latinos or immigrants did not significantly affect respondents' support for the three policy positions, except the Limit All Muslim Immigration statement. Here, significant differences in support for this policy can be seen in those exposed to the positive immigrant treatment compared to its negative counterpart. Perhaps, again, this is due to respondents linking immigrants with Muslims. On the whole, though, no significant differences can be seen between the positive and negative Latino treatments, and between the positive and negative immigrant treatments, regarding respondents' support for the three policy positions. These results indicate that it is negative coverage of Muslims and Muslim Americans specifically that leads to increased support for more punitive policy preferences.

Finally, this chapter examines whether exposure to positive and negative Latino and immigrant treatments impacts individuals' feeling thermometers toward Latinos and illegal immigrants, respectively. Table 6.9 displays respondents' within-subject differences after exposure to each of these four treatments, and shows that exposure to positive coverage of immigrants significantly increases an individual's feeling thermometer rating toward-illegal immigrants. It also shows that exposure to negative coverage about Latinos significantly decreases an individual's feeling thermometer rating toward Latinos. As there are no systematic trends, it is difficult to draw conclusions about the role of the media in shaping attitudes toward these groups. However, this may simply be due to the fact that the dependent variables do not represent a perfect measure of attitudes toward either group, and they should perhaps be replaced by more specific and tailored questions.

The same can be said about racial resentment as a dependent variable. Table 6.10 displays differences in respondents' racial

Table 6.9. *How Exposure to Coverage on Latinos or Immigrants Affects Anti-Immigrant and Anti-Latino Sentiment*

Condition	Obvs.	Pre-FT	Post-FT	Diff.
Positive Treatments				
T1. Latino	n = 387	71.53	71.34	0.1860
				p = 0.7763
T2. Immigrant	n = 395	46.04	47.41	1.36
				p = 0.0752
Negative Treatments				
T3. Latino	n = 377	69.00	67.56	1.437
				p = 0.0401
T4. Immigrant	n = 384	45.51	45.23	0.276
				p = 0.6731

Note: The feeling thermometers (FT) asked respondents to rate Latinos and illegal immigrants, respectively, from 0–100. The reported FTs for the Latino treatments are toward Latinos, whereas the reported FTs for the immigrant treatments are toward illegal immigrants.
Source: July 2018 Lucid survey.

Table 6.10. *July 2018 Study: CCES Racial Resentment Scale Does Not Adequately Measure Movement in Attitudes Toward Other Racialized Groups*

Positive Condition	CCES RR Score	Negative Condition	CCES RR Score	Diff.
T1. Muslim American	3.41	T4. Muslim American	3.362	0.055
				p = 0.534
T2. Muslim American (alt.)	3.423	T4. Muslim American	3.362	0.0613
				p = 0.481
T3. Muslim	3.37	T5. Muslim	3.36	0.0110
				p = 0.898
T6. Latino	3.37	T8. Latino	3.38	0.0108
				p = 0.904
T7. Immigrant	3.43	T9. Immigrant	3.37	0.0661
				p = 0.451

Note: The CCES Racial Resentment Scale is based on the average of four statements, which were each measured on a 1–6 Likert scale. The reported differences are between the positive and negative conditions.
Source: July 2018 Lucid survey.

resentment after having viewed positive versus negative coverage of a particular group. Across the board, no significant differences can be seen, arguably indicating that a measure scholars have long relied on does not sufficiently capture resentment toward particular groups.

6.9   IMPLICATIONS

This chapter has shown that discourse about Muslims and Muslim Americans has serious consequences for how public attitudes are shaped. Exposure to negative media coverage about Muslims and Muslim Americans increases resentment toward the domestic group, as well as increasing support for punitive policies targeting them. Positive coverage, meanwhile, had mixed effects and does not appear to work in the same way. Importantly, these results move beyond the descriptive literature concerning stereotypical depictions of Muslims and Muslim Americans in American news media coverage, and in doing so present two new innovations. First, they causally demonstrate that exposure to negative media coverage of Muslims and Muslim Americans increases individual-level resentment toward Muslim Americans, thereby enabling the proliferation of negative public attitudes. Second, they demonstrate that negative media coverage has tangible effects on the American public's support for policies that directly and negatively harm Muslims and Muslim Americans.

The results also demonstrate that the status of Muslim Americans has been particularly harmed by the media's treatment of Muslims as a foreign group, coverage of whom has increased markedly since 2001, becoming more negative and more commonplace compared to other marginalized groups. This is noteworthy, and indicates that such negative coverage may be resulting in increased support for policies limiting the freedoms of Muslims in America.

Moreover, scholarship has found that media coverage has the ability to communicate hierarchies to the public through a myriad of channels, such as segregation of races in images and through physical intimacy (Entman and Rojecki, 2001). This book proposes that one additional way such stereotypes are being presented to the public is through the language used by the news media. Volume, sentiment, and tone are particularly important, especially when news media stories contain traces of essential racial difference (Entman and Rojecki, 2001). Finally, it should be noted that respondents are reading only a short block of text and are not actually watching a longer video, as they would in a typical broadcast. They are not receiving the visual and sound aids that work with the content of a news broadcast to deliver information to the mass public. The treatment here, in contrast, is very mild. As such the effects might be understating how much the news media can actually shape attitudes.

Taken together, these results confirm that the news media matters for shaping public opinion. It is an institution that is actively processing information about Muslim Americans along racialized lines, and perpetuating their framing as troublesome constituents. The news media's coverage therefore has important consequences for how the public evaluates, processes, and contextualizes Muslim Americans as the "other."

7 Muslim American Representation: Outsiders in Their Own Country?

Previous chapters have demonstrated that negative attitudes toward Muslim Americans influence the public's vote choice and policy preferences. They have also established that the sentiment of media coverage of Muslims, both foreign and domestic, has attitudinal and policy consequences for the domestic group. Equally important for evaluating the status of Muslim Americans in the U.S. sociopolitical context is understanding how legislators treat and value them.

Chapter 3 argued that the prospects for substantive representation of Muslim Americans were slim, given that those with higher MAR preferred candidates and policies that were hostile to both foreign and domestic Muslims. This chapter tests whether this statement is in fact true. One form of substantive representation that legislators can provide is meeting and addressing constituency requests (Pitkin, 1967). This chapter, therefore, assesses how political elites treat their Muslim constituents, and in doing so explores U.S. Muslims' prospects for inclusion in the political process.

As noted several times throughout this volume already, the 2016 presidential campaign highlighted that not only were legislators aware of the U.S. Muslim community, but that the group were front and center of the national discourse. This raises the question of how well Muslim American citizens are being served by their elected representatives. Do representatives discriminate against Muslim Americans in the context of hiring? Does a representative's political affiliation play a role in how they treat their Muslim constituents? Are Muslim Americans with high socioeconomic status able to escape discrimination in this context? And does discrimination against Muslim American individuals extend to community leaders seeking legislative visits? The sparse empirical literature on Muslim American representation means very little is known about the support those from the group can expect to receive from elected officials, particularly during a time when they have become increasingly marginalized.

Evidence that elected officials underrepresent particular constituents along racialized lines is pervasive, with audit studies having found them racially biased in whether and how they respond to constituent communications (e.g. Broockman, 2013; Butler, 2014; Butler and Broockman, 2011; Butler, Karpowitz, and Pope, 2012; Carnes and Holbein, 2015; Distelhorst and Hou, 2014; Einstein and Glick, 2017; Grose, Malhotra, and Parks van Houweling, 2015; White, Nathan, and Faller, 2015). Given Muslim Americans have become increasingly racialized since 9/11, a similar lack of responsiveness might be expected from legislators.

There is a surprising dearth of studies examining the responsiveness of America's elected officials to their Muslim constituents, particularly given that Muslim Americans are an unpopular and arguably racialized religious minority group (Dana et al., 2018; Jamal, 2009). It is also a critical omission, given the role that legislators play in providing constituent services to their electorates. The rate and manner in which legislators offer – or do not offer – Muslim Americans opportunities to integrate into the political process could be a marker of the widespread discrimination they face.

Chapter 7, therefore, explores the quality of Muslim American representation through two audit studies on state legislators, using putatively identifiable white and Muslim names. The first study tests whether Muslim Americans can integrate and find work in America's political system, and finds that elected officials across all 50 states are significantly less likely to respond to Muslim Americans compared to Whites, regardless of the Muslim's socioeconomic status or the legislator's party identification. The second study explores whether Muslim leaders have more success than other group individuals in accessing politics on behalf of their communities. While bias against individual voters is both antidemocratic and discriminatory, an even more concerning problem exists if representatives are also excluding and ignoring community leaders, such as religious figures. Bias – or differential responsiveness – against these leaders may indicate an entire group has very little access to the political arena and shaping representational outcomes. The study does indeed find such a bias exists, with Muslim leaders significantly less successful than their Christian counterparts at securing opportunities to integrate their communities into the political process.

Across both studies, the results reveal legislators largely ignore the Muslim American community. Indeed, anecdotal evidence and observable signs of discrimination are just the tip of the iceberg, with Muslim Americans underserved by elected officials across the country. Moreover, assimilation does not help Muslims: even the "successful" ones do not matter. This, of course, has profound implications for Muslim Americans hoping to integrate into politics, particularly at a time when elected representatives are increasingly adopting policies targeting the group.

Taken together, the two audit studies present several important findings, as well as offering advantages over previous scholarship. This is for a number of reasons. First, they assess the representation of Muslim Americans, a group previously understudied in the literature. Second, they measure responsiveness in new domains of constituent representation, namely access to politics in the form of internships and legislative visits. Third, they use a novel, qualitative, and nonrandomized dependent variable in the literature: the helpfulness of the legislator's response. Finally, and perhaps most importantly, in addition to assessing the experiences of individuals, they add a new dimension to audit studies by testing political discrimination against a racialized community.

7.1 BACKGROUND AND THEORY

Extant research on Muslim American representation is limited (Calfano et al., 2019), with only one published study to date assessing the substantive representation of the group (Martin, 2009). Aside from identifying the size of the Muslim population as an important determinant of Muslim substantive representation, this area of scholarly work lacks rigorous theoretical development and quantitative testing.

Despite the dearth of scholarship, there is substantial evidence that the prospects for Muslim inclusion in American democracy appear slim. Literature on the representation of other unpopular minority groups in American politics provides a strong foundation from which expectations can be drawn about legislator responsiveness toward Muslim Americans. Audit studies on legislators, in particular, have served as an important tool for testing political inclusion and incorporation. Responding to constituents is one of the regular duties of legislators and their staff. When they do so, reelection-motivated legislators communicate that they are capable of fulfilling the needs of those in their districts (Mayhew, 1974). Those legislators who please their constituents are ultimately able to win their support, or at least temper negative perceptions. While Fenno's landmark 1978 work suggested that legislators do not discriminate against constituents residing within their congressional districts, other work has identified the importance of descriptive representation as a conduit for a marginalized group's substantive representation (Mansbridge, 1999; Pitkin, 1967).

Across a wide range of areas, audit experiments have demonstrated sizable gaps in responsiveness between Whites and racialized minorities (e.g. Adida, Laitin, and Valfort, 2010; Lavergne and Mullainathan, 2004; Pager, Bonikowski, and Western, 2009; Schulman et al., 1999). In political science, the scholarship has largely shown that minorities are often ignored and underrepresented by elected officials (Broockman, 2013; Butler, 2014; Butler and Broockman, 2011; Butler et al., 2012; Carnes and Holbein, 2015; Distelhorst and Hou, 2014; Einstein and Glick, 2017; Grose et al., 2015; White et al., 2015).

Nevertheless, this body of work has overlooked Muslim Americans, an unpopular group that has moved from a nonsalient and religious group to a salient and racialized outgroup reporting heightened societal and political discrimination (Oskooii, 2016; Westfall et al., 2017, 2016). Understanding the political incorporation of U.S. Muslims is especially important today, as there is growing evidence that in recent elections candidates and campaigns have largely either ignored them or else characterized them as threats. In 2008, the executive director of the Muslim Public Affairs Council stated that presidential candidates "are not willing to have their photo taken, they don't meet with Muslim organizations, and they shy away from any issue that may link them to the Muslim community" (Zoll, 2008). They have not been recruited by Democrats or Republicans in recent times, despite the great lengths many candidates and their campaigns go to in reaching out to other small but politically relevant constituency groups (e.g. American Jews). Even worse than simply being ignored, Muslim Americans have been treated as political scapegoats and liabilities (Zoll, 2008).

In a context of heightened public discrimination, it is unsurprising that elected officials may also be systemically discriminating against Muslim Americans. This therefore leads to the following hypothesis:

Hypothesis 1: All else equal, legislators will be less responsive to Muslim Americans than they are to their white constituents.

Even so, hundreds of thousands if not millions of Muslims participate in American elections (CAIR, 2016a), the great majority of whom are concentrated in battleground states such as Michigan, Pennsylvania, Florida, and Virginia.[1] Furthermore, an October 2016 Council on American–Islamic Relations report found that 74% of Muslims surveyed intended to vote in the 2016 presidential election (CAIR, 2016b). Also, while the number of Muslim voters is still small, the population is expected to double by 2050, increasing their electoral relevance.[2]

Broadly, it is anticipated that strategic politicians will pay less attention to issues that are only important to small numbers of their constituencies. Legislators are reelection motivated (Fenno, 1978), and have limited resources, and so must strategically decide how to win the most votes with the least amount of resources (Butler, 2014). As Bartels (1998, p. 68) reminds us: "rational candidates are impelled by the goal of vote maximization to discriminate among prospective voters, appealing primarily to those who either are likely to vote and susceptible to partisan conversion or reliable supporters susceptible to mobilization."

This chapter posits that legislators may be incentivized to privately court high-propensity Muslim voters. While candidates and legislators may not publicly be meeting with Muslim constituents, there is some evidence they have been quietly courting the Muslim American community for years (Zoll, 2008). This is due, in part, to the fact that most Muslim Americans mirror the socioeconomic dimensions of Whites. Many are wealthy professionals who came to the United States to earn advanced degrees in engineering, medicine, and business (Zoll, 2008); who tend to report college education rates and household incomes above the national median (Barreto and Bozonelos, 2009; Bukhari and Nyang, 2004); and who regularly report participating in politics.[3]

Given legislators likely view Muslims with high socioeconomic status as politically useful, it is anticipated that they will be more responsive to these Muslims as a means of privately recruiting them. This leads to the following hypothesis:

Hypothesis 2: All else equal, legislators will be more responsive to Muslim Americans from a higher socioeconomic status than their low socioeconomic status counterparts.

A legislator's party identification may likewise be an important determinant for Muslim American representation. Prior to 9/11, a nonnegligible portion of Muslim Americans were aligned with the Republican Party, with the 2000 presidential election seeing many Muslim Americans closing ranks behind President Bush and the Republican Party (Barreto and Bozonelos, 2009; Dana et al., 2011;

Findley, 2001). The 9/11 attacks prompted many Muslims to radically shift their partisan identification away from the Republicans to the Democrats. When Muslim Americans vote in elections today, they overwhelmingly support Democrats (Ayers, 2007; Jalalzai, 2009; Jamal, 2005), with their allegiance to the Democratic Party only strengthening over time (see Barreto and Bozonelos, 2009, Table 1; CAIR, 2016a). In no other contest was this as visible as when the Democratic nominee in the 2016 presidential election ran on a platform of "standing up to anti-Muslim hatred and bigotry."[4]

This relationship, however, is nuanced at best. Since 9/11, legislators across the ideological aisle have made numerous negative statements about Muslim Americans, though the vast majority of these have come from Republicans, who have openly critiqued and assigned blame to Muslim Americans. Democrats, meanwhile, have largely done little to publicly embrace or encourage American Muslims to join their coalition. Despite these poor representational prospects, Muslims view Democrats as being more aligned with their interests (CAIR, 2016a).

Given that elected officials who want to maximize their chances of winning reelection are more responsive to constituent members of their own party, and given that Muslim Americans are aligned with the Democratic Party, vote at high rates, and are expected to double in number in the next three decades, the following hypothesis is posited:

Hypothesis 3: All else equal, Democratic legislators will be more responsive to Muslims than are Republicans.

7.2   DATA AND METHODS

For the two audit experiments, state legislators were randomly sent requests to their email addresses from fictional constituents. In the first study, responses to applications for an internship at a state legislator's office by prospective Muslim and white applicants are examined, in order to explore the opportunities Muslim Americans have to be incorporated into the political pipeline. Like members of Congress, state legislators hire interns to conduct their day-to-day business (van Horn, 1989), and one way that political internships are procured in state legislatures is through direct contact via the representative's email address, with some even posting bulletins inviting students to apply.[5]

One question concerning external validity is whether it is unusual for legislators to have Muslim staffers. While the U.S. Congress is more institutionalized than many state legislatures, it serves as a useful starting point. Congress has a number of Muslim staffers, some of whom join the Congressional Muslim Staffer Association (CMSA), an employee association within Congress representing their interests and concerns. Given that Muslims do in fact seek political careers to the extent that a formal organization is required to meet their staffing needs, it is not much of a stretch to assume that some also seek similar positions in state legislative offices.

In the second study, responses to requests for a legislative visit are examined. In particular, it evaluates the ability of Muslim leaders – rather than individuals – to procure a response regarding a proposed legislative visit to discuss integrating the congregation into the district. In Study 2, I only include legislators from states with large Muslim populations, as greater responsiveness (and less discrimination) to Muslim religious leaders is anticipated in states where this is the case.

7.2.1 Who Replies?

Who replies to the emails? Thousands of constituents contact legislators each year, who possess only limited resources to respond to such requests. In 2004, members collectively received more than 200 million emails and letters (Fitch et al., 2005, p. 7). In 2015, when the audit experiments were conducted, that figure had almost certainly risen considerably with the advent and more widespread usage of internet technologies. While the number of communications has risen, the numbers of staff in member offices have remained static since the 1980s, with Fitch et al. (2005, p. 7) writing, "[i]n other words, congressional offices are trying to do more work with roughly the same number of staff they had in the late 1970s." As such, members are not keeping pace with the exponentially increasing number of requests coming from constituents.

State legislators are also facing a rising number of communications from constituents. Compared to the Senate and House of Representatives, however, the resources available to respond to constituent requests, for example regarding internships, are generally much more limited. The U.S. Senate is the most professionalized body in the United States, and can afford to pay their pages (interns). The U.S. House of Representatives is the next most professionalized assembly and, while they do not pay their interns, gaining employment in their offices is much more difficult and competitive. In these two bodies, those who call or email legislators are funneled through low-level staff or interns. State legislatures have much more variation, depending on the level of professionalization.

The National Conference of State Legislatures (NCSL) has classified state legislatures as being either full-time, hybrid, or part-time.[6] Legislators in full-time assemblies treat their position in elected office as a full-time job, and as such are compensated at higher rates, as well as being equipped with large numbers of staff. These assemblies are more similar to Congress than other state legislatures. Next, representatives in hybrid legislatures spend about two-thirds of their work hours being legislators. Their incomes from elected office are typically insufficient to sustain their households and they usually have other sources of income. These representatives have an intermediate number of staff. Part-time legislatures are the least "professionalized" assemblies, with lawmakers spending about half their work hours on legislative work. They are typically not compensated much, and thus rely on other sources of income to make a living. These legislators also have very small numbers of staff, with much of the responsibilities of elected office falling on the legislators themselves.

Finally, it should be noted that part-time legislatures are more Republican-leaning than professional ones. The National Conference of State Legislators lists 14 states[7] as being part-time legislatures – of these, nine have both assemblies dominated by Republicans.[8] Moreover, while in session, the legislative calendar for these bodies is much more intense than that of full-time bodies, which are able to spread out and address the needs of constituents year-round.

The two studies presented in this chapter were conducted on state legislators who come from assemblies with varying levels of professionalization. In the first study, 162 out of 521 (31.09%) responses received by the fictional constituent were sent by the legislators themselves. Legislators from Idaho (13), New Hampshire (11), Pennsylvania (11), Maine (8), Arkansas (8), Connecticut (7), and New York (7) sent the bulk of these emails. Overall, most of these emails – 134 of 162 (82.72%) – were sent by legislators in states that had hybrid or part-time legislatures. In the second study, only 52 of 279 (18.64%) responses were sent by legislators, with legislators from Virginia (17), Illinois (11), Michigan (8), New York (6), and Texas (6), forming the bulk of these.

In the remaining cases, staffers emailed the fictional constituent on behalf of the legislator. As Madonna and Ostrander (N.d., p. 4) write, "[w]hile they may have influence, staff do not dictate outcomes. Staff serve at the pleasure of the member of Congress they serve and are held accountable through a variety of mechanisms (Romzek, 2000)." Thus, staff are responsible for a great deal of contact between legislators and their constituents, even at the state level. The exercise of contacting legislators might then reflect the racial bias of the lowest-ranked staffer tasked with replying to communications.

7.3   ACCESS TO POLITICS FOR INDIVIDUALS: STUDY I

Study 1 tests state legislators' responsiveness to individual constituents requesting an application for a political internship and evaluates the hypotheses articulated above. Testing the availability of access to a political career is compelling, as it demonstrates how the country's representatives integrate groups into the political process, and is a unique form of participation infrequently studied in American politics. Though a sizable amount of research concerns elites and political participation, little attention has been paid to appointed public officials working at the pleasure of Congresspeople. Working in one of these offices offers tremendous contact with and potential influence on political elites, while access to politics through a political career can serve as a gateway through which individuals can affect policies relevant to their groups. Without it, groups face an additional obstacle in securing their rights and having their preferences reflected.

Public service internships began during the Second World War, and despite interns now being staples in political offices and agencies (Gryski, Johnson, and O'Toole, 1987; Hennessy, 1970), scholars have largely ignored questions on the scope, structure, and strategies of these internship programs. As there is no central office managing access to internships at the state, local, or national levels, there is no systemic way to allocate political internships to prospective interns (Hedlund, 1973). Rather, hiring decisions are subjective, with interested applicants relying mostly on informal channels of communication (Hedlund, 1973).

Academics and professionals agree that the internship experience should be an essential part of public service education, as early internship programs have shown promising results regarding the development of administrative skills (Chauhan, 1978). While legislative internships are the least coveted positions due to the clerical tasks entailed, they are temporary and provide the intern with unprecedented access to the legislator and a potential political career. This work can have important policy and career implications; for many individuals, a legislative internship is a rung on the political career ladder, signaling the representative trusts them as a member of their work group (Romzek and Utter, 1996).

However, as with women (Palmer and Simon, 2010), the slow integration of minorities into state legislatures and Congress is likely due in part to the "pipeline theory." The pipeline theory underscores how structural forces – such as the dearth of women or, in this case, minorities in the pipeline (e.g. in internships) – affect the emergence of candidates from these groups in politics (Burrell, 1994; Darcy, Welch, and Clark, 1994; Donovan, 2007; Hardy-Fanta et al., 2007; Thomsen, 2015). Internships serve as a springboard into state legislatures that, in turn, yield the requisite experience to run for congressional office.

Again, as with women compared to men, minorities may be more likely than Whites to consider themselves insufficiently qualified to run for office, and therefore more likely to feel the need to go through the traditional political pipeline (e.g. internships). Thus, in order that marginalized groups attain representation in legislative positions, it is critical they be represented among the pool of interns in legislator offices. In other words, to increase the descriptive representation of a group, it is necessary that more people from that group are incorporated into the pipeline.

Finally, scholarship notes that traditionally disadvantaged groups are penalized by lawmakers, who are less likely to share their political opinions than they are with wealthy and white constituents (Bartels, 2016; Gilens, 2005; Griffin and Newman, 2008). In the first study, therefore, education is used as a proxy for socioeconomic status to test whether it aids Muslim Americans in overcoming the setbacks that result from their racial/religious identity.

7.3.1 *Experimental Design*

To assess whether Muslims face political discrimination, an audit study of state legislators was conducted in February 2015. It was possible to obtain email addresses for 6,630 of the 7,383 state legislators.[9] Moreover, because, as previously noted, American Muslims have historically hailed from high socioeconomic backgrounds, by varying both the religion/race and education level of the fictional applicant, it was assessed whether Muslims with high levels of education can more easily access a political career.

A putatively white and a putatively Muslim alias were used to vary race/religion (Butler and Broockman, 2011), namely "Jake Thompson" and "Abdul Al-Nawad," respectively. The name "Abdul Al-Nawad" was selected as it connotes gendered, racial, and religious cues. Abdul is a common Muslim male first name, while Al-Nawad is a common Middle Eastern, Arab, and Muslim surname. A simple Google image search of the name "Abdul Al-Nawad" reveals a Middle Eastern or South Asian looking male in most, if not all, of the pictures. It is also entirely possible that the name could be construed as "Arab," signaling an Arab Christian or non-Middle Eastern Muslim name. Thus, any evidence of discrimination could therefore be interpreted as legislators exhibiting anti-Arab and not necessarily anti-Muslim bias. Likewise "Jake Thompson" also sends gendered and racial signals, with a Google image search of the name yielding mostly pictures of white men.

Education was used as a proxy for socioeconomic status, with the putative alias either being assigned a degree from a local community college or a degree from Harvard University. Having a degree from Harvard arguably signals high socioeconomic status, while, conversely, having a degree from a community college signals a lower socioeconomic status. The fictional aliases also indicate that they reside in the legislator's state, in order to convey that they are a potential constituent. Many legislators exhibit "in-district bias," whereby they expend resources on and reply to those who are from their districts, and are therefore more likely to be part of a group of citizens who can hold them accountable. In general, we might expect a decrease in responsiveness to individuals who are not from, or who are suspected to not be from, a member's district. However, as treatment states that the applicant is indeed from the member's district, it would be expected any bias would be equal across all treatments.

Figure 7.1 displays the template used, with the experimental manipulations — education level and religion/race — in bold. All treatments ask state legislators for an internship application in the legislator's office.

Table 7.1. *Experimental Design*

Fictional Alias	Block 1 Republican Legislators	Block 2 Democratic Legislators
White high education	945 legislators	718 legislators
White low education	939 legislators	723 legislators
Muslim high education	938 legislators	724 legislators
Muslim low education	939 legislators	704 legislators
Total	3,761 legislators	2,869 legislators

(ABDUL AL-NAWAD / JAKE THOMPSON)

Attn: Hiring Staff

Re: An Internship Position for Summer 2015

To Whom It May Concern:

My name is (**Abdul Al-Nawad** / **Jake Thompson**). I am 22 years old and (**recently finished community college** / **graduated from Harvard University**) with a degree in Political Science. I was born and raised in ___**(legislator's state)**___ and I am very interested in working in your office as an intern to gain more experience in politics; as it is a career I would like to pursue in Washington in the coming years. I believe that an internship in your office would be an invaluable opportunity towards attaining that goal.

Can you please email me an application for an internship position in your local office for summer 2015?

Best regards,

(**Abdul Al-Nawad** / **Jake Thompson**)

FIGURE 7.1 Study 1 experimental template

The four treatment groups are as follows: (1) Treatment 1: white and low education; (2) Treatment 2: Muslim and low education; (3) Treatment 3: white and high education; (4) Treatment 4: Muslim and high education. Table 7.1 displays the experimental design. To test the effect of partisanship, the legislator's party identification was labeled as Block 1 (Republican) and Block 2 (Democrat), with one of the four treatments randomly assigned to state legislators within each block.[10]

Emails were sent to each of the state legislators, with several different email addresses employing variations of the aliases' names in order to increase external validity that the emails were sent from real individuals. To obtain the legislators' email addresses, a list was compiled from each state's Assembly and Senate website. These email addresses are the direct points of contact where legislators have indicated they can be reached. Each office received only one email from one of the four groups.

7.3.2   Results and Discussion

Six months after the experiment was concluded, two coders collected the data on responsiveness. The delay in collecting the data was to account for the fact that the legislative sessions of state legislatures vary from state to state, with some states in session for as little as 50% of the time.[11]

When the fictional constituent received a particularized response from the contacted representative, the "response" variable was assigned a value of 1. When they did not receive a response, the variable was assigned a value of 0.[12]

Overall, state legislators were significantly more likely to discriminate against the Muslim alias compared to the white alias. Table 7.2 displays the mean aggregated results for the key dependent variable – an email response from the contacted representative – and thereby evaluates Hypothesis 1's thesis that legislators will be less responsive to Muslim Americans than to white constituents.

Table 7.2. *Experimental Results: Aggregate Responsiveness Rate by Race/Religion Alias*

Fictional Alias	Response Rate
White	10.16%
	(338/3325)
Muslim	5.44%
Difference	4.7%***

Note: $^{+}$ p < 0.10, * p < 0.05, ** p < 0.01, *** p < 0.001

The results indicate widespread discrimination against Muslims seeking access to a political career, with legislators responding to the white alias almost twice as often as the Muslim alias, thereby confirming Hypothesis 1.

While these response rates may at first glance appear low compared to other audit studies,[13] there are two reasons to believe that the legislators' email addresses were in fact treated. First, in Study 2, in which the same email addresses were utilized, responses were just as high, if not higher, than most audit experiments in political science (Costa, 2017a). Second, asking for an internship is not the same type of request as simply asking a service-related question, as it may demand additional resources from legislators. It should therefore be expected that the response rate would be lower than is the case in other audit studies.

Table 7.3 displays results assessing if socioeconomic status played a role in whether legislators responded to Muslim Americans or not. Models 1 and 2 assess the responsiveness of those legislators who only received either a Muslim high education or a Muslim low education treatment, while Models 3 and 4 assess the responsiveness of those who only received either a white low education or a white high education treatment. In the four models, the white low education and Muslim low education indicators are binary variables connoting whether a legislator responded to an email from the respective disaggregated treatment. As Models 1 and 2 demonstrate, there were no significant differences in responsiveness to the Muslim treatments, regardless of their educational status. Similarly, Models 3 and 4 suggest that responsiveness to the white treatments did not significantly differ from one either, regardless of whether the individual graduated from a local community college or Harvard.

Hypothesis 2 posited that all else being equal, legislators will be more responsive to Muslim Americans from a higher socioeconomic status than their low socioeconomic status counterparts. As Figure 7.2 shows, however, the white high education alias and white

Table 7.3. *Responsiveness of Those Legislators Who Received Muslim Treatments and Those Who Received White Treatments*

	(1) Response	(2) Response	(3) Response	(4) Response
Muslim low education	0.00426	0.00347		
	(0.00575)	(0.00601)		
White low education			−0.00595	−0.00679
			(0.0109)	(0.0109)
Republican		0.000506		−0.00196
		(0.0101)		(0.0131)
Black population size		0.000436		0.0000805
		(0.000786)		(0.00130)
Asian population size		0.000141		−0.000611
		(0.00201)		(0.00151)
Hispanic population size		0.00158		0.000336
		(0.00136)		(0.00201)
Obama margin of victory (2012)		0.00105		0.00135
		(0.000835)		(0.00129)
State Muslim pop. size		$1.90e-09$		$2.41e-09$
		$(1.42e-09)$		$(2.36e-09)$
Constant	0.0523***	−0.0320	0.105***	0.0211
	(0.00823)	(0.0423)	(0.0133)	(0.0619)
n	3305	3305	3325	3325
adj. R^2	−0.000	0.014	−0.000	0.005

Note: Standard errors in parentheses and clustered by state in all models.
Note: $^{+}$ $p < 0.10$, * $p < 0.05$, ** $p < 0.01$, *** $p < 0.001$
Note: Models 1 and 2 include only those legislators who received emails from one of the two Muslim treatments.
Note: Models 3 and 4 include only those legislators who received emails from one of the two White treatments.

low education alias received response rates of 10.46% and 9.87%, respectively, while the Muslim high education and Muslim low education treatments received response rates of 5.23% and 5.66%, respectively. In other words, the results provide little support for Hypothesis 2, with the signal sent by the fictional treatment's name, conveying the individual's religion/race, a far more powerful indicator of responsiveness than their socioeconomic status.

Ultimately, the findings are clear, with legislators less responsive to Muslim treatments than white treatments, irrespective of education levels. High-status Muslim Americans were no more advantaged than their low-status Muslim counterparts in receiving a response about pursuing a political career in a state legislative office, showing that signaling a Muslim American's socioeconomic mobility

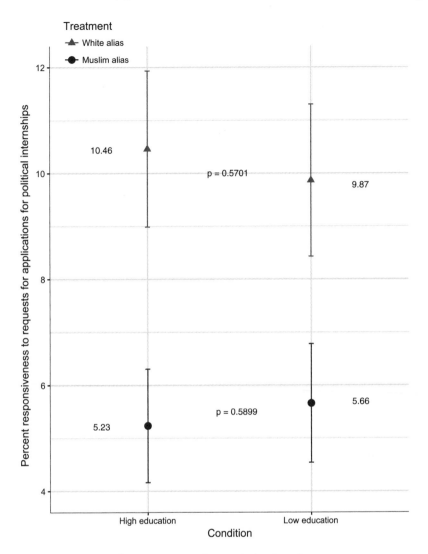

FIGURE 7.2 Aggregate responsiveness to treatment groups

does not offset the "otherizing" connotations conveyed by culture. Finally, and relatedly, low socioeconomic status did not hinder Whites seeking integration into the political labor market. This, of course, has widespread implications for differences in group mobility, with low education not appearing to impede Whites from applying to gain access to a political career. Conversely, high-status Muslims are unable to benefit from their academic achievements, and are only almost half as likely as Whites to be afforded this opportunity.

Next, differences in legislators' partisanship are explored to examine whether Democrats are privately responsive to American Muslims, despite having done little to publicly embrace them. Surveys have found that a majority of Muslim Americans voted for the Democratic nominee in 2008 and 2012; approved of the way Barack Obama handled his job as president; believe the Democratic Party is friendly toward Muslims; and expect that the Democratic Party is more aligned with their interests. A Pew Research Center poll, for instance, found that, in June 2011, 76% of Muslim Americans approved of Obama's performance as president, compared to 46% of the general public.[14] A natural extension, then, is to explore whether Democrats reciprocate the allegiance offered them by Muslim Americans.

Hypothesis 3 posited that, all else being equal, Democratic legislators will be more responsive to Muslims than Republicans. Table 7.4 displays the disaggregated responsiveness rates by party identification. Contrary to the expectation that Democrats may be privately more responsive to Muslim Americans than their Republican counterparts, the results show that not only do both Democrats and Republicans discriminate against the two Muslim treatments, but that they are equally likely to do so. Republicans responded

Table 7.4. *Disaggregated Responsiveness by Party*

Fictional Alias	Republican Legislators	Difference (from WH)	Democratic Legislators	Difference (from WH)
White high education	10.37% (98/945)		10.58% (76/718)	
White low education	9.05% (85/939)	1.32%	10.93% (79/723)	−0.34%
Muslim high education	4.79% (45/938)	5.57%***	5.80% (42/724)	4.78%***
Muslim low education	5.43% (51/939)	4.93%***	5.97% (42/704)	4.62%**

Note: $^{+}$ p < 0.10, * p < 0.05, ** p < 0.01, *** p < 0.001

to the white high education treatment 10.37% of the time and to the white low education treatment 9.05% of the time, compared to responding to the Muslim high education and the Muslim low education treatments 4.79% and 5.43% of the time, respectively.

Similarly, Democrats responded to the white treatments equally – 10.58% to the white high education treatment and 10.93% to the white low education treatment – while significantly discriminating against the Muslim treatments, replying to the Muslim high education and the Muslim low education treatments 5.8% and 5.97% of the time, respectively. Contrary to the expectations of Hypothesis 3, Democrats are no more likely than Republicans to provide Muslim Americans with opportunities for representation, even in a private domain.

Heterogeneous Effects: The Size of a State's Muslim Population
Building off Martin (2009), this section explores whether the size of a state's Muslim population has any moderating effect on responsiveness outcomes. As contact with Muslims is generally rare for many Americans,[15] Muslims may be receiving more attention in these states where the group is more populous, and therefore legislators and their staff are more familiar with them. Extant research has demonstrated that knowing someone from a religious group is linked with having relatively more positive views of that group. As previously discussed, eight states in the U.S. have Muslim populations of higher than 100,000 Muslims, and it is therefore to be expected that in these states contact with Muslims will be more common.

Table 7.5 explores whether responsiveness to Muslims improves in states with large Muslim populations (about 16.15% of legislators in this sample). In Models 1, 3, and 5, the sample is limited to legislators in states where the number of Muslims in the state exceeds 100,000 people, while Models 2, 4, and 6 limit the sample to legislators in states where the number of Muslims is below 100,000 people. Across most model specifications, Muslims continue to face widespread discrimination in states with both large

Table 7.5. *Legislator Responsiveness in States with Large and Small Muslim Populations*

	(1) Response	(2) Response	(3) Response	(4) Response	(5) Response	(6) Response
Muslim	-0.0449*	-0.0470***				
	(0.0175)	(0.00880)				
White low education			0.00305	-0.00806	0.0111	-0.00901
			(0.0296)	(0.0116)	(0.0282)	(0.0114)
Muslim high education			-0.0383	-0.0540***	-0.0315	-0.0547***
			(0.0276)	(0.0107)	(0.0255)	(0.0112)
Muslim low education			-0.0480*	-0.0478***	-0.0412*	-0.0506***
			(0.0200)	(0.0124)	(0.0165)	(0.0132)
Republican					0.0605+	-0.0128
					(0.0296)	(0.00934)
Black population size					-0.00881	-0.000310
					(0.00667)	(0.00109)
Asian population size					-0.00529	-0.000805
					(0.00888)	(0.000824)
Hispanic population size					0.00773*	0.00219
					(0.00325)	(0.00161)
Obama margin of victory (2012)					0.0107+	0.000489
					(0.00469)	(0.00106)
State Muslim pop. size					-1.01e-08+	6.21e-09**
					(4.28e-09)	(1.89e-09)
Constant	0.144***	0.0932***	0.142**	0.0972***	-0.319	0.0459
	(0.0238)	(0.0122)	(0.0316)	(0.0146)	(0.236)	(0.0555)
n	1071	5561	1071	5559	1071	5559
adj. R^2	0.004	0.008	0.002	0.008	0.032	0.016

Note: Standard errors in parentheses.

Note: $^+$ $p < 0.10$, * $p < 0.05$, ** $p < 0.01$, *** $p < 0.001$

Table 7.6. *Responsiveness by Legislators in Small versus Large Muslim Population States*

Fictional Alias	Legislators LMP	Difference (from White or WH)	Legislators SMP	Difference (from White or WH)
White	14.39% (80/556)		9.32% (258/2769)	
Muslim	9.90% (51/515)	4.48%**	4.62% (129/2792)	4.70***
White, high education	14.23% (39/274)		9.72% (135/1389)	
White, low education	14.53% (41/282)	0.3%	8.91% (123/1380)	0.8%
Muslim, high education	10.4% (26/250)	3.83%	4.32% (61/1412)	5.4%***
Muslim, low education	9.43% (25/265)	4.8%*	4.93% (68/1378)	4.78%***

Note: $^+$ p < 0.10, * p < 0.05, ** p < 0.01, *** p < 0.001

and small Muslim populations. In Models 3 and 5, however, the Muslim high education alias loses its negative significance. This could be due to decreased discrimination against Muslims who signal a high socioeconomic status, due to the results possibly being underpowered, or due to legislators from large Muslim population states being more likely to work in full-time or hybrid legislatures and therefore more likely to be in session.

To unpack this further, Table 7.6 displays the raw responsiveness rates to each of the treatments in states with large and small Muslim populations. While these are nonrandomized results, the evidence is nevertheless suggestive that the study is underpowered, and that discrimination against high socioeconomic status Muslims is likely taking place. Looking at the aggregate results, legislators in both small and large Muslim population states were significantly less likely to respond to the Muslim aliases compared to the white aliases. In states with large Muslim populations, legislators responded to the white alias 14.39% of the time, compared to 9.9% for the Muslim alias. In states with small Muslim populations, legislators were more than twice as likely to respond to the white aliases compared to the Muslim aliases, replying to 9.32% and 4.62% of these communications, respectively.

The disaggregated results, moreover, indicate that Muslims are less likely than their white counterparts to receive a response from legislators in states with both small and large Muslim populations, irrespective of their socioeconomic status. Legislators from states with large Muslim populations responded to the white high education alias 14.23% of the time and to the Muslim high education alias 10.4% of the time, while the Muslim low education treatment received a response rate of 9.43%. The differences between the white high education alias and the two Muslim treatments are marginal: 3.83% for the Muslim high education treatment and 4.8% for the Muslim low education treatment. When the sample is subsetted to explore whether the difference in responsiveness to the two Muslim treatments is significant, it becomes nowhere near statistically significant. While this heterogeneous evidence is inconclusive, it indicates that the extent to which Muslim Americans receive representation in states where they constitute large numbers remains an open question.

Finally, one concern that should be highlighted about the conclusions drawn is that perhaps legislators are not offering internships to the fictional aliases simply because they do not have positions available in their offices. Even so, as Costa (2017a) finds in her meta-analysis of the more typical responsiveness outcome, the literature supports the conclusion that the legislative behavior highlighted by the study is driven by personal bias, rather than strategic, electoral considerations. If state legislators are indeed driven by bias in not responding to internship application requests, it could be the case that they do not treat Muslims equally in other respects as well. This finding comes with its limitations, however, as the evidence lacks generalizability. Nevertheless, no matter the intention behind legislators' behavior — for example whether it is due to strategic considerations or bias — the implications are the same: in this context, Muslims are disadvantaged compared to Whites and to Christians.

Exploring the Helpfulness of a Legislator's Response

The results thus far only assess one dimension of discrimination: whether or not the fictional constituent received a response. This, however, ignores the wide variety of services a legislator can provide their constituents. For example, beyond simply replying, a legislator might potentially devote a great deal of time and energy to producing a helpful response.

One important contribution of this work is to introduce a somewhat new, qualitative, and nonrandomized dependent variable to the literature: the helpfulness of the legislator's response. While responsiveness is an appropriate variable to examine in the first instance, it lacks information on whether the response actually helped the fictional constituent to achieve their desired goal. A lack of response reveals very little about the quality of representation a constituent receives, and can just as easily be interpreted as a legislator's negligence as revealing their malice. In contrast, the helpfulness of a legislator's response tests the level of effort put in by those who did in fact reply to the constituent. A helpful response is worth examining, as it has the power to encourage further political participation and engagement, while unhelpful responses (or a lack of a response) can potentially stifle future political behavior.

In Study 1, a helpful response was an email that actually aided the fictional constituent in attaining the internship application they asked for, rather than merely being a reply. For instance, a representative from California wrote, "Thank you for your interest in the internship program here at Assembly member XXX's District Office. As requested, I have attached an application for an intern position with this email. Please send me the application completed and with a copy of your resume via email, fax, or mail."

The literature has previously operationalized several ways of measuring whether the legislator and their staff have provided the constituent with a "good" response (Costa, 2017b). White, Nathan, and Faller (2015), for instance, focus on the accuracy of the response, while Einstein and Glick (2017) assess the tone of the response. These two measures do not, however, assess whether the legislator's response meaningfully assisted the constituent. Overall, legislators sent 521 responses to all fictional aliases, 306 of which were helpful. Prior scholarship has estimated the effect of friendliness in emails conditioned on a response (e.g. White et al., 2015), but recent work has argued that such an approach is flawed.

Coppock (2018) points out that because a reply is a post-treatment outcome in the context of an audit experiment, conditioning on a post-treatment outcome "de-randomizes" an experiment, such that the resulting treatment and control groups no longer have equivalent potential outcomes. The helpfulness dependent variable explored here helps tease out who the legislators actually assisted. Helpful responses are those that aid the fictional alias in attaining the service they asked for, while unhelpful responses are those that do not. In this case, those legislators whose response to the fictional alias assisted them in procuring an application for a political internship are coded as 1, while a 0 indicates that either a response was not received or that it was not helpful.

Table 7.7 displays the heterogeneous effects and does not condition on a response. Of those who responded, the most helpful responses came from legislators in Florida (82.3%), Illinois (86.6%), Indiana (76.9%), Massachusetts (71.4%), Maine (90.9%), New Jersey (86.9%), New York (89.2%), Texas (92.8%), Virginia (85.7%), and Wisconsin (88.9%). What is particularly noteworthy is that these states are not necessarily among the most professionalized state legislatures, according to the NCSL. With the exception of New York, these states are "full-time lite," "hybrid," and "part-time lite" state legislatures. The results show that even some of the legislators who sent a reply, and therefore appear at first glance not to be discriminating against the Muslim treatments, actually were discriminating once their responses are evaluated. As depicted in Models 1 and 2 in Table 7.7 the white treatments were significantly more likely to receive a helpful response than their Muslim counterparts.

In Table 7.7, the dependent variable "Response Helpful" is operationalized such that 1 corresponds to a helpful response and 0

Table 7.7. *Study 1 Exploring the Helpfulness of a Legislator's Response*

	RH	RH	RH	RH
Muslim alias	−0.0341***	−0.0342***		
	(0.00670)	(0.00680)		
White low education			0.00124	0.000443
			(0.00840)	(0.00812)
Muslim low education			−0.0339***	−0.0349***
			(0.00856)	(0.00878)
Muslim high education			−0.0331***	−0.0330***
			(0.00822)	(0.00850)
Republican		0.00476		0.00477
		(0.00701)		(0.00700)
Black population size		−0.000286		−0.000285
		(0.000452)		(0.000453)
Asian population size		−0.0000366		−0.0000345
		(0.00110)		(0.00110)
Hispanic population size		0.000152		0.000150
		(0.000951)		(0.000952)
Obama margin of		0.00138*		0.00138*
victory (2012)		(0.000551)		(0.000552)
State Muslim pop. Size		3.94e−09***		3.94e−09***
		$(8.84e - 10)$		$(8.81e - 10)$
Constant	0.0632***	−0.0319	0.0625***	−0.0322
	(0.00896)	(0.0243)	(0.0103)	(0.0238)
n	6632	6630	6630	6630
adj. R^2	0.006	0.030	0.006	0.030

Note: Standard errors in parentheses.
Note: [+] $p < 0.10$, [*] $p < 0.05$, [**] $p < 0.01$, [***] $p < 0.001$
Note: RH is the "helpfulness of the response" dependent variable, where 1 indicates a helpful response and 0 indicates that no response was received or that the response was not helpful.

indicates that either a response was not received or that it was not helpful. The disaggregated Muslim low and high education treatments in Models 3 and 4 in Table 7.7 together lead to an important finding: Muslims receive less helpful responses than their white high education counterparts. The disaggregated results in Models 3 and 4 reveal that this discriminatory result is significantly connected to both the Muslim high education and Muslim low education treatments. Muslim aliases, regardless of their socioeconomic background, were significantly less likely to receive helpful responses from elected officials compared to their white high education counterparts. All of this suggests that the socioeconomic background of the Muslim constituent likely does not matter for the quality of representation they experience, nor does it offset the negative racial/religious signal sent to the legislator by their name.

Importantly, these findings are suggestive of more widespread discrimination than previous studies have measured. As most audit studies have stopped short of exploring whether their treatments have been provided with meaningful assistance, it could very well be the case that discrimination against minorities is much greater than scholarship has previously found.

The results from Study 1 point to a couple of important conclusions. First, that ordinary American Muslims are unable to access a political career at the same rate as their white counterparts, regardless of socioeconomic status. While this finding may not be surprising, it is troubling, as Muslim integration does not increase even with upward socioeconomic mobility. Second, though Muslims strongly identify with the Democratic Party today, they do not have strong allies among Democratic representatives. These conclusions raise questions about the prospects Muslims have for representation in American democracy, especially since numerous states are rapidly introducing legislation, such as anti-Islam and anti-sharia laws, that specifically target Muslims.

7.4   ACCESS TO POLITICS FOR COMMUNITIES: STUDY 2

A second audit experiment on state legislators was run in August 2015 to address two lingering questions on the ability of Muslim Americans to access politics. First, do legislators discriminate against group leaders as they do against individuals? Second, do Muslims experience representation when they send a clear and direct signal of their faith? In Study 2, these questions are addressed by evaluating the ability of the Muslim leaders – rather than individuals – to procure a response when asking for a legislative visit to discuss integrating their congregation into the district.

This is important because, while legislators may reason away their dismissal of a lone individual, members of marginalized groups are truly hindered from integrating into the political arena when their community leaders are ignored. When such leaders are unable to reach representatives to discuss the pressing issues facing their members, representation opportunities become scant. A legislator's conduct toward leaders of marginalized communities may therefore reveal the inherent inability of individual members of that community to gain representation.

Unlike Study 1, a clear and direct signal of the fictional constituent's faith is sent in Study 2, to address the issue of race and religion being conflated. In Study 1, the fictional constituent's name connoted a "Muslim" identity through a name that was ostensibly Middle Eastern-, Arab-, or Muslim-sounding. The four treatments were not, however, explicitly linked to religion, whether Islam or Christianity. In Study 2 either "Pastor John Rogers" or "Imam Yassir Siddiqui" – individuals identifying as religious leaders – requests a legislative visit to better integrate their respective "congregations" into the legislator's district.

Additionally, Study 2 is solely conducted on legislators from those states with large Muslim populations, as greater responsiveness (and less discrimination) to Muslim religious leaders is anticipated in states where the Muslim community forms a large proportion of the population. In these states, it is anticipated that contact between legislators and the Muslim community takes place more frequently and is more normalized. Legislators, then, may be willing to court Muslim leaders – and by extension, their community – to broaden their electoral constituencies. This leads to the following hypothesis:

Hypothesis 4: Legislators in states with large Muslim populations will be equally responsive to Muslims and Christian religious leaders, all else being equal.

7.4.1 Experimental Design

In Study 2, randomized emails asking for a legislative visit were sent to state legislators' email addresses from two fictional religious leaders in eight states with large Muslim populations. This scenario

Table 7.8. *Study 2 Template*

(1) Dear Representative _____,
(2) My name is **(Pastor John Rogers /Imam Yassir Siddiqui)**.
(3) I am a local **(Christian/Muslim)** leader, here in __(insert state)__.
(4) I am writing you to ask for a moment of your time and to schedule a legislative visit so that I can come discuss ways to better integrate my congregation in the district.
(5) Any assistance in this matter is greatly appreciated.
(6) Sincerely,
(7) **(Pastor John Rogers/Imam Yassir Siddiqui)**

Note: Bolded items were manipulated.

was chosen for several reasons. First, legislative visits are a service that legislators provide to their constituents that benefit members of both parties. Second, legislative visits provide elected officials with information pertaining to constituents represented by community leaders and PAC organizers (Chin, Bond, and Geva, 2000). During a legislative visit, elected officials can gather valuable information about their constituents' opinions and preferences (Butler, 2014). Third, scheduling a legislative visit is revealing, as the legislator and his staff must decide not only whether to respond to the person asking for the visit, but also whether to expend a scarce and strategic resource: their time. Given the community leader aliases ask for a legislative visit to integrate their members into the district, by extension, the study is testing whether Muslim communities can procure legislators' time in order to gain representational benefits. Table 7.8 displays the text of the emails sent to elected officials in Study 2.

In sum, 1,244 emails were randomly assigned and sent to state legislators and blocked according to the legislator's party identification (Table 7.9). Legislators responded to 35.5% of the emails sent, a much higher aggregated response rate than in Study 1 (7.8%). As noted previously, the same email addresses were used for state legislators in Study 1 as were used in Study 2, with the difference in

Table 7.9. *Study 2 Experimental Design*

Fictional Alias	Block 1 Republican Legislators	Block 2 Democratic Legislators
Christian Pastor	314 legislators	308 legislators
Muslim Imam	314 legislators	308 legislators
Total	628 legislators	616 legislators

Table 7.10. *Responsiveness by Religion Alias*

Fictional Alias	Responsiveness
Christian Pastor	42.12 %
Christian Pastor	(262/622)
Muslim Imam	28.94%
Difference	13.18%***

Note: $^{+}$ p < 0.10, * p < 0.05, ** p < 0.01, *** p < 0.001

response rates possibly due in part to differences in the nature of the requests. Moreover, while the aggregated response rate in Study 1 was 7.8%, across states with large Muslim populations this increased to 12.23% (which, of course, is still much lower than 35.5%). The high aggregate response rate in Study 2 compared to Study 1 may indicate that political leaders are much more likely to respond to leaders of constituent communities than they are to individual constituents.

7.4.2 Results: Study 2

Despite the fact that across both studies legislators appear to be more attentive to group leaders, the Muslim community continues to encounter barriers when attempting to access politics and politicians. As Table 7.10 indicates, the pastor treatment received a 42.12% response rate compared to the imam treatment's 28.94% response rate. These results remain consistent even when controlling for other variables and clustering standard errors by state. The differences in responsiveness to the Muslim leader treatment compared to that of the Christian leader treatment are striking: even in states with large Muslim populations and even when the contacting constituent is a community leader, Muslims continue to face widespread discrimination.

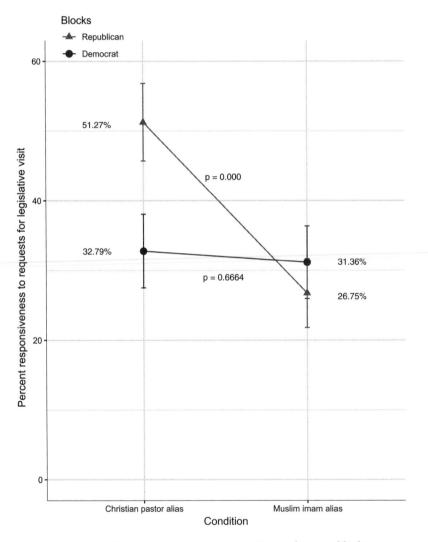

FIGURE 7.3 Percent responsiveness to treatments by party blocks

However, when the legislator's party affiliation is examined, variations in responsiveness can be seen, the results of which are displayed in Figure 7.3.

Democrats did not significantly differ in their responses to the imam and pastor treatments, responding to the pastor treatment 32.79% of the time and the imam treatment 31.36% of the time, a difference that is statistically insignificant. Republicans, on the other hand, were 1.9 times more likely to court the Christian congregation (51.27% response rate) compared to their Muslim counterparts (26.75% response rate).

Republicans, though, did not wholly ignore the Muslim community, with their response rate to the imam treatment (26.75%) not significantly different from that of the Democrats (31.36%). There are several ways of interpreting this. On the one hand, the 26.75% response rate seen in Study 2 is significantly higher than the 5.44% response rate to the Muslim treatments seen in Study 1. On the other hand, Republicans were almost twice as likely to respond to non-Muslim treatments as Muslim treatments. It might also be the case that Republicans are much more likely to respond to church-based inquiries as this is typically part of their support base. Future studies should therefore observe whether responsiveness to Muslim treatments is similar to other racialized minorities, such as Hispanics, Asian Americans, and African Americans. The results indicate that in these states, Muslim communities are, by and large, equally likely to be courted by legislators from both parties.

Unpacking this finding further, the helpfulness of the legislator's response used in Study 1 is again introduced. A helpful response, coded as 1, is recorded if the legislator's reply assists the fictional alias in scheduling a legislative visit, while an unhelpful response, coded as 0, is recorded if it does not. The results show that while the Christian treatment received more replies overall from state legislators, when the Muslim treatment did receive responses from legislators, they were significantly more likely to be helpful compared to their Christian counterparts. Of the 1,244 emails sent in total,

Table 7.11. *Study 2 Exploring the Helpfulness of a Legislator's Response: Experimental Effects*

Fictional Alias	Overall	Block 1 Republican Legislators	Block 2 Democratic Legislators
Christian pastor	21.06% (131/622)	27.71% (87/314)	14.28% (44/308)
Muslim imam	23.79% (148/622)	21.97% (69/314)	25.65% (79/308)

622 responses were received. Of the 180 responses received by the imam treatment, 148 (82.22%) were helpful. By contrast, of the 262 responses the pastor treatment received, only 131 (50%) were helpful. Importantly, this trend extends to state legislators from both parties.

As with Study 1, bias is introduced into the analysis through examining only those legislators who replied to an email (Coppock, 2018). To address this potential threat, the analyses in Tables 7.11 and 7.12 code the dependent variable as follows: 1 indicates a helpful response and 0 indicates that either a response was not received or that it was not helpful. In Study 2, a helpful response was an email that actually aided the fictional constituent in arranging a meeting with the legislator, with one example being the response from a legislator in the Michigan assembly, part of which read, "Would you be able to meet in Lansing on October 6th at 11:30 a.m.?" This email was deemed helpful because it proposed a meeting soon after (seven days) being contacted, and provided an in-person meeting time within a month of the original email being sent.

Tables 7.11 and 7.12 demonstrate much smaller differences in helpful responses than would be the case if 0 only corresponded to those who had replied but were not helpful. The results show that discrimination does not exist in the aggregate, and only appears when the legislator's party identification is examined. Models 3 and 4 in Table 7.12 demonstrate that Republicans only discriminate slightly against the imam treatment, but that Democrats are significantly likelier to provide a helpful response. As Table 7.11 denotes,

Table 7.12. *Study 2 Exploring the Helpfulness of a Legislator's Response*

	RH	RH	RH (Rep. Legislators)	RH (Dem. Legislators)
Muslim leader treatment	0.0273	0.0314	−0.0553[+]	0.118*
	(0.0269)	(0.0255)	(0.0272)	(0.0371)
Republican		0.0312		
		(0.0215)		
Black population size		0.0139***	0.0105***	0.0160**
		(0.00130)	(0.00183)	(0.00436)
Asian population size		0.0219***	0.0237***	0.0241**
		(0.00134)	(0.00249)	(0.00495)
Hispanic population size		−0.00587***	−0.00250[+]	−0.0107***
		(0.000624)	(0.00124)	(0.00184)
Obama margin of victory (2012)		−0.0114***	−0.0105***	−0.0138***
		(0.000624)	(0.00139)	(0.00209)
State Muslim pop. size		5.99e−09***	1.82e−09	1.05e−08**
		(6.33e−10)	(2.02e−09)	(2.23e−09)
Constant	0.211***	0.532***	0.596***	0.601**
	(0.0288)	(0.0621)	(0.0609)	(0.126)
n	1244	1244	628	616
adj. R^2	0.000	0.015	0.009	0.035

Note: Standard errors in parentheses.
Note: [+] p < 0.10, * p < 0.05, ** p < 0.01, *** p < 0.001
Note: RH is a different operationalization of the "helpfulness of the response" dependent variable, where 1 indicates a helpful response and 0 indicates that no response was received or that the response was not helpful.

Republicans and Democrats were helpful to the imam treatment in over 20% of all cases (21.97% and 25.65%, respectively). While Republicans were significantly more likely to reply to the pastor treatment, when they did reply to the imam treatment, they were still somewhat helpful.

Taken together, these findings indicate that efforts by Muslim leaders to gain access to politics are often ignored by legislators, even in states where they form a large proportion of the population. However, in instances where Muslim community leaders are not ignored and do in fact receive a response from legislators, they are significantly more likely than their Christian counterparts to be offered an opportunity to meet with elected representatives to discuss the integration of their congregation into the political process. This counterintuitive finding provides some hope that when they are given access to legislators, their representation will be meaningful. Nonetheless, these results could also be an indication of the fact that the legislators perceive (in a negative sense, and perhaps based on stereotypes) that Muslim congregations are not currently "integrated" into the wider community compared to Christians, and so perceive some "intervention" at a legislator level is required.

7.5   IMPLICATIONS AND CONCLUSION

Understanding differences in responsiveness by elected officials to their constituencies along racialized lines is critical, as it reveals the quality of representation that groups can expect to receive. This is a particularly important gap to fill given how little is known about the prospects for political incorporation of understudied groups, such as Muslim Americans. This chapter has shown that legislators discriminate against American Muslims, regardless of their socioeconomic status and irrespective of whether group leaders, as opposed to individual members, seek assistance. In most cases, legislators' party identification does not matter for responsiveness to Muslim Americans, with the only instance in the studies revealing a positive story for the Muslim American community being that when legislators did reply to Muslim community leaders, they were equally (Republicans) and significantly more likely (Democrats) to provide a helpful response.

One explanation for the widespread discrimination by members of both political parties found in this study is that, as with African Americans, Democrats are able to electorally capture (Frymer, 1999) Muslims without having to be responsive to or inclusive of them in the political process. In other words, as the Muslim vote is already solidly in favor of Democrats, Democrats feel free to ignore Muslims. Voter demands may also play another role in moderating how representatives treat Muslim constituents and community leaders. As previously discussed, negative attitudes toward Muslim Americans are pervasive among both Republican and Democratic voters, and it could be the case that legislators of both parties reason that they have more to lose than gain vote-wise by engaging with Muslim Americans.

All of this raises questions about the prospects of Arab and Muslim American political power and inclusion in the political process, especially given that the language and protections of liberalism may be excluding U.S. Muslims (Gutterman and Murphy, 2014). Prospects for Muslim American inclusion in American politics may well be contingent on descriptive – rather than substantive – representation. Today, three Muslims serve in the House of Representatives, two of whom are women. Not all Muslim candidates are successful, and as highlighted in the Introduction, performing assimilation does not necessarily grant Muslims access to politics. Abdul El-Sayed ran as a Democratic candidate in Michigan's 2018 gubernatorial race, but despite running in a state with a large Muslim population, was unable to secure the nomination. Thus, Arab and Muslim political power may lie in the hands of their own community through civic engagement.

A robust scholarship has shown, of course, that U.S. Muslims are motivated toward greater political participation when they perceive greater political or institutional discrimination and threat (Oskooii, 2016; Schoettmer, 2015). This mobilizing capacity, motivated in large part through mosques (Dana, Wilcox-Archuleta, and Barreto, 2017; Jamal, 2005), cannot be underscored enough, and may serve as the defining path forward for Muslims seeking increased political incorporation. All the while, policies affecting the Muslim American population are being introduced and enacted by elected representatives, from state legislators all the way up to the president himself. When the voices of Muslim Americans are muted to such an extent, scholars, practitioners, and policymakers alike should consider whether and how Muslim Americans can hope to attain representation in American democracy.

8   The Flipside: Muslim American Experiences of Discrimination

Prior chapters have demonstrated the pervasiveness of Muslim American resentment and discrimination. There is an abundance of evidence that Muslim Americans are portrayed negatively in the media, treated differently by legislators, and viewed with resentment by the masses. It remains an open question, however, whether Muslim Americans are aware of their positioning. This chapter, therefore, examines how much discrimination Muslim Americans perceive, whether this changes how they behave politically, and what their anxieties are for the future. Specifically, the chapter asks if Muslim Americans are aware of such discrimination.

Because of the numerous constraints on surveying representative populations of Muslim Americans, the chapter relies on convenience samples of those who identify themselves as "Muslim." Ascribing the panethnic "Muslim" label to individuals is problematic for several reasons: (1) the category may mistakenly include individuals who phenotypically embody the traditional markers of the "Muslim" person, but who are not in fact Muslim; (2) the category may include numerous "secular" Muslims whose families originate from Muslim-majority countries, yet who themselves do not (a) identify as Muslims, or (b) practice the religion; or (3) the category may fail to incorporate many individuals who are "Muslim" due to the Census not collecting information on the group and many MENA-originating individuals who are instead counted grouped under another category.

As such, analyses in this chapter are only conducted on those who themselves identify as Muslims. To paint a baseline picture of U.S. Muslims' sociopolitical experiences from their own perspective, the chapter first provides a brief sketch of policies that may explain why (1) trust in governmental institutions might be low;

and (2) why perceptions of societal discrimination might be high. Next, and because U.S. Muslims report that discrimination, racism, prejudice, and policies targeting them are among the most important problems facing Muslims today, the chapter explores Muslim American (1) anxiety and fear of catastrophic events, and (2) experiences with institutional and societal discrimination. The results of the research indicate that U.S. Muslims' trust in government is low; that they experience heightened levels of anxiety and discrimination; and that they report having retreated from the public sphere.

As touched upon in Chapters 1 and 5, navigating which group to evaluate is a difficult task, and begs the questions: How do Muslim Americans see themselves? Do those grouped under the "Muslim American" label feel they belong to the group? There is a great deal of anecdotal evidence that, prior to 9/11, many immigrant Muslims did not identify as Muslim first, but were rather much more likely to identify with their national origin. In many respects, this is intuitive, given that the discrimination many experienced was mainly disseminated along racial or national origin lines. In the 1960s, Black Muslims rallied for racial causes and were prominent players in the Civil Rights movement under the leadership of individuals such as Malcolm X. Meanwhile, Iranians in America were targeted along national origin lines and referred to as "camel jockeys." The ongoing conflict between the Palestinians and the Israelis, the 1993 World Trade Center bombing, and the Gulf Wars also gave rise to discrimination against Arab Americans along ethnic lines, many of whom worried that such events would bring to the surface anti-Arab sentiment.[1]

As discussed in Chapter 5, there is considerable evidence that the media has, in the years since the attacks of September 11, 2001, settled on the "Muslim American" panethnic label to refer to the group in question (see Figure 5.1). However, resistance among some to being labeled as part of this "group" might be expected for several reasons.

First, when imposed by the public, the "Muslim American" label may include those who appear Muslim because they phenotypically embody the traditional markers of the "Muslim" person, but who are in fact secular, atheists, or perhaps even from other religious groups. Members of the Sikh community, who are often mistaken for Muslims because of their beards and turbans, have become targets for zealots seeking revenge since the 9/11 attacks. In August 2012, for example, a shooter entered a Sikh temple in Wisconsin and killed six people. In response, one member of the Wisconsin Sikh community told the *New York Times*, "Everyone here is thinking this is a hate crime for sure ... People think we are Muslims."[2]

Second, there are numerous "secular" individuals born into Muslim families who would inadvertently be classified under the "Muslim American" label. Often, their families originate from Muslim-majority countries, despite the fact that the individuals themselves do not (a) identify as Muslims; nor do they (b) practice the religion.

Third, race is a difficult category to rely on as a proxy for the "Muslim American" label. As Chapter 1 explains, the Census has instructed those originating from Middle Eastern countries that they are white. Historically, when the white classification failed them, national origin and ancestry – and not religious background – became their default identity. Therefore, the all-encompassing "Muslim American" label ignores the historical rivalries among those classified as such. As Maghbouleh (2017) reminds us, Iranians were taught by their families that they were the original Aryans, and are distinguishable from Arabs. Part of this distancing practice is rooted in historical Middle Eastern conflicts spanning millennia, but part of the practice is also an active effort to escape hostilities arising in a post-9/11 world that holds Sunni and Muslim "Arabs" responsible for the instability, conflict, and violence taking place in that region of the world.

Of course, there is also the looming fact that it does not really matter in terms of public perception how individuals covered under any umbrella group actually feel about the panethnic label they are grouped into. For the most part, these distinct and diverse identities are conflated in the public's mind, and individuals will be coded without much thought or knowledge. The February 2017 shooting of two Indian men at a Kansas bar underscores this point. The 9-1-1 call later revealed that a white man had admitted to shooting two "Iranian" people. One's Islamic religion per se perhaps does not matter for being identified as Muslim by the masses, but, rather, one's phenotypic distinctiveness relative to Whites is a determinant for how many are treated.

8.1 MUSLIM AMERICANS' TRUST IN GOVERNMENT IS LOW

Trust in institutions, such as the police, among minority communities generally is relatively low. This is no different among Muslim Americans, with Black Muslims especially having historically had a strained relationship with law enforcement (Karam, 2012). Even prior to the 9/11 attacks, mistrust had translated to a lack of communication on both sides, with orthodox Muslims and those from the Nation of Islam hesitating to report hate crimes to officers and law enforcement. For example, Karam describes how law enforcement officers allegedly entered a New York City mosque with guns drawn in response to a bogus 911 call regarding an ongoing burglary (Karam, 2012). Karam also details another example of pre-9/11 tensions in which 30 Newark police officers invaded a Muslim couple's home without a warrant, interrupting 40 worshipers who were attending Ramadan celebrations. During the intrusion, one police officer responded to complaints by stating "he didn't give a fuck" what month it was. Later, the officers realized they were at the wrong address.

In the aftermath of 9/11, the relationship between police officers and the Muslim community only worsened. The NYPD launched a program whereby plainclothes officers were dispatched to Muslim neighborhoods and mosques in order to eavesdrop on conversations and build detailed casefiles on where individuals ate, prayed, and shopped.[3] The police department's own published work on the surveillance program demonstrates that law enforcement conflated the practice of counterradicalization with the behaviors of millions of American Muslims leading ordinary lives (Kalin and Lajevardi, 2017; Shamas and Arastu, 2010): common markers of religiosity, such as wearing Islamic clothes, having a beard, becoming involved in social activism and community issues, and giving up drinking and smoking, were viewed as "typical signatures" of latent Islamic extremism (Shamas and Arastu, 2010). From U.S. Muslims' perspective, this program indicated that the police viewed their every action with suspicion. Activist Linda Sarsour, quoted by the *New York Times*, expressed the effect the program had on the community:

> "[t]he Demographics Unit created psychological warfare in our community ... Those documents, they showed where we live. That's the cafe where I eat. That's where I pray. That's where I buy my groceries. They were able to see their entire lives on those maps. And it completely messed with the psyche of the community."[4]

The Institute for Social Policy and Understanding (ISPU), a research organization focused on the American Muslim community and its place in American democracy, found that in setting up "community outreach" meetings with Muslims, rather than simply wanting to create trust, government officials had more duplicitous aims (Aziz, 2012). During the Bush and Obama years, millions of dollars were spent flying federal agency bureaucrats across the country in order to meet Muslim leaders. Unbeknownst to those they were meeting, however – some of whom years later found themselves under investigation – the government representatives were secretly recording their meetings, as well as taking notes on personal information, even in instances where there was no evidence of terrorism. These community outreach meetings were later revealed to be nothing more than a "fishing expedition" among Muslim communities nationwide, laying the foundation for future sting operations (Aziz, 2012). As such, the government arguably alienated its most important counterterrorism ally: the Muslim American community (Aziz, 2012).

The NSA also launched a warrantless national surveillance program that lasted from 2001 to 2007. Years after the unlawful program launched, the Intercept reported that the NSA and FBI had been covertly monitoring the emails of prominent Muslim Americans,[5] confirming many Muslims' suspicions that their calls and email communications had been subject to warrantless searches.

Unlawful detentions of Muslims gave rise to panic among the American Muslim community, and, in 2005, the American Civil Liberties Union released a Human Rights Watch report revealing that:

> since the attacks of September 11, 2001, at least seventy men living in the United States – all Muslim but one – have been thrust into a Kafkaesque world of indefinite detention without charges, secret evidence, and baseless accusations of terrorist links. They have found themselves not at Guantnamo Bay or Abu Ghraib but in America's own federal prison system, victims of the misuse of the federal material witness law in the U.S. government's fight against terrorism. (Human Rights Watch, 2005)

FBI training teaches counterterrorism agents that "main stream" [sic] American Muslims are likely to be terrorist sympathizers; that the Prophet Mohammed was a "cult leader"; and that the Islamic practice of giving charity is no more than a "funding mechanism for combat."[6] At the Bureau's training ground in Quantico, Virginia, agents are shown a chart contending that the more "devout" a Muslim, the more likely he is to be "violent." Those destructive tendencies cannot be reversed, with an FBI instructional presentation claiming: "Any war against non-believers is justified" under Muslim law; and a "moderating process cannot happen if the Koran continues to be regarded as the unalterable word of Allah."[7]

Even President Obama, who was often incorrectly labeled as a Muslim himself, did little to support the constitutional rights of U.S.

Muslims, and in fact the Obama era saw the implementation of the Countering Violent Extremism (CVE) program (Tekelioglu, 2019). In March 2017, the Brennan Center revealed that, in practice, CVE programs almost exclusively targeted American Muslim communities (Brennan Center, 2017), relying primarily on debunked methodologies that aim to identify potential terrorists based on their supposedly radical views. The result was that innocent people were implicated and distrust was sown between Muslim American communities and law enforcement (Brennan Center, 2017). This perpetual myth that U.S. Muslims pose a threat and so should be subject to suspicion has had enduring effects on the community (Kalin and Lajevardi, 2017), with a 2013 qualitative survey finding that a spy program had a "chilling effect" on the community's mobilization capacity (Shamas and Arastu, 2010).

It also does not appear that U.S. Muslims' trust in government has increased in the almost two decades since 9/11. As a 2017 Pew Research Center survey on American Muslims demonstrates, the group remain mistrustful of law enforcement officials and skeptical of the integrity of government sting operations, with almost a third of respondents believing law enforcement had arrested mostly people who were tricked and did not pose a real threat (Pew, 2017). Moreover, U.S. Muslims are not convinced that such covert monitoring policies have ended (Gillum, 2019), with a third of respondents in the Pew survey stating that they were either very worried (15%) or somewhat worried (20%) that the government monitors their phone calls and emails because of their religion.

The U.S. Muslim community's anxieties likely increased substantially with the election of Donald Trump as president and, subsequently, when the first travel ban executive order was enacted. Just weeks after the 2016 election, Muslims across the country feared they were being surveilled – rather than merely surveyed – when asked to indicate their religion on an automated telephone poll conducted by a nonprofit organization (Calfano et al., 2019; Kalin and Lajevardi, 2017).[8] U.S. Muslims' reactions to surveillance, monitoring, and detention should not come as a surprise to observers; the group are uniquely aware that the cost of not acting as the country's "eyes and ears" can potentially result in the wholesale monitoring and policing of their everyday lives. In effect, the Muslim ban executive order was simply further proof of what they were afraid of: that what had been happening in secret regarding monitoring the community was now openly touted as national policy.

All of this suggests that scholars investigating Muslim Americans should be wary of inadvertently inducing fear, social desirability bias, or anxiety by partnering with organizations, and should avoid conducting surveys in such a way that might frighten the population into self-censorship and segregation.

8.2 MEASUREMENT LIMITATIONS

While some surveys have indicated that Muslim Americans report experiencing societal and institutional discrimination (Oskooii, 2016; Rippy and Newman, 2006; Westfall et al., 2017), research on Muslim Americans is limited by the fact that researchers cannot be certain what a nationally representative sample should even look like because the U.S. Census does not collect information on religion. Moreover, information on Middle Eastern Muslims is further muddied by the fact that those from the Middle East and North Africa must indicate that they are white.[9]

Surveying nationally representative samples of Muslims is thus both extremely costly and extremely difficult (Barreto and Dana, 2019; Calfano et al., 2019; Dana et al., 2017, 2018; Hobbs and Lajevardi, 2019; Kalin and Lajevardi, 2017). Representative, rich, systematic, and aggregate data on Muslim American sociopolitical attitudes and behaviors is simply not as readily available as it is for other stigmatized groups (Calfano et al., 2019). This is exacerbated by the fact that Muslim Americans often fear they are being surveilled when asked to participate in polls.[10]

Data limitations also restrict researchers' abilities to study the effects of heightened discrimination. Without panel data or frequently conducted large-scale surveys of Muslims, it is not possible to measure shifts in perception of discrimination, self-esteem, or political participation. Much of the extant literature on the behavior and attitudes of racial and religious minorities encounters challenges in recruiting minority participants, and even once participants are recruited, results can be plagued by social desirability bias. In the face of these restraints, therefore, researchers often combine qualitative and quantitative evidence to build a portrait of minority attitudes and behavior. These data and measurement constraints have limited our understanding of how the current sociopolitical environment has affected Muslim American behavior, and much more scholarship on how the group fares in the country today is required.

Even so, the legitimate fear is that there is a great deal of discrimination currently affecting Muslim Americans on profound dimensions. As previewed in Chapter 2, Hobbs and Lajevardi (2019) have introduced a macro-level measurement of Arab and Muslim American behavior, and provided aggregate-level evidence that the group shifted its behavior and retreated in light of the discrimination faced in the 2016 presidential election. In fact, the evidence demonstrates that heightened political discrimination has resulted in isolating and restrictive behaviors among Arab and Muslim Americans, who have reduced their online visibility and reported fading from the public sphere (Hobbs and Lajevardi, 2019).

Thus, on the one hand, the behavior and attitudes of Muslim Americans are difficult to observe and measure, while on the other hand, anecdotal evidence suggests that the country's surveillance programs during the Bush and Obama years, as well as the 2016 election season, have led to negative – and arguably antidemocratic – outcomes for the group. This makes it all the more important to understand how Muslim Americans have responded to their marginalization.

8.3 ARE MUSLIMS AWARE OF THEIR POSITIONING IN THE U.S. SOCIOPOLITICAL CONTEXT?

How do Muslims view their positioning within U.S. society? How much discrimination do they perceive? These are important questions, made all the more pressing given that Muslims are aware the government is infiltrating their communities with sting operations and imposing prolonged detentions that come with gag orders.

To explore these questions, scholars can turn to data collected by research institutes, such as the Pew Research Center or ISPU. Both of these research centers conduct surveys on Muslims in America, and both go to considerable efforts to ensure that their samples are as representative as possible. Scholars may also interview or survey Muslims themselves in order to acquire data, though these will usually not be representative. Below, findings are presented from Pew and ISPU in order to establish how Muslim Americans perceive levels of discrimination against their group in recent times.

Pew's 2017 survey of 1,001 Muslim Americans[11] demonstrates that the community is facing numerous challenges,[12] with three-quarters of Muslim respondents (compared to 69% of the American public) reporting there was "a lot" of discrimination against Muslims in the U.S. Over two-thirds (68%) reported that Donald Trump made them feel worried, while half (50%) agreed that it had become more difficult to be a Muslim in the U.S. in recent years. As Pew's survey results show, Muslims are mostly concerned about discrimination, with all of the cited top ten "most important problems facing Muslims today" pertaining to the issue.

Pew concludes there is no doubt that U.S. Muslims are experiencing concerns and worries about the future of the country and their place in American society, especially in the wake of Trump's election.[13] Most are dissatisfied with the direction of the country, a reversal of opinion compared to 2011, during the Obama years. A majority of Muslims in America see the Republican Party and the president as unfriendly toward their community, with these concerns being most pronounced among women and U.S.-born individuals.

ISPU also surveyed a nationally representative sample of 2,389 U.S. Muslims in 2017, with their summary revealing that Muslim Americans disproportionately report experiencing negative effects as a result of the political climate (ISPU, 2017): "Muslims (38%) and

Jews (27%) are most likely to express fear for their personal safety or that of their family from white supremacist groups as a result of the 2016 elections." The report also finds that among the faith groups examined, Muslims were the most likely to report religious-based discrimination (60%) over the past year, compared to 38% of Jews (ISPU, 2017).

8.4   HOW DOES DISCRIMINATION AFFECT WHAT U.S. MUSLIMS DO?

Having established that Muslim Americans perceive a great deal of discrimination, the next question is whether such perceptions of discrimination affect how they behave in the American sociopolitical context.

To explore this, the chapter turns to a survey fielded through Survey Sampling International in February 2017 on a convenience sample of 203 Muslim Americans. While not representative, this survey has the advantage of being fielded after the 2016 campaign, in the midst of heightened discrimination, and also of including key variables worthy of exploration.

8.4.1   Muslim American Responses to an Era of Increased Discrimination

Respondents' anxieties over future catastrophic events were evaluated by asking them to answer the following question:

> In your opinion, what is the likelihood that you or other Muslims you know will experience the following events in the next 12 months? 1 – *Unlikely*, 2 – *Somewhat unlikely*, 3 – *Neither likely nor unlikely*, 4 – *Somewhat likely*, and 5 – *Very likely*.
>
> 1. Being unfairly fired or denied a job promotion.
> 2. Being unfairly targeted by the police and other law enforcement.
> 3. Being singled out by airport security.
> 4. Treated unfairly or with less respect at restaurants or stores.
> 5. Be hurt in a terror attack.

6. Become the victim of a violent crime.
7. Be negatively affected by one of President Donald Trump's executive orders.
8. Be forced to turn over information on your phone to airport security or border patrol.
9. Become target of verbal abuse or physical threat.

Table 8.1. *Descriptive Statistics from February 2017 Survey on Muslim Americans*

Variables	SSI Survey February 2017
% Male	48.77
Age (mean)	34.96
Income (1–6 Likert)	3.49
Education (1–6 Likert)	4.55
% White	46.80
% Black	16.26
% Hispanic	1.48
% Asian	26.11
% Mixed Race	0.99
% Middle Eastern	7.88
% Other Race	0.49
% Citizen	90.15
n	203

An individual's level of attachment to their Muslim American identity, the size of their Muslim social networks (including the percentage of their friends that come from the group), and religiosity are all likely to impact how they perceive their treatment in American society and what the future holds for them. Muslim American identity was measured using similar questions to those typically used to measure "national identity," an inclusive construct highlighting the importance of nationality in defining an individual's identity and their belonging to a national "us" (Collingwood et al., 2018; Gustavsson, 2017; Oskooii, Lajevardi, and Collingwood, 2019). The "Muslim American identity" scale builds on Huddy and

Khatib's (2007) national identity measures and Verkuyten's (2005, 2007) group identification measures.

Muslim American identity, then, captures a subjective or internalized sense of belonging to the Muslim American collective (Citrin, Wong, and Duff, 2001; Huddy, 2001, 2015; Ocampo, Dana, and Barreto, 2018). The Muslim American identity independent variable employed here is an additive scale of four items:

> Muslim American Identity (additive scale): To what extent do you agree or disagree with the following statements: 1 – *Strongly disagree*, 2 – *Somewhat disagree*, 3 – *Neither agree nor disagree*, 4 – *Somewhat agree*, or 5 – *Strongly agree*? The scale runs from 5 (low Muslim American identity) to 20 (high Muslim American identity):
>
> 1. My Muslim American identity is an important part of my "self."
> 2. Being a Muslim American is an important part of how I see myself.
> 3. I am proud to be a Muslim American.
> 4. Sometimes, I dislike being a Muslim American *(reverse coded)*.

Those who fell in the 75th percentile and above were coded as having a high Muslim American identity, the expectation being that this will be associated with increased anxiety and reports of societal discrimination. Conversely, it is anticipated that those with a low Muslim American identity will report less anxiety and institutional discrimination.

Religiosity is another variable shaping Muslim American behavior and perceptions of discrimination. Numerous studies have explored the relationship between religiosity and mosque attendance, and have found religiosity is associated with increased social and political incorporation (Bagby, 2009; Dana et al., 2011, 2017, 2018; Jamal, 2005; Oskooii and Dana, 2018).

In the February 2017 survey, respondents were asked, "How often do you attend religious services at the mosque or masjid?" Possible answers were: (1) Never; (2) Only on religious holidays; (3) Once a month; (4) Once a week; and (5) More than once a week. From here, a "religious" variable was created whereby a value of 1 indicated that the respondent attended religious services "once a week" or "more than once a week," and a 0 indicated the subject attended the mosque or masjid "never," "only on religious holidays," or "once a month." In sum, 96 respondents (47.29%) fell into the religious category and 107 respondents (52.71%) into the nonreligious category.

Regarding an individual's Muslim social network, the survey asked respondents to answer the following question on a percentage scale of 1,100: "What percent of your close friends are Muslim?" The mean response was 54.78%; those in the 25th percentile reported having 35% of their close friends be Muslims, while those in the 75th percentile responded with 81%. Those in the 75th percentile and above were coded as having a large Muslim social network. It is anticipated that those who have higher percentages of Muslim friends will express more anxiety, perceive more discrimination, and fear more catastrophic events because of the "telephone effect." That is, they are more aware of discrimination due to engaging in regular conversations with peers and therefore being more likely to share anecdotes about negative experiences.

Finally, given that so many Muslims cite discrimination and prejudice as the most important problems facing their community today, the survey explored the extent to which U.S. Muslims in the study had had personal experiences with societal and institutional discrimination (Oskooii, 2016), and whether these experiences were shaped by Muslim American identity, religiosity, or large Muslim social networks. Thus, respondents were asked to rate the following statements regarding their personal experiences with discrimination due to their Muslim identity:

> In the past 12 months, how often have any of the following things happened to you because you are a Muslim? 1 – *Never*, 2 – *Once in awhile*, 3 – *Somewhat often*, and 4 – *Very often*.
>
> 1. You have received poorer service than other people at restaurants and stores.
> 2. People act as if they are afraid of you.

3. People act as if they are suspicious of you.
4. People called you offensive names or treated you with less respect.
5. You were physically threatened or attacked.
6. You were singled out or treated unfairly by airport security.
7. You were singled out or treated unfairly by other government officials or institutions such as the police.
8. You heard or saw your local government officials or politicians make negative comments about Muslims.

These items take into account a nuanced form of societal versus political discrimination. Not all discrimination is alike, and, as Oskooii (2016) indicates, the conflation of different types of discrimination can obscure and understate how racial, ethnic, and religious groups respond to such mistreatment. Societal discrimination occurs when individuals have been exposed to mistreatment and intimidation in social/interpersonal contexts on the basis of race, ethnicity, or religious affiliation (Oskooii, 2016). Political – or institutional – discrimination instead occurs when discriminatory laws, campaign messages, policies, or practices are carried out by state or private institutions and/or their affiliated actors (Oskooii, 2016). These two phenomena must therefore be evaluated separately. Some scholars have found discrimination to mobilize members of racialized groups (e.g. Barreto and Woods, 2005; Pantoja et al., 2001; Ramakrishnan, 2005), but evaluating whether this discrimination is societal or institutional is important, as it is also possible that individuals may also be retreating in light of discrimination (Hobbs and Lajevardi, 2019). Oskooii (2016, p. 636) suggests that to overcome this measurement problem, scholars should generate "more creative and detailed survey questions and other methods." The above questions, curated with the help of Oskooii himself, attempt to do just that. Five of the statements capture forms of social discrimination, while three capture experiences of institutional discrimination.

The rampant political and societal discrimination that Muslim Americans faced throughout the 2016 election campaign may have resulted in isolating and restrictive behaviors, despite the prevailing wisdom in political science leading us to expect members of stigmatized communities to take action rather than resign from the public sphere in light of such discrimination. Evaluating whether retreat from public spaces has occurred is thus important to tease out whether or not this prevailing wisdom holds true for Muslim Americans, who in recent times have seen members of their religion from across the globe negatively communicated to the U.S. public more than any other group.

Table 8.2 demonstrates that respondents with high levels of Muslim American identity (MAMID) were less likely than the rest of the sample and other subsets of the sample – such as those with high levels of religiosity and those with large Muslim social networks – to report experiences of societal and institutional discrimination.

At first glance, this is a striking result. Those with high Muslim American identity are the same age, are no more likely to be U.S. citizens, and have comparable levels of income and education, as the rest of the sample. One would perhaps expect those with strong levels of Muslim American identity to feel the impact of discrimination more deeply as they are more tied to their identity. However, another plausible explanation is perhaps at play here, namely that it could be those individuals with high levels of Muslim American identity who are most likely to hold their heads up high and express pride in being Muslim despite the rampant discrimination seen in the United States today. As a result, it could be that they refuse to allow discrimination to affect them, and reject any negative connotations placed upon their identity or religion. This possibility, however, should be further unpacked in future experiments and research.

8.4.2   Perceptions of Future Catastrophic Events

The February 2017 survey also evaluated how fears of future instances of discrimination – or catastrophic events – vary by subsets of Muslim identity. Respondents were asked: "In your opinion, what is the

Table 8.2. Responses to Perceptions of Discrimination

Variables	Sample: Aggregate	Sample: Religiosity	Sample: MAMID	Sample: Social Network
Societal Discrimination				
1. You have received poorer service than other people at restaurants and stores	2.04	2.42	1.83	2.19
2. People act as if they are afraid of you	2.19	2.50	1.97	2.36
3. People act as if they are suspicious of you	2.26	2.56	1.9	2.5
4. People called you offensive names or treated you with less respect	2.18	2.56	1.90	2.19
5. You were physically threatened or attacked	1.82	2.26	1.4	2.11
Institutional Discrimination				
6. You were singled out or treated unfairly by airport security	2.12	2.44	1.83	2.36
7. You were singled out or treated unfairly by other government officials or institutions such as the police	2.02	2.43	1.58	2.23
8. You heard or saw your local government officials or politicians make negative comments about Muslims	2.27	2.59	2.15	2.33
N	203	96	60	52

Note: 2/2017 survey asked, "In the past 12 months, how often have any of the following things happened to you because you are a Muslim?"

Note: Range of answer responses: Never (1), Once in Awhile (2), Somewhat Often (3), Very Often (4).

Note: Figures above are the means for the samples indicated.

likelihood that you or other Muslims you know will experience the following events in the next 12 months?" and then told to evaluate (on a scale of 1 to 5) five statements on respondents' fears of future societal discrimination and four statements on institutional discrimination.

Table 8.3 displays the mean responses to the nine statements in the full sample, among those who are highly religious, those with high levels of Muslim American identity, and those who have large Muslim social networks. It shows that across the board, the sample on average rated each of these statements as between "Neither Likely nor Unlikely" and "Somewhat Likely" to occur, with respondents with high levels Muslim American identity no less likely than others to express fears of future instances of societal and institutional discrimination. This raises further questions about those with high levels of Muslim American identity, suggesting that future research is critical in order to reconcile how those who are confident in their identity express low levels of societal and institutional discrimination, but still believe that harm can occur in the future.

8.5 IMPLICATIONS

Having established in previous chapters that the sociopolitical positioning of Muslim Americans is low, two important questions remained: Are Muslim Americans aware of their treatment in the United States? And, how pervasive are perceptions of societal and institutional discrimination? This chapter has shown that the answer to the former question is "yes"; while the answer to the latter question is more nuanced, though it is clear that perceptions of discrimination are highly pervasive.

Researchers should be cautious when evaluating U.S. Muslims as research subjects. The group is already under a great deal of governmental surveillance and scrutiny, and is therefore legitimately afraid of escalation. Muslim Americans are acutely aware of their positioning and report anxieties, but what we do not yet know is how detrimental and paralyzing these anxieties are. Has an individual's

Table 8.3. *Fears of Future Instances of Discrimination by Measures of Identity*

Variables	Sample: Aggregate	Sample: Religiosity	Sample: MAMID	Sample: Social Network
Societal Discrimination				
1. Being unfairly fired or denied a job promotion	3.44	3.60	3.48	3.44
2. Treated unfairly or with less respect at restaurants or stores	3.59	3.69	3.57	3.62
3. Be hurt in a terror attack	3.39	3.62	3.2	3.46
4. Become the victim of violent crime	3.55	3.66	3.50	3.61
5. Become target of verbal abuse or physical threat	3.80	3.97	3.95	3.88
Institutional Discrimination				
6. Being unfairly targeted by the police and other law enforcement	3.68	3.79	3.6	3.75
7. Being singled out by airport security	3.96	3.94	4.05	3.85
8. Be negatively affected by one of President Donald Trump's executive orders	3.93	3.96	4.02	4
9. Be forced to turn over information on your phone to airport security or border patrol	3.63	3.75	3.82	3.73

Note: 2/2017 survey asked, "In your opinion, what is the likelihood that you or other Muslims you know will experience the following events in the next 12 months?"
Note: Range of answer responses: Unlikely (1), Somewhat Unlikely (2), Neither Likely nor Unlikely (3), Somewhat Likely (4), Very Likely (5).

health been affected? Have they reduced their mosque attendance? Are their children experiencing discrimination and bullying, and how do these children communicate with their peers? Have they reduced their international travel? Do they continue to fear that more policies targeting them will be enacted by the president? How fearful are they of white supremacists? Have they changed their routes to avoid instances of discrimination? Have Muslim women removed their hijab?

These are some of the questions that linger, and that are realistic and potential consequences of the political climate Muslim Americans are experiencing today. In the February 2017 survey, Muslim respondents were asked to free-write a response to the following question: "In your own words, please describe what effects, if any, you think the recent immigration and visa ban has had on you or other Muslims in the United States." The answers varied but even so illuminate the struggles that Muslim Americans face in the current sociopolitical climate. Below, 51 of their answers are listed.

1. If extended family want to make a life here they cant because of the ban.
2. We want defend our selves and not get out of USA because of Donald trump.
3. I might need to go back to my country.
4. There is fear that anti Muslim sentiment and violence will be on the rise and people will act on it, feeling more free to do so.
5. I think it has everyone on edge. We are worried about traveling back and forth to our home countries to visit friends and family.
6. It has put a big spotlight on Muslims, especially from people who already didn't like Muslims.
7. making people stressed.
8. Feel unsafe in this country.
9. People are so angry about that, because their have family living abroad.
10. I am worried that if I ever leave the country, I won't be able to come back, even though I was born and raised here.
11. It painted a bigger target on our backs.
12. It has affected Muslims who were in America legally, because they couldn't enter the US if they traveled outside. A 70 year old Muslim

lady was stopped in an airport, and was not allowed to enter, and ended up having a heart attack and dying.

13. there will be extremely high number of racial crime will emerge.

14. This would make traveling very hard. Many of our relatives and family members are back home, and we cannot go visit them without worrying if you could come back or not.

15. if leaders want to put anyone out the country the same could have happen to me.

16. Makes us feel scared.

17. I believe that the Mosque fire in Florida was a direct result of the discriminatory action of the policies of this administration.

18. I'm afraid to travel to Pakistan even though I'm a natural born American citizen. I'm sad for my family members in Pakistan that may not be able to visit me in the U.S.

19. I think it's made Muslims more aware of the political process and of their rights as Americans.

20. People have became more supportive of Muslim American.

21. MAKES US SOMEHOW APPREHENSIVE OF OUR OWN FUTURE IN THIS COUNTRY OTHER CHILDREN IN MY KIDS' CLASSES WERE ASKING THEM IF THEY WERE GOING TO BE DEPORTED NOW THAT TRUMP HAS BEEN ELECTED.

22. It makes me feel unwanted and unsafe.

23. I think that it's enabling islamaphobes to keep hating. My mom's own cousin has been spewing filth about how they just want to get over here to bomb us.

24. It vilifies all Muslims. It makes us all the unnecessarily the bad guys. It makes the country more divisive. To true believers of Islam these terrorists are not considered Muslims.

25. a lot of people are worried about their families and traveling.

26. Some people weren't able to pursue a higher education here because of the ban. A lot of people weren't able to see their families. Some terrorists were actually caught.

27. many were targeted for wearing hijabs.

28. I think there is a lot of confusion and mistrust due to blanket statements insinuating that Muslims are dangerous and it in turn makes Muslims fear for their safety/expect mistreatment in this country.

29. Not allowing families from war torn countries a safe place.

30. It makes people more suspicious.
31. Unwisely, some Muslims have began to isolate themselves out of fear.
32. very bad effect because most of the muslim in the USA were not given enough time to receive the green card.
33. feeling like something bad is going to happen to all of us.
34. it is causing racism vibes.
35. It prevented us from being able to freely leave when we want.
36. They feel not included in American Society inspite of their contribution to all aspect of American life.
37. Depression leaving family behind. Its not right its disgusting Trump and his parents are immigrants so why let a specific group not have the same right of liberty of hope.
38. The recent ban has effected our sense of security and has often casted doubt as to whether we can afford to really stay in our own country. I'm really disappointed and worried that this will create more friction between the US and the middle east.
39. I think overall travel is a problem especially when it comes to religious right such as hajj travel to Mecca.
40. actually my uncle was trying to get into america but they didnt let him in I was missing him so much but they didnt let him in and he was sent back.
41. its offensive and scary.
42. It has normalized people bullying or singling out muslims. This encourages hate attacks.
43. it has made some of my friends afraid to travel outside of U.S. for fear of not being able to get back to family.
44. its made us feel rejected by our government. but at the same time, the number of people who came out to support us was tremendous. It was heartwarming to see and made me less scared.
45. It has created fear in the Muslim community. Not only did a mosque in my hometown get burnt, but the mosque that I grew up going to got vandalized twice. My family was targeted by white males. They were walking out of a restaurant and three males in a car starting swearing and saying racial slurs to them. When I meet a white person now, all I wonder is if they voted for Trump or not.
46. it has caused the public attitudes towards muslims to change in a bad way it creates stereotypes

47. This ban has not effected me and my family directly, but it has effected a lot of other Muslims in this country. Tearing apart families, having Muslims humiliated in airports being detained for no reason whatsoever. This ban is turning this country into a bad place, and the rest of the world is watching this.
48. more hate crimes against innocent muslims.
49. we don't feel good and safe.
50. became very careful and reserved.
51. it makes us more likely to die.

Many Muslims in America do not understand how they became so racialized and wish they could escape the spotlight focused on the group. Even with the 2017 Muslim ban protests, some feared that highlighting issues related to the ban made the group more visible and therefore more susceptible to being targeted. Some even see their lives as being at stake, linking this increased visibility with hate crimes. Future studies should examine how other emotions, such as anger and sadness, rather than just anxiety and fear, shape Muslims' perceptions about their sociopolitical status.

9 Conclusion

The sociopolitical status of Muslims in today's United States is of great concern. Fifteen years after the attacks on September 11, 2001, the country elected a president who ran on a platform targeting Muslims, both foreign and domestic, and vowing to take away their freedoms. Supporters of these policies were no longer on the fringes of society – their voices now amplified by those in the White House (Muslim Advocates, 2018).

Meanwhile, the past decade has seen a refugee crisis in the Middle East that has resulted in millions being displaced, numerous wars in the region, and the rise of ISIS. It has also seen numerous terrorist attacks in the U.S., in western Europe, and across the world. At the same time, America has witnessed increases in hate crimes against Muslims, a proliferation in the number of anti-sharia bills introduced and enacted in state legislatures across the country, and three versions of a Muslim ban instituted.

This context begs the question: "How do Muslim Americans fare in American democracy?" Answering such a complex and broad question requires a multifaceted approach. This book provides empirical evidence of the degenerating situation of Muslim Americans, and argues that it has occurred rapidly, while yielding devastating political consequences. Using news broadcast data spanning over 20 years, the book has demonstrated that the United States has a dynamic sociopolitical hierarchy in which groups enter and exit mainstream news cycles, and are discussed differently at various times. The book has further evaluated the status of Muslim Americans through survey research, field experiments, and text-as-data methods. The results reveal the rampant discrimination faced by Muslims in American politics today.

More recently, the 2018 midterm campaigns saw rampant Islamophobia apparent in a U.S. election once again.[1] For instance, Republican Duncan Hunter ran a campaign ad accusing his multiracial Democratic opponent Ammar Campa-Najjar, a candidate of Palestinian and Mexican descent, of having ties to Islamic terrorism. Campa-Najjar was characterized as "a Palestinian, Mexican, millennial Democrat" who was cooperating with the Muslim Brotherhood as a part of a "well-orchestrated plan" to infiltrate the U.S. government.[2]

Muslim Advocates, a legal organization studying outcomes related to U.S. Muslims, traced office-seekers who ran on anti-Muslim campaigns throughout the 2018 election. The group identified 80 candidates, 64% of whom were seasoned elected or appointed officials. Among these potential officeholders, 40 ran for Congress, 15 sought municipal or county office, 15 ran for governor or other statewide office, and 10 ran for a seat in a state legislature (Muslim Advocates, 2018). A majority, however, lost the election they were running in. While analyses by Muslim Advocates could not pinpoint anti-Muslim rhetoric being the cause of such losses, in a separate experiment, the organization showed that fictional candidates who vilified American Muslims lost more votes than they gained, even among conservatives (Muslim Advocates, 2018).

The comprehensive analysis of political discrimination against Muslim Americans conducted in this book demonstrates that the group's situation is far worse than previously imagined. Such discrimination has not gone unnoticed and is not inconsequential: Muslim Americans are deprived of fair treatment in the sociopolitical context and are acutely aware of their worsening situation in the American political arena.

There are a number of lingering issues that should be addressed in future studies. First, scholarship on the treatment of Muslim Americans cannot be conducted in a vacuum, and the status of Muslim Americans should be compared to that of other religious and racialized groups. Another outstanding question is whether rainbow

coalitions can be formed between U.S. Muslims and other racialized and negatively situated groups. The literature has shown that
building rainbow coalitions is one possible way to make strides in
U.S. politics, especially given today's context in which so many
groups are suffering discrimination and harm (Butler and Murray,
1989; Gilliam Jr. and Kaufmann, 1998; Kaufmann, 2003; Meier and
Stewart Jr., 1991). Alone, these groups may not have much leverage,
but together they may be able to gain sufficient voting power to
elect leaders of their choice and thereby sway policies (Kreppel and
Tsebelis, 1999). This may, however, be difficult due to many minorities holding Muslims in low esteem (Lajevardi and Oskooii, 2018),
as well as the fact that groups tend to view other groups as below
their own. Blacks, Latinos, and Asian Americans all viewed other
minority groups as being more than 5 points below their own (on a
0–100 scale), suggesting that dehumanization is not solely limited to
how American Muslims are viewed.

There is, though, some evidence that Muslims – especially
younger ones – may be finding allies among communities of color.
Latinos, Pakistanis, Ghanaians, Asians, and African Americans are
all described by Maghbouleh (2017) as serving as important allies
to young Iranian Americans as they navigate a post-9/11 climate of
Islamophobia. Extending this line of thinking, opportunities may be
ripe for Muslim Americans to find allies among other marginalized
communities.

Foreign and domestic policy shifts have also created opportunities for coalition building. The election of Ilhan Omar and Rashida
Tlaib to the House of Representatives has seen an alliance being
formed with two other powerful women of color in Congress: Alexan-
dria Ocasio-Cortez and Ayanna Pressley. Commonly scapegoated by
Republicans, President Trump, and even the leader of their own
party in the House, two Muslim women in Congress are emerging
as powerful voices at the center of an influential coalition. Moreover,
the decade following 2010 has seen the decline of a number of divisive
issues – such as the Palestinian–Israeli debate, the Iraq War, and the

surge policy in Afghanistan – in the national consciousness. This has resulted in these issues becoming not only less important and divisive for Muslim Americans, but also for other stigmatized groups who are more conservative on foreign policy.

During George W. Bush's presidency, Muslims stood apart from other racialized minorities in their stance on the War on Terror, support for Israel, the USA Patriot Act, and unlawful detentions. Latinos and African Americans have traditionally been conservative on foreign policy issues, with many enlisting in the military to fight battles abroad. With Obama's election, however, Americans had chosen a president who had taken public stances supporting U.S. Muslims, meaning the group became less situated against the nation on these foreign policy issues. There was no need for a rainbow coalition at that time, with groups on the same "side" for different reasons: Blacks turned out in large numbers for the 2008 election due to the prospect of electing the first Black president, while Latinos supported Obama due to his stance on immigration policies.

The context shifted in 2015, when the 2016 presidential campaign began. First, a policy space emerged whereby a coalition could be built among groups. By this time, the Palestinian–Israeli debate had died down, the U.S. combat presence in the Iraq/Afghanistan wars was ending, many racialized groups were being publicly attacked by those on the right, and marginalized communities were experiencing increased incidence of hate crimes across the board (especially among the LGBT community, Jews, Blacks, Muslims, and Latinos). The seeds of possible coalitions can already be seen to have been planted, among Muslims and Jews in particular. American Jews showed up in record numbers to support Muslims at travel ban marches in January 2017, while Muslims raised money for Jewish cemeteries that had been destroyed in the wake of hate crimes after the election. It is also possible to imagine that these groups will attribute more positive favorability scores to one another, as well as adopt more liberal stances on policies affecting one another.

Scholarship on the substantive representation of Muslim Americans remains grossly underexplored. We simply have very little understanding of how legislators represent the policy preferences of Muslim Americans, nor do we have much information on the symbolic representation of Muslim Americans. In an October 2015 visit to Washington D.C., just as the 2016 presidential campaign was beginning to take a markedly discriminatory turn, I had a meeting on Capitol Hill with a staffer from a Congressman's office. Interested in the symbolic and substantive representation of Muslim Americans, I asked how the Congressman highlighted his Muslim identity and appealed to his Muslim constituency. The staffer indicated that the Congressman's activities were mostly centered on his Black identity and relationship to the Congressional Black Caucus. Why would one of only two Muslim members of Congress at the time appear to suppress his religious identity at such an important juncture in the treatment of Muslims? Could it be electorally harmful to him? These are the sort of questions that need to be answered.

Finally, future work needs to further unpack how MAR and support for candidates and policies affecting Muslim Americans grew so rapidly. Tesler (2018), Lajevardi and Oskooii (2018), and Lajevardi and Abrajano (2019) have begun this task, but much more scholarship on the priming and activation of old-fashioned racism is likely necessary. Weighing the likelihood of a registry of Muslims who are U.S. citizens – a policy espoused by Trump – becoming law, Aziz (2017) writes that such a program would be unlikely to pass constitutional muster, especially if the program were to be explicitly set up on the basis of religion. A registry of Muslim immigrants is possible, however, especially if courts apply an apparently neutral national security justification that would almost be guaranteed to pass a rational basis test (Aziz, 2017). But as, Aziz (2017) writes, this could very well be a precursor to internment, especially if there is another large-scale terrorist attack on U.S. soil.

Appendices

Table A1. *Summary Statistics – Dataset 1: May 2016 MTurk Survey*

Variable	Mean	SD	Min.	Max.	N
MAR	.376988	.23798	0	1	619
MAR (alt.)	.3887837	.2385357	0	1	619
Racial resentment	.4972403	.3013933	0	1	616
Age	40.33764	12.81676	21	82	619
Married	.457189	.4985667	0	1	619
Income	2.969305	1.431509	1	6	619
Education	4.185784	1.31067	1	6	619
Male	.4862682	.5002156	0	1	619
White	.8029079	.3981242	0	1	619
Asian	.0597738	.2372591	0	1	619
Black	.0759289	.2650986	0	1	619
Hispanic	.0339257	.1811843	0	1	619
Other race	.0274637	.1635623	0	1	619
Republican	.2277868	.4197435	0	1	619
Democrat	.447496	.4976378	0	1	619
Independent	.2859451	.4522288	0	1	619
Support Trump in 2016 primary	.3030588	.362077	0	1	595
Favorability of Muslim Americans	.5441419	.2856968	0	1	606
Muslim ban policy	.367541	.345074	0	1	610
Limit Muslim immigration policy	.4846788	.3500295	0	1	607
Patrol Muslim neighborhoods policy	.4955665	.3330433	0	1	609

Table A2. *Summary Statistics – Dataset 2: October 2016 CCAP Survey*

Variable	Mean	SD	Min.	Max.	N
MAR	.4257642	.2389827	0	1	916
MAR (alt.)	.4266687	.231948	0	1	916
Racial resentment	.5306587	.3248583	0	1	916
Age	49.74017	15.74351	19	95	916
Married	.5251092	.4996419	0	1	916
Income	6.025253	3.31405	1	17	792
Education	3.406114	1.433756	1	6	916
Male	.4312227	.4955176	0	1	916
White	.7751092	.4177385	0	1	916
Asian	.0098253	.0986885	0	1	916
Hispanic	.069869	.2550654	0	1	916
Other race	.0458515	.2092773	0	1	916
Republican	.2849345	.4516298	0	1	916
Democrat	.4072052	.4915821	0	1	916
Independent	.2772926	.4479067	0	1	916
Trump vote in 2016	.4191617	.4937176	0	1	835
Favorability of Muslims	.4432099	.3513837	0	1	810

Table A3. *Summary Statistics – Dataset 3: December 2016 SSI Survey*

Variable	Mean	SD	Min.	Max.	N
MAR	.3604679	.2010188	0	1	1261
MAR (alt.)	.3670352	.1941645	0	1	1261
Age	42.6465	18.04892	18	95	1256
Income	3.046788	1.508768	1	6	1261
Education	3.651864	1.397324	1	6	1261
Male	.334655	.4720569	0	1	1261
White	.6502776	.4770714	0	1	1261
Asian	.0459952	.2095579	0	1	1261
Black	.1205393	.3257202	0	1	1261
Hispanic	.1451229	.3523645	0	1	1261
Other race	.038065	.1914292	0	1	1261
Republican	.2466297	.4312203	0	1	1261
Democrat	.3727201	.4837203	0	1	1261
Independent	.2125297	.4092599	0	1	1261
Support Trump	.29659	.4569354	0	1	1261
Favorability of Muslims	.6450139	.2778251	0	1	1083
Muslim ban policy	.3983981	.3397949	0	1	1261

Table A4. *Summary Statistics – Dataset 4: January 2017 MTurk Survey*

Variable	Mean	SD	Min.	Max.	N
MAR	.3523355	.2426408	0	1	402
MAR (alt.)	.3661158	.2426435	0	1	402
Age	39.74627	13.07413	19	83	402
Income	3.112219	1.514885	1	6	401
Education	2.616915	.8749848	1	4	402
Male	.539801	.4990344	0	1	402
White	.818408	.3859883	0	1	402
Black	.0671642	.250618	0	1	402
Other race	.1144279	.3187269	0	1	402
Republican	.2835821	.451298	0	1	402
Democrat	.4129353	.4929749	0	1	402
Independent	.261194	.4398328	0	1	402
Trump approval	.5572139	.4973347	0	1	402
Favorability of Muslims	.6005528	.2972632	0	1	398

Table A5. *Summary Statistics – Dataset 5: June 2017 MTurk Survey*

Variable	Mean	SD	Min.	Max.	N
MAR	.329898	.218723	0	1	1035
MAR (alt.)	.3385783	.2159689	0	1	1035
Racial resentment	.4249274	.2791974	0	1	1033
Age	37.32527	13.11173	19	99	1033
Married	.4125604	.4925329	0	1	1035
Income	3.038647	1.468052	1	6	1035
Education	4.227053	1.288111	1	6	1035
Male	.4714976	.4994283	0	1	1035
White	.7758454	.417226	0	1	1035
Black	.1111111	.3144216	0	1	1035
Other race	.1130435	.316799	0	1	1035
Republican	.2470588	.4315128	0	1	1020
Democrat	.4901961	.5001491	0	1	1020
Independent	.2627451	.440341	0	1	1020
Trump vote in 2016	.2630029	.4404802	0	1	1019
Favorability of Muslims	.5908341	.2862389	0	1	1031
Muslims: Patriotic	.5434995	.2626095	0	1	1023
Muslims: Intelligent	.5480613	.3440045	0	1	1023
Muslims: Foreign	.2420984	.2705689	0	1	1023
Muslims: Lazy	.3594005	.3092655	0	1	1023
Muslims: Violent	.4548713	.2887691	0	1	1023
Muslims: Trustworthy	.3515803	.2947195	0	1	1023

Table A6. *Summary Statistics – Dataset 6: July 2018 Lucid Survey*

Variable	Mean	SD	Min.	Max.	N
MAR	.401638	.1989823	0	1	4009
MAR (alt.)	.4106386	.193298	0	1	4009
Racial resentment	.480101	.2422515	0	1	3764
Age	44.80469	17.16557	18	93	4009
Married	.4567224	.4981857	0	1	4009
Income	2.789973	1.521073	1	6	4009
Education	3.385383	1.395171	1	6	4009
Male	.4320279	.49542	0	1	4009
White	.7565478	.4292193	0	1	4009
Asian	.040908	.1981017	0	1	4009
Black	.126216	.3321341	0	1	4009
Hispanic	.0219506	.1465406	0	1	4009
Other race	.0543777	.2267897	0	1	4009
Republican	.3110501	.462981	0	1	4009
Democrat	.3826391	.4860919	0	1	4009
Independent	.291095	.4543239	0	1	4009
Trump vote in 2016	.322163	.4673644	0	1	3939
Favorability of Muslim Americans	.5880768	.2891652	0	1	4009
Muslims: Patriotic	.3909596	.3182253	0	1	3783
Muslims: Intelligent	.5759979	.2932494	0	1	3783
Muslims: Foreign	.5438365	.3441026	0	1	3783
Muslims: Lazy	.2954445	.3002791	0	1	3783
Muslims: Violent	.3954534	.3177947	0	1	3783
Muslims: Trustworthy	.4586307	.3073555	0	1	3783
Muslim ban policy	.4030704	.3258919	0	1	3892
Limit Muslim immigration policy	.4789954	.3373138	0	1	3892
Patrol Muslim neighborhoods policy	.4419483	.303321	0	1	3906

Table A7. *Summary Statistics – Dataset 7: October 2018 CCES Survey*

Variable	Mean	SD	Min.	Max.	N
MAR	.3751389	.2443203	0	1	1000
MAR (alt.)	.3845	.2385646	0	1	1000
Racial resentment	.5144	.1810429	0	1	1000
Age	48.022	17.69273	18	90	1000
Married	.486	.5000541	0	1	1000
Income	6.129032	3.286104	1	16	899
Education	3.647	1.534518	1	6	1000
Male	.439	.4965134	0	1	1000
White	.74	.4388537	0	1	1000
Asian	.031	.1734044	0	1	1000
Black	.098	.2974634	0	1	1000
Hispanic	.088	.2834367	0	1	1000
Other race	.043	.2029586	0	1	1000
Republican	.238	.4260722	0	1	1000
Democrat	.379	.4853809	0	1	1000
Independent	.382	.4861196	0	1	1000
Trump approval	.47725	.3254241	0	1	1000
Muslims: Patriotic	.511	.2910562	0	1	1000
Muslims: Hardworking	.694	.2503531	0	1	1000
Muslims: Trustworthy	.5855	.2835404	0	1	1000
Muslims: Violent	.7155	.2334293	0	1	1000

Table A8. *Summary Statistics – Dataset 8: October 2018 Lucid Survey*

Variable	Mean	SD	Min.	Max.	N
MAR	.4110566	.2033447	0	1	713
MAR (alt.)	.40558	.1959607	0	1	713
Racial resentment	.4863254	.2619789	0	1	713
Age	45.73625	16.93756	18	90	709
Married	.4431978	.4971118	0	1	713
Income	3.01122	1.64808	1	6	713
Education	3.614306	1.445126	1	6	713
Male	.4810659	.4999921	0	1	713
White	.7096774	.4542298	0	1	713
Asian	.0448808	.2071876	0	1	713
Black	.1164095	.3209405	0	1	713
Hispanic	.0813464	.2735583	0	1	713
Other race	.0476858	.2132503	0	1	713
Republican	.371669	.4835899	0	1	713
Democrat	.3702665	.483215	0	1	713
Independent	.2580645	.4378769	0	1	713
Trump support 2016	.454418	.4982675	0	1	713
Favorability of Muslim Americans	.5737307	.2860111	0	1	713
Muslim ban policy	.5098453	.365658	0	1	711
Limit Muslim immigration policy	.6297335	.3447533	0	1	713
Patrol Muslim neighborhoods policy	.5285211	.3552646	0	1	710

Table A9. *Summary Statistics – Dataset 9: March 2019 Lucid Survey*

Variable	Mean	SD	Min.	Max.	N
MAR	.4228319	.2056407	0	1	1212
MAR (alt.)	.4214698	.1982176	0	1	1212
Racial resentment	.5103135	.2585688	0	1	1212
Age	45.56436	16.92081	18	88	1212
Income	2.851485	1.540338	1	6	1212
Education	3.584158	1.393158	1	6	1212
Male	.4793729	.4997806	0	1	1212
White	.720297	.4490385	0	1	1212
Asian	.0486799	.2152867	0	1	1212
Black	.1188119	.3237006	0	1	1212
Hispanic	.0676568	.2512597	0	1	1212
Other race	.0445545	.2064086	0	1	1212
Republican	.3217822	.4673528	0	1	1212
Democrat	.4257426	.4946592	0	1	1212
Independent	.2524752	.4346117	0	1	1212
Trump approval	.3993399	.4899649	0	1	1212
Favorability of Muslim Americans	.5408993	.2897576	0	1	1212
Muslim ban policy	.4766914	.3409549	0	1	1212
Limit Muslim immigration policy	.5614686	.3393059	0	1	1212
Patrol Muslim neighborhoods policy	.4971122	.3367951	0	1	1212

Table A10. *Summary Statistics – Dataset 10: June 2019 Lucid Survey*

Variable	Mean	SD	Min.	Max.	N
MAR	.4055639	.2081987	0	1	3988
MAR (alt.)	.4092904	.200264	0	1	3988
Racial resentment	.5236514	.273052	0	1	3689
Age	44.68669	16.96245	15	89	3712
Married	.4633621	.498723	0	1	3712
Income	2.81127	1.536493	1	6	3709
Education	3.430305	1.390873	1	6	3709
Male	.4752155	.4994526	0	1	3712
White	.6484453	.4775156	0	1	3988
Asian	.0363591	.1872055	0	1	3988
Black	.1236209	.3291898	0	1	3988
Hispanic	.0712136	.2572136	0	1	3988
Other race	.1203611	.3254241	0	1	3988
Republican	.3128219	.4637053	0	1	3689
Democrat	.4255896	.4944991	0	1	3689
Independent	.2615885	.4395593	0	1	3689
Trump vote in 2016	.4023268	.4904335	0	1	3696
Favorability of Muslim Americans	.5683467	.2993204	0	1	3750
Muslims: Patriotic	.4183036	.3222719	0	1	3920
Muslims: Trustworthy	.4760204	.2988435	0	1	3920
Muslims: Intelligent	.6047194	.2754118	0	1	3920
Muslims: Foreign	.5397959	.3401427	0	1	3920
Muslims: Lazy	.2110969	.3003644	0	1	3920
Muslim ban policy	.4233325	.3497182	0	1	3988
Limit Muslim immigration policy	.5219408	.3491651	0	1	3988
Patrol Muslim neighborhoods policy	.4441327	.3312969	0	1	3920

Table A11. *Summary Statistics of MAR Variable across Datasets*

Dataset	MAR Mean	Std. Dev.	Min.	Max.	N
5/2016 (MTurk)	0.377	0.238	0	1	619
10/2016 (CCAP)	0.426	0.239	0	1	916
12/2016 (SSI)	0.360	0.201	0	1	1261
1/2017 (MTurk)	0.352	0.243	0	1	402
6/2017 (MTurk)	0.330	0.219	0	1	1035
7/2018 (Lucid)	0.402	0.199	0	1	4009
10/2018 (CCES)	0.375	0.244	0	1	1000
10/2018 (Lucid)	0.411	0.203	0	1	713
3/2019 (Lucid)	0.423	0.206	0	1	1212
6/2019 (Lucid)	0.406	0.208	0	1	3989

Table A12. *Summary Statistics of Trump Support Variable across Datasets*

Dataset	Variable	Mean	Std. Dev.	Min.	Max.	N
5/2016 (MTurk)	Support DT in 2016 primary	0.303	0.362	0	1	595
10/2016 (CCAP)	Trump vote in 2016	0.419	0.494	0	1	835
12/2016 (SSI)	Support Trump in 2016	0.281	0.45	0	1	1329
1/2017 (MTurk)	Trump approval	0.553	0.498	0	1	414
6/2017 (MTurk)	Trump vote in 2016	0.263	0.44	0	1	1019
7/2018 (Lucid)	Trump vote in 2016	0.322	0.467	0	1	3939
10/2018 (CCES)	Trump approval	0.477	0.325	0	1	1000
10/2018 (Lucid)	Trump support in 2016	0.447	0.498	0	1	751
3/2019 (Lucid)	Trump approval	0.399	0.49	0	1	1212
6/2019 (Lucid)	Trump vote in 2016	0.402	0.49	0	1	3697

Table A13. *Bivariate Relationship between MAR and Trump Support*

	(1) 5/2016 (MTurk)	(2) 10/2016 (CCAP)	(3) 12/2016 (SSI)	(4) 1/2017 (MTurk)	(5) 6/2017 (MTurk)	(6) 7/2018 (Lucid)	(7) 10/2018 (CCES)	(8) 10/2018 (Lucid)	(9) 3/2019 (Lucid)	(10) 6/2019 (Lucid)
MAR	0.784***	1.385***	0.783***	1.173***	1.024***	0.756***	0.999***	0.948***	0.958***	0.968***
	(0.0532)	(0.0527)	(0.0601)	(0.0836)	(0.0547)	(0.0354)	(0.0423)	(0.0847)	(0.0627)	(0.0350)
Constant	0.00531	−0.168***	0.0145	−0.0434	−0.0726***	0.0187	−0.0428*	0.0649	−0.00583	0.0114
	(0.0239)	(0.0257)	(0.0248)	(0.0362)	(0.0215)	(0.0159)	(0.0189)	(0.0389)	(0.0295)	(0.0159)
n	595	835	1261	354	1019	3939	973	713	1212	3696
adj. R^2	0.266	0.453	0.118	0.357	0.256	0.104	0.364	0.148	0.161	0.171

Note: Standard errors in parentheses.

* $p < 0.05$, ** $p < 0.01$, *** $p < 0.001$

Table A14. *Exploring the Relationship between MAR, Racial Resentment, and Favorability of Muslims and Trump Support*

	(1) 5/2016 (MTurk)	(2) 10/2016 (CCAP)	(3) 12/2016 (SSI)	(4) 1/2017 (MTurk)	(5) 6/2017 (MTurk)	(6) 7/2018 (Lucid)	(7) 10/2018 (CCES)	(8) 10/2018 (Lucid)	(9) 3/2019 (Lucid)	(10) 6/2019 (Lucid)
MAR	0.355***	0.774***	0.808***	1.166***	0.574***	0.451***	0.830***	0.659***	0.642***	0.542***
	(0.0787)	(0.0840)	(0.0847)	(0.115)	(0.0926)	(0.0512)	(0.0660)	(0.104)	(0.0757)	(0.0584)
Racial resentment	0.505***	0.540***			0.471***	0.636***	0.500***	0.560***	0.573***	0.544***
	(0.0523)	(0.0487)			(0.0532)	(0.0336)	(0.0654)	(0.0734)	(0.0562)	(0.0294)
Favorability MAM	-0.0114					0.0103		0.0888	0.0876	-0.0138
	(0.0577)					(0.0294)		(0.0687)	(0.0484)	(0.0306)
Favorability Muslims		-0.111*	-0.105	-0.0125	-0.0356					
		(0.0549)	(0.0616)	(0.0945)	(0.0583)					
Muslims: Patriotic					0.0427	-0.0283	-0.114*			
					(0.0605)	(0.0306)	(0.0527)			
Muslims: Intelligent					0.00931	-0.00373	0.00791			
					(0.0424)	(0.0315)	(0.0639)			
Muslims: Foreign					-0.00347	0.00660				
					(0.0552)	(0.0248)				
Muslims: Lazy					0.0641	-0.0432				
					(0.0576)	(0.0296)				
Muslims: Violent					0.0367	-0.0137				
					(0.0617)	(0.0306)				
Muslims: Trustworthy					-0.0432	0.0903**	0.136*			
					(0.0522)	(0.0344)	(0.0601)			
Muslims: Hardworking							0.00803			
							(0.0643)			
Constant	-0.0791	-0.131*	0.122	-0.0318	-0.156**	-0.204***	-0.268***	-0.155*	-0.212***	-0.108**
	(0.0562)	(0.0566)	(0.0649)	(0.0918)	(0.0574)	(0.0364)	(0.0635)	(0.0753)	(0.0514)	(0.0398)
n	591	741	1083	350	1019	3764	973	713	1212	3689
adj. R^2	0.368	0.556	0.146	0.353	0.308	0.185	0.403	0.211	0.227	0.255

Note: Standard errors in parentheses.

* $p < 0.05$, ** $p < 0.01$, *** $p < 0.001$

Table A15. Full Models Exploring the Relationship between MAR and Trump Support

	(1) 5/2016 (MTurk)	(2) 10/2016 (CCAP)	(3) 12/2016 (SSI)	(4) 1/2017 (MTurk)	(5) 6/2017 (MTurk)	(6) 7/2018 (Lucid)	(7) 10/2018 (CCES)	(8) 10/2018 (Lucid)	(9) 3/2019 (Lucid)	(10) 6/2019 (Lucid)
MAR	0.309***	0.706***	0.541***	0.722***	0.375***	0.261***	0.503***	0.350***	0.404***	0.291***
	(0.0742)	(0.0839)	(0.0693)	(0.110)	(0.0841)	(0.0431)	(0.0643)	(0.0812)	(0.0703)	(0.0477)
Age	−0.00142	0.00156	0.000683	0.000760	0.00147	0.00222***	0.000919	0.000777	−0.000776	0.000584
	(0.000887)	(0.000824)	(0.000627)	(0.00139)	(0.000826)	(0.000367)	(0.000579)	(0.000808)	(0.000715)	(0.000387)
Married	0.0548*	−0.0408			0.00364	0.0516***	0.0320	0.0175	−0.0674**	−0.0391**
	(0.0247)	(0.0263)			(0.0223)	(0.0124)	(0.0208)	(0.0275)	(0.0241)	(0.0127)
Income	−0.00141	0.00659	−0.00513	0.00887	0.0157*	0.00943*	−0.000764	0.0176	0.00840	0.00397
	(0.00897)	(0.00409)	(0.00815)	(0.0132)	(0.00783)	(0.00431)	(0.00335)	(0.00963)	(0.00853)	(0.00420)
Education	−0.00315	−0.0164	0.00300	0.0109	−0.00987	0.0214***	0.00208	0.00686	0.00920	0.00261
	(0.00907)	(0.00907)	(0.00881)	(0.0240)	(0.00867)	(0.00463)	(0.00692)	(0.0103)	(0.00910)	(0.00463)
Male	0.0321	0.00405	0.0125	−0.00740	0.00847	0.0337**	0.0352	0.0443	0.0873***	0.0428***
	(0.0228)	(0.0247)	(0.0232)	(0.0368)	(0.0210)	(0.0116)	(0.0195)	(0.0256)	(0.0226)	(0.0116)
Asian	−0.0262	−0.164	−0.0409			0.00798	0.0350	−0.124*	−0.0303	−0.0650*
	(0.0492)	(0.136)	(0.0517)			(0.0299)	(0.0571)	(0.0624)	(0.0527)	(0.0298)
Black	−0.0327	−0.138**	−0.145***	−0.110	−0.0425	−0.0602**	−0.0200	−0.0992*	0.0259	−0.0793***
	(0.0437)	(0.0451)	(0.0348)	(0.0794)	(0.0339)	(0.0184)	(0.0326)	(0.0425)	(0.0368)	(0.0182)
Hispanic	−0.0469	−0.0941*	−0.112***			−0.00115	−0.0241	−0.139**	0.0133	−0.0537*
	(0.0620)	(0.0477)	(0.0319)			(0.00199)	(0.0335)	(0.0489)	(0.0461)	(0.0220)
Other race	0.0384	0.0741	−0.164*	0.00625	−0.0662*	−0.0321	0.0340	−0.156*	0.0300	−0.0465
	(0.0709)	(0.0603)	(0.0695)	(0.0607)	(0.0330)	(0.0264)	(0.0500)	(0.0611)	(0.0547)	(0.0257)
Democrat	−0.309***	−0.362***	−0.586***	−0.521***	−0.477***	−0.547***	−0.428***	−0.658***	−0.471***	−0.613***
	(0.0324)	(0.0344)	(0.0271)	(0.0496)	(0.0305)	(0.0155)	(0.0282)	(0.0337)	(0.0294)	(0.0155)
Independent	−0.168***	−0.179***	−0.390***	−0.292***	−0.367***	−0.441***	−0.294***	−0.479***	−0.334***	−0.468***
	(0.0319)	(0.0327)	(0.0292)	(0.0512)	(0.0306)	(0.0155)	(0.0260)	(0.0340)	(0.0312)	(0.0157)
Racial resentment	0.294***	0.282***			0.210***	0.238***	0.308***	0.124*	0.347***	0.235***
	(0.0542)	(0.0528)			(0.0504)	(0.0302)	(0.0631)	(0.0607)	(0.0543)	(0.0253)
Favorability MAM	−0.0116					0.00655		−0.0592	0.0643	0.000161
	(0.0542)					(0.0243)		(0.0539)	(0.0433)	(0.0247)

Table A15. Continued

	(1) 5/2016 (MTurk)	(2) 10/2016 (CCAP)	(3) 12/2016 (SSI)	(4) 1/2017 (MTurk)	(5) 6/2017 (MTurk)	(6) 7/2018 (Lucid)	(7) 10/2018 (CCES)	(8) 10/2018 (Lucid)	(9) 3/2019 (Lucid)	(10) 6/2019 (Lucid)
Favorability Muslim	-0.0690 (0.0545)	-0.0224 (0.0498)		-0.0122 (0.0835)	-0.0464 (0.0522)					
Muslims: Patriotic					0.0465 (0.0538)	-0.0274 (0.0253)	-0.0974* (0.0490)			-0.0132 (0.0261)
Muslims: Intelligent					-0.00993 (0.0378)	-0.0115 (0.0260)	0.0555 (0.0597)			0.0491 (0.0269)
Muslims: Foreign					0.0348 (0.0490)	-0.00277 (0.0205)				0.0290 (0.0200)
Muslims: Lazy					0.0568 (0.0513)	0.0148 (0.0246)				0.00619 (0.0277)
Muslims: Violent					0.0713 (0.0553)	0.00556 (0.0254)				0.0354 (0.0280)
Muslims: Trustworthy					-0.0446 (0.0467)	0.0632* (0.0285)	0.0881 (0.0571)			-0.0226 (0.0287)
Muslims: Hardworking						-0.0286	(0.0613)			
Constant	0.273*** (0.0817)	0.188* (0.0861)	0.528*** (0.0697)	0.343** (0.132)	0.290*** (0.0752)	0.195*** (0.0413)	0.152* (0.0727)	0.542*** (0.0846)	0.271*** (0.0798)	0.475*** (0.0435)
n	591	640	1080	350	1017	3764	878	709	1212	3689
adj. R²	0.460	0.632	0.458	0.517	0.460	0.447	0.521	0.552	0.388	0.517

Note: Standard errors in parentheses.

* p < 0.05, ** p < 0.01, *** p < 0.001

Table A16. *Bivariate Relationship between MAR and Support for the Muslim Ban*

	(1) 5/2016 (MTurk)	(2) 12/2016 (SSI)	(3) 7/2018 (Lucid)	(4) 10/2018 (Lucid)	(5) 3/2019 (Lucid)	(6) 6/2019 (Lucid)
MAR (alt.)	1.118***	1.084***	0.983***	1.096***	1.022***	0.979***
	(0.0370)	(0.0387)	(0.0219)	(0.0566)	(0.0398)	(0.0229)
Constant	−0.0696***	0.000667	−0.000294	0.0654*	0.0460*	0.0226*
	(0.0170)	(0.0161)	(0.00992)	(0.0255)	(0.0185)	(0.0104)
n	610	1261	3892	711	1212	3988
adj. R^2	0.600	0.383	0.342	0.345	0.352	0.314

Note: Standard errors in parentheses.

* $p < 0.05$, ** $p < 0.01$, *** $p < 0.001$

Table A17. *Exploring the Relationship between MAR, Racial Resentment, and Favorability of Muslims and Support for the Muslim Ban*

	(1) 5/2016 (MTurk)	(2) 12/2016 (SSI)	(3) 7/2018 (Lucid)	(4) 10/2018 (Lucid)	(5) 3/2019 (Lucid)	(6) 6/2019 (Lucid)
MAR (alt.)	0.882***	1.007***	0.751***	0.895***	0.834***	0.590***
	(0.0587)	(0.0533)	(0.0321)	(0.0716)	(0.0483)	(0.0382)
Racial resentment	0.204***		0.167***	0.284***	0.270***	0.101***
	(0.0383)		(0.0204)	(0.0478)	(0.0346)	(0.0190)
Favorability MAM	−0.0842		−0.0166	−0.0208	−0.0148	−0.0774***
	(0.0431)		(0.0181)	(0.0460)	(0.0301)	(0.0198)
Favorability Muslim		−0.104**				
		(0.0375)				
Muslims: Patriotic			−0.0147			−0.0160
			(0.0188)			(0.0210)
Muslims: Intelligent			0.0129			0.0505*
			(0.0193)			(0.0217)
Muslims: Foreign			0.0324*			0.117***
			(0.0152)			(0.0161)
Muslims: Lazy			0.0332			0.0900***
			(0.0181)			(0.0220)
Muslims: Violent			0.0598**			0.137***
			(0.0187)			(0.0222)
Muslims: Trustworthy			−0.0602**			−0.0112
			(0.0211)			(0.0233)
Constant	−0.0316	0.0962*	−0.00791	0.0131	−0.00496	0.0281
	(0.0423)	(0.0405)	(0.0230)	(0.0511)	(0.0324)	(0.0269)
n	604	1083	3764	711	1212	3689
adj. R^2	0.622	0.403	0.368	0.376	0.383	0.378

Note: Standard errors in parentheses.

* $p < 0.05$, ** $p < 0.01$, *** $p < 0.001$

Table A18. Full Models Exploring the Relationship between MAR and Support for the Muslim Ban

	(1) 5/2016 (MTurk)	(2) 12/2016 (SSI)	(3) 7/2018 (Lucid)	(4) 10/2018 (Lucid)	(5) 3/2019 (Lucid)	(6) 6/2019 (Lucid)
MAR (alt.)	0.874***	0.987***	0.716***	0.845***	0.804***	0.561***
	(0.0591)	(0.0539)	(0.0326)	(0.0716)	(0.0498)	(0.0382)
Age	0.000462	0.00209***	0.00128***	0.000442	0.000682	0.00116***
	(0.000696)	(0.000465)	(0.000271)	(0.000680)	(0.000494)	(0.000309)
Married	0.0223		0.0236**	0.0571*	-0.0330*	-0.0309**
	(0.0194)		(0.00912)	(0.0230)	(0.0167)	(0.0101)
Income	0.00671	-0.00167	-0.00329	0.00612	0.00340	-0.00110
	(0.00704)	(0.00604)	(0.00319)	(0.00810)	(0.00590)	(0.00336)
Education	-0.0175*	-0.00760	-0.0120***	0.00787	0.00383	-0.0105**
	(0.00730)	(0.00653)	(0.00342)	(0.00869)	(0.00630)	(0.00370)
Male	-0.00605	0.000112	-0.0128	0.0401	0.00254	0.000916
	(0.0179)	(0.0172)	(0.00860)	(0.0216)	(0.0156)	(0.00928)
Asian	-0.0232	0.0393	0.0684**	-0.119*	-0.00462	0.00315
	(0.0376)	(0.0384)	(0.0221)	(0.0525)	(0.0364)	(0.0239)
Black	0.0174	-0.0162	0.0426**	0.0282	0.00134	0.00160
	(0.0335)	(0.0259)	(0.0136)	(0.0357)	(0.0254)	(0.0146)
Hispanic	0.0293	0.0250	-0.00163	-0.0588	-0.00168	-0.00259
	(0.0490)	(0.0236)	(0.00147)	(0.0413)	(0.0319)	(0.0176)
Other race	0.0144	-0.0376	0.0247	-0.0581	-0.0339	-0.0157
	(0.0530)	(0.0515)	(0.0195)	(0.0514)	(0.0378)	(0.0206)
Democrat	-0.0637*	-0.0545**	-0.0384***	-0.114***	-0.0747***	-0.0528***
	(0.0252)	(0.0200)	(0.0114)	(0.0282)	(0.0203)	(0.0124)
Independent	-0.0902***	-0.0679**	-0.0306**	-0.0912**	-0.0791***	-0.0577***
	(0.0248)	(0.0216)	(0.0115)	(0.0285)	(0.0215)	(0.0125)
Racial resentment	0.145***		0.135***	0.191***	0.215***	0.0555**
	(0.0424)		(0.0222)	(0.0512)	(0.0372)	(0.0202)
Favorability MAM	-.101*		-0.0173	-0.0638	-0.0211	-0.0774***
	(0.0431)		(0.0180)	(0.0461)	(0.0299)	(0.0197)

Table A18. Continued

	(1) 5/2016 (MTurk)	(2) 12/2016 (SSI)	(3) 7/2018 (Lucid)	(4) 10/2018 (Lucid)	(5) 3/2019 (Lucid)	(6) 6/2019 (Lucid)
Favorability Muslim		-0.0836* (0.0375)				-0.0000375 (0.0210)
Muslims: Patriotic			-0.0167 (0.0187)			0.0471* (0.0216)
Muslims: Intelligent			0.00865 (0.0192)			0.119*** (0.0160)
Muslims: Foreign			0.0352* (0.0151)			0.103*** (0.0221)
Muslims: Lazy			0.0403* (0.0181)			0.103*** (0.0221)
Muslims: Violent			0.0686*** (0.0187)			0.139*** (0.0221)
Muslims: Trustworthy			-0.0525* (0.0210)			-0.00777 (0.0232)
Constant	0.0903 (0.0647)	0.0698 (0.0534)	0.0207 (0.0313)	0.0687 (0.0728)	0.0555 (0.0556)	0.0922** (0.0356)
n	604	1080	3764	707	1212	3689
adj. R^2	0.630	0.419	0.378	0.414	0.395	0.389

Note: Standard errors in parentheses.

* $p < 0.05$, ** $p < 0.01$, *** $p < 0.001$

Table A19. *Bivariate Relationship between MAR and Support for Limiting Immigration from Muslim Countries*

	(1) 5/2016 (MTurk)	(2) 7/2018 (Lucid)	(3) 10/2018 (Lucid)	(4) 3/2019 (Lucid)	(5) 6/2019 (Lucid)
MAR (alt.)	1.085***	1.045***	0.910***	0.913***	0.951***
	(0.0401)	(0.0223)	(0.0565)	(0.0416)	(0.0231)
Constant	0.0598**	0.0501***	0.261***	0.177***	0.133***
	(0.0184)	(0.0101)	(0.0254)	(0.0194)	(0.0105)
n	607	3892	713	1212	3988
adj. R^2	0.547	0.361	0.266	0.284	0.298

Note: Standard errors in parentheses.
* $p < 0.05$, ** $p < 0.01$, *** $p < 0.001$

Table A20. *Exploring the Relationship between MAR, Racial Resentment, and Favorability of Muslims and Support for Limiting Immigration from Muslim Countries*

	(1) 5/2016 (MTurk)	(2) 7/2018 (Lucid)	(3) 10/2018 (Lucid)	(4) 3/2019 (Lucid)	(5) 6/2019 (Lucid)
MAR (alt.)	0.824***	0.719***	0.609***	0.618***	0.530***
	(0.0624)	(0.0314)	(0.0674)	(0.0487)	(0.0382)
Racial resentment	0.302***	0.377***	0.510***	0.444***	0.267***
	(0.0407)	(0.0200)	(0.0448)	(0.0349)	(0.0190)
Favorability MAM	−0.00822	0.0168	0.0371	−0.00554	−0.0546**
	(0.0459)	(0.0177)	(0.0432)	(0.0303)	(0.0198)
Muslims: Patriotic		−0.0544**			−0.0908***
		(0.0184)			(0.0210)
Muslims: Intelligent		0.0180			0.0495*
		(0.0189)			(0.0217)
Muslims: Foreign		0.0779***			0.136***
		(0.0148)			(0.0161)
Muslims: Lazy		−0.00189			−0.00337
		(0.0177)			(0.0220)
Muslims: Violent		0.0158			0.0744***
		(0.0183)			(0.0222)
Muslims: Trustworthy		−0.0438*			−0.0149
		(0.0206)			(0.0233)
Constant	0.0154	−0.0391	0.0994*	0.0773*	0.114***
	(0.0449)	(0.0225)	(0.0480)	(0.0327)	(0.0269)
n	602	3764	713	1212	3689
adj. R^2	0.583	0.436	0.378	0.369	0.380

Note: Standard errors in parentheses.
* $p < 0.05$, ** $p < 0.01$, *** $p < 0.001$

Table A21. *Full Models Exploring the Relationship between MAR and Support for Limiting Immigration from Muslim Countries*

	(1) 5/2016 (MTurk)	(2) 7/2018 (Lucid)	(3) 10/2018 (Lucid)	(4) 3/2019 (Lucid)	(5) 6/2019 (Lucid)
MAR (alt.)	0.804***	0.662***	0.556***	0.598***	0.476***
	(0.0625)	(0.0314)	(0.0634)	(0.0493)	(0.0376)
Age	0.00159*	0.00134***	0.00204***	0.00209***	0.00152***
	(0.000737)	(0.000262)	(0.000601)	(0.000490)	(0.000305)
Married	−0.00216	0.0277**	0.0462*	−0.0178	−0.0247*
	(0.0205)	(0.00881)	(0.0204)	(0.0165)	(0.00998)
Income	0.0106	−0.00301	−0.00108	0.00511	0.00120
	(0.00746)	(0.00307)	(0.00716)	(0.00585)	(0.00331)
Education	−0.00858	−0.00457	0.00843	0.00105	−0.00409
	(0.00772)	(0.00330)	(0.00769)	(0.00624)	(0.00365)
Male	−0.0167	−0.00985	0.0117	0.00779	−0.00945
	(0.0189)	(0.00830)	(0.0190)	(0.0155)	(0.00913)
Asian	−0.0270	0.0224	−0.110*	−0.0554	−0.0197
	(0.0397)	(0.0213)	(0.0464)	(0.0361)	(0.0235)
Black	0.0342	0.0268*	−0.00130	−0.0195	0.0260
	(0.0358)	(0.0131)	(0.0316)	(0.0252)	(0.0144)
Hispanic	−0.00313	−0.000159	−0.110**	−0.0127	0.00316
	(0.0518)	(0.00142)	(0.0364)	(0.0316)	(0.0174)
Other race	−0.0259	0.0181	−0.114*	−0.00662	0.0343
	(0.0561)	(0.0188)	(0.0455)	(0.0375)	(0.0203)
Democrat	−0.110***	−0.111***	−0.208***	−0.101***	−0.134***
	(0.0267)	(0.0110)	(0.0250)	(0.0201)	(0.0122)
Independent	−0.0898***	−0.0931***	−0.142***	−0.103***	−0.101***
	(0.0262)	(0.0111)	(0.0252)	(0.0213)	(0.0123)
Racial resentment	0.228***	0.295***	0.324***	0.346***	0.193***
	(0.0448)	(0.0214)	(0.0452)	(0.0369)	(0.0199)
Favorability MAM	−0.0177	0.0160	−0.00494	−0.0144	−0.0534**
	(0.0457)	(0.0174)	(0.0407)	(0.0296)	(0.0194)
Muslims: Patriotic		−0.0555**			−0.0566**
		(0.0181)			(0.0207)
Muslims: Intelligent		0.0130			0.0404
		(0.0185)			(0.0212)
Muslims: Foreign		0.0793***			0.139***
		(0.0146)			(0.0158)
Muslims: Lazy		0.0124			0.0186
		(0.0175)			(0.0217)
Muslims: Violent		0.0248			0.0720***
		(0.0180)			(0.0217)
Muslims: Trustworthy		−0.0422*			−0.0141
		(0.0203)			(0.0228)
Constant	0.0911	0.0425	0.227***	0.108	0.197***
	(0.0685)	(0.0302)	(0.0643)	(0.0551)	(0.0350)
n	602	3764	709	1212	3689
adj. R^2	0.596	0.458	0.483	0.401	0.409

Note: Standard errors in parentheses.

* p < 0.05, ** p < 0.01, *** p < 0.001

Table A22. *Bivariate Relationship between MAR and Support for Patrolling Muslim Neighborhoods*

	(1) 5/2016 (MTurk)	(2) 7/2018 (Lucid)	(3) 10/2018 (Lucid)	(4) 3/2019 (Lucid)	(5) 6/2019 (Lucid)
MAR (alt.)	0.881***	0.845***	1.053***	0.972***	0.936***
	(0.0438)	(0.0211)	(0.0554)	(0.0401)	(0.0217)
Constant	0.151***	0.0950***	0.102***	0.0873***	0.0616***
	(0.0201)	(0.00958)	(0.0249)	(0.0187)	(0.00990)
n	609	3906	710	1212	3920
adj. R^2	0.399	0.291	0.337	0.327	0.321

Note: Standard errors in parentheses.
* $p < 0.05$, ** $p < 0.01$, *** $p < 0.001$

Table A23. *Exploring the Relationship between MAR, Racial Resentment, and Favorability of Muslims and Support for Patrolling Muslim Neighborhoods*

	(1) 5/2016 (MTurk)	(2) 7/2018 (Lucid)	(3) 10/2018 (Lucid)	(4) 3/2019 (Lucid)	(5) 6/2019 (Lucid)
MAR (alt.)	0.620***	0.708***	0.878***	0.742***	0.595***
	(0.0695)	(0.0311)	(0.0695)	(0.0481)	(0.0358)
Racial resentment	0.268***	0.144***	0.332***	0.327***	0.126***
	(0.0454)	(0.0198)	(0.0461)	(0.0345)	(0.0178)
Favorability MAM	−0.0444	0.0174	0.0515	−0.0232	−0.0768***
	(0.0511)	(0.0175)	(0.0445)	(0.0300)	(0.0185)
Muslims: Patriotic		0.00795			−0.0205
		(0.0182)			(0.0196)
Muslims: Intelligent		−0.00322			0.0246
		(0.0187)			(0.0203)
Muslims: Foreign		0.0737***			0.110***
		(0.0147)			(0.0151)
Muslims: Lazy		−0.0343			0.0878***
		(0.0175)			(0.0207)
Muslims: Violent		0.0559**			0.140***
		(0.0182)			(0.0208)
Muslims: Trustworthy		−0.0161			0.0825***
		(0.0204)			(0.0218)
Constant	0.143**	0.0193	−0.0275	0.0300	0.0112
	(0.0501)	(0.0223)	(0.0494)	(0.0323)	(0.0252)
n	604	3764	710	1212	3689
adj. R^2	0.431	0.316	0.381	0.374	0.392

Note: Standard errors in parentheses
* $p < 0.05$, ** $p < 0.01$, *** $p < 0.001$

Table A24. *Full Models Exploring the Relationship between MAR and Support for Patrolling Muslim Neighborhoods*

	(1) 5/2016 (MTurk)	(2) 7/2018 (Lucid)	(3) 10/2018 (Lucid)	(4) 3/2019 (Lucid)	(5) 6/2019 (Lucid)
MAR (alt.)	0.608***	0.681***	0.785***	0.707***	0.583***
	(0.0702)	(0.0316)	(0.0670)	(0.0496)	(0.0358)
Age	0.000871	0.000350	0.000163	0.000444	0.000158
	(0.000827)	(0.000263)	(0.000636)	(0.000493)	(0.000290)
Married	0.0470*	0.0187*	0.0528*	−0.0454**	−0.0214*
	(0.0231)	(0.00886)	(0.0215)	(0.0166)	(0.00949)
Income	0.00860	−0.00214	−0.00863	−0.00138	0.00584
	(0.00837)	(0.00309)	(0.00757)	(0.00588)	(0.00315)
Education	−0.000841	0.00334	0.0184*	0.00656	0.00391
	(0.00871)	(0.00332)	(0.00811)	(0.00628)	(0.00347)
Male	−0.0294	−0.0204*	0.0334	0.0131	−0.0225**
	(0.0212)	(0.00835)	(0.0201)	(0.0156)	(0.00868)
Asian	0.0549	0.0726***	−0.0367	−0.0220	0.0845***
	(0.0446)	(0.0215)	(0.0490)	(0.0363)	(0.0224)
Black	0.0523	0.0450***	0.0535	0.0290	0.0195
	(0.0398)	(0.0132)	(0.0335)	(0.0254)	(0.0137)
Hispanic	0.0900	0.00177	−0.0708	−0.0111	0.0205
	(0.0582)	(0.00143)	(0.0386)	(0.0318)	(0.0165)
Other race	0.0755	0.0197	−0.0897	−0.00923	0.0548**
	(0.0630)	(0.0189)	(0.0479)	(0.0377)	(0.0193)
Democrat	−0.0426	−0.0356**	−0.217***	−0.0601**	−0.0462***
	(0.0300)	(0.0111)	(0.0264)	(0.0202)	(0.0116)
Independent	−0.0104	−0.0241*	−0.145***	−0.0663**	−0.0724***
	(0.0294)	(0.0111)	(0.0266)	(0.0214)	(0.0117)
Racial resentment	0.228***	0.137***	0.196***	0.293***	0.107***
	(0.0504)	(0.0215)	(0.0477)	(0.0371)	(0.0189)
Favorability MAM	−0.0643	0.0159	0.0141	−0.0271	−0.0810***
	(0.0515)	(0.0175)	(0.0430)	(0.0298)	(0.0184)
Muslims: Patriotic		0.00383			−0.00849
		(0.0182)			(0.0197)
Muslims: Intelligent		−0.00261			0.0245
		(0.0187)			(0.0202)
Muslims: Foreign		0.0727***			0.110***
		(0.0147)			(0.0150)
Muslims: Lazy		−0.0292			0.0911***
		(0.0176)			(0.0206)
Muslims: Violent		0.0598***			0.138***
		(0.0182)			(0.0207)
Muslims: Trustworthy		−0.0169			0.0742***
		(0.0204)			(0.0217)
Latino			−0.0708	−0.0111	0.0205
			(0.0386)	(0.0318)	(0.0165)
Constant	0.122	0.0214	0.137*	0.0839	0.0391
	(0.0770)	(0.0304)	(0.0680)	(0.0555)	(0.0333)
n	604	3764	706	1212	3689
adj. R^2	0.438	0.322	0.460	0.384	0.404

Note: Standard errors in parentheses.

* p < 0.05, ** p < 0.01, *** p < 0.001

CHAPTER 4 APPENDIX

Table B1. *Study 1 Heterogeneous Treatment Effects*

	(1) Vote for Candidate B (Rep. Subjects)	(2) Vote for Candidate B (Dem. Subjects)	(3) Vote or Candidate B (Ind. Subjects)
Candidate B: Muslim	−0.163* (0.0681)	−0.0595 (0.0527)	−0.115 (0.0796)
Constant	0.424*** (0.0592)	0.600*** (0.0454)	0.569*** (0.0699)
n	244	466	223
adj. R^2	0.020	0.001	0.005

Note: Standard errors in parentheses.
* $p < 0.05$, ** $p < 0.01$, *** $p < 0.001$

Table B2. *Exploring How Partisanship Shapes Candidate Support in Fictional Republican Elections*

	(1) Vote for Candidate B (Rep, Subjects)	(2) Vote for Candidate B (Dem. Subjects)	(3) Vote for Candidate B (Ind. Subjects)
Candidate B: Muslim	−0.174 (0.0980)	−0.0549 (0.0753)	−0.0831 (0.103)
Constant	0.433*** (0.0837)	0.692*** (0.0664)	0.594*** (0.0887)
N	111	234	126

Note: Standard errors in parentheses
* $p < 0.05$, ** $p < 0.001$

Table B3. *Experimental Effects on Vote Choice and Likelihood of Winning in Study 2*

Disaggregated Treatments	Vote Choice Candidate B	Diff. with White Treatment	Candidate B Likely to Win	Diff. with White Treatment
Stephen Johnson v. Eric Miller	40.81%		45.92%	
Stephen Johnson v. Dean Abdul-Qaadir (white Muslim)	35.00%	5.82%	20.00%	25.91%***
Stephen Johnson v. Richard Porter	36.08%	4.73%	40.21%	5.71%
Stephen Johnson v. Ahmed Al-Akbar (Arab Muslim)	43.87%	−3.06%	18.37%	27.55%***
Stephen Johnson v. Neil Richardson (white)	37.62%	3.19%	38.61%	7.30%
Stephen Johnson v. Louis Muhammad (Black Muslim)	51.00%	−10.18%	22.00%	23.91%***
Stephen Johnson v. Joe Buckner (Black)	47.50%	−6.69%	42.57%	3.34%

Note: $^{+}$ p < 0.1, * p < 0.05, ** p < 0.01, *** p < 0.001

CHAPTER 5 APPENDIX

Table C1. *Search Terms Used to Subset Groups in Broadcast Transcripts*

Muslim: muslim, moslem

Muslim American: muslim american, muslim-american, american muslim, american-muslim, amer muslim, amer. muslim, muslims in america, muslim in america

African American: african american, african americans, african-american, african-americans

Latino: latino, latina, latinos, latinas, hispanic, hispanics

Asian American: asian american, asian-american, american asian, american asian, amer asian, amer. asian

Middle Eastern: middle easterner, middle-easterner, middle eastern american, middle-eastern american, middle easterners, middle-easterners, middle eastern americans, middle-eastern americans

Arab American: arab american, arab americans, arab-american, arab-americans, american arab, american arabs, american-arabs, amer arab, amer. arab

National Origin American: libyan-american, libyan american, american libyan, kuwaiti-american, kuwaiti american, american kuwaiti, tunisian-american, tunisian american, american tunisian, bahraini-american, bahraini american, american bahraini, egyptian-american, egyptian american, american egyptian, iraqi-american, iraqi american, american iraqi, yemeni-american, yemeni american, american yemeni, turkish-american, turkish american, american turk, moroccan-american, moroccan american, american moroccan, jordanian-american, jordanian american, american jordanian, iranian-american, iranian american, american iranian, lebanese-american, lebanese american, american lebanese, armenian-american, armenian american, american armenian, omani-american, omani american, american omani, saudi arabian-american, saudi arabian american, american saudi arabian, syrian-american, syrian american, american syrian, algerian-american, algerian american, american algerian, palestinian-american, palestinian american, american palestinian

---

Table C2. *Frequency Table for CNN Broadcasts*

Year	Muslim n	Muslim Prop.	Muslim Std. Sent.	Muslim Am. n	Muslim Am. Prop.	Muslim Am. Std. Sent.	Black n	Black Prop.	Black Std. Sent.	Latino n	Latino Prop.	Latino Std. Sent.	Asian Am. n	Asian Am. Prop.	Asian Am. Std. Sent.	Total Trans. n	Total Trans. Std. Sent.
1992	503	0.0217	-0.5585	2	0.0001	-0.3817	496	0.0214	-0.3009	613	0.0264	-0.3334	137	0.0059	-0.4307	23,223	-0.1327
1993	1,354	0.0499	-0.499	12	0.0004	-0.7831	484	0.0178	-0.3315	504	0.0186	-0.3804	168	0.0062	-0.3731	27,146	-0.1127
1994	853	0.0362	-0.4552	8	0.0003	-0.3999	628	0.0267	-0.4881	330	0.014	-0.3831	91	0.0039	-0.3274	23,542	-0.157
1995	741	0.0271	-0.4509	11	0.0004	-0.4677	1,371	0.0502	-0.4526	436	0.016	-0.4036	182	0.0067	-0.4215	27,309	-0.1272
1996	449	0.0158	-0.5111	4	0.0001	-0.3122	766	0.0269	-0.3553	351	0.0123	-0.2479	144	0.0051	-0.1483	28,476	-0.1258
1997	423	0.0135	-0.3935	3	0.0001	-0.0884	764	0.0243	-0.3104	342	0.0109	-0.3012	253	0.0081	-0.2937	31,380	-0.1368
1998	408	0.0157	-0.4453	12	0.0005	-0.4203	545	0.021	-0.2736	342	0.0132	-0.1677	120	0.0046	-0.2484	25,919	-0.1483
1999	692	0.0219	-0.3062	13	0.0004	-0.6479	710	0.0225	-0.1469	537	0.017	-0.0113	148	0.0047	-0.1674	31,563	-0.041
2000	942	0.0195	-0.2643	30	0.0006	-0.159	2,019	0.0417	0.0782	1,402	0.029	0.1864	249	0.0051	0.1098	48,367	0.0812
2001	1,464	0.0514	-0.3198	69	0.0024	-0.1152	884	0.0311	-0.0769	474	0.0166	0.0303	121	0.0043	0.0917	28,470	0.0068
2002	1,339	0.0583	-0.3381	78	0.0034	-0.3247	657	0.0286	-0.0558	406	0.0177	-0.0645	54	0.0024	-0.1131	22,973	0.0014
2003	1,514	0.0637	-0.2731	28	0.0012	-0.5603	605	0.0255	-0.0216	398	0.0168	-0.0186	63	0.0027	-0.0999	23,755	0.0195
2004	1,822	0.1754	-0.2153	67	0.0065	-0.2722	915	0.0881	0.0923	668	0.0643	0.1742	71	0.0068	0.1121	10,387	0.5257
2005	1,596	0.184	-0.1629	46	0.0053	-0.4381	792	0.0913	0.0394	592	0.0683	-0.0345	59	0.0068	-0.2064	8,672	0.7244
2006	2,291	0.2841	-0.3728	106	0.0131	-0.4421	865	0.1073	-0.0937	773	0.0959	-0.2532	94	0.0117	-0.3188	8,064	0.4061
2007	1,356	0.1973	-0.3054	107	0.0156	-0.5799	1,174	0.1708	-0.2175	873	0.127	-0.2207	171	0.0249	-0.459	6,873	0.479
2008	860	0.1198	0.1887	39	0.0054	0.2241	2,371	0.3303	0.5382	1,500	0.2089	0.6543	117	0.0163	0.5789	7,179	1.482
2009	1,390	0.1934	0.1221	169	0.0235	0.0813	1,745	0.2428	0.3829	1,381	0.1922	0.3398	166	0.0231	0.2923	7,187	1.2431
2010	1,201	0.1692	0.1428	185	0.0261	0.079	1,223	0.1723	0.2647	1,096	0.1544	0.2842	88	0.0124	0.4298	7,100	1.2957
2011	1,534	0.1957	0.0141	218	0.0278	-0.1012	828	0.1056	0.1205	615	0.0785	0.1444	92	0.0117	0.436	7,838	0.8771
2012	1,315	0.1624	-0.0738	35	0.0043	-0.2352	1,319	0.1629	0.1942	1,604	0.198	0.2888	143	0.0177	0.224	8,099	1.0092
2013	1,186	0.1085	-0.3508	33	0.003	-0.5222	1,128	0.1032	-0.2453	900	0.0823	-0.109	120	0.011	-0.0765	10,934	0.235
2014	1,341	0.1197	-0.4812	23	0.0021	-0.6564	1,567	0.1398	-0.3813	793	0.0708	-0.2976	94	0.0084	-0.4887	11,206	0.0362
2015	2,740	0.2567	-0.4177	347	0.0325	-0.2013	1,914	0.1793	-0.3513	1,295	0.1213	0.0197	120	0.0112	-0.3467	10,675	0.1398
2016	3,614	0.2846	0.3319	527	0.0415	0.3443	3,645	0.287	0.576	3,118	0.2455	0.751	193	0.0152	0.7824	12,699	1.3864

Table C3. *Frequency Table for Fox Broadcasts*

Year	Muslim n	Muslim Prop.	Muslim Std. Sent.	Muslim Am. n	Muslim Am. Prop.	Muslim Am. Std. Sent.	Black n	Black Prop.	Black Std. Sent.	Latino n	Latino Prop.	Latino Std. Sent.	Asian Am. n	Asian Am. Prop.	Asian Am. Std. Sent.	Total Trans. n	Total Trans. Std. Sent.
1998	31	0.0153	-0.4566	0	0	.	96	0.0473	-0.2918	75	0.0370	-0.1538	28	0.0138	-0.058	2,028	0.0449
1999	112	0.0248	-0.3707	2	0.0004	-0.3949	259	0.0574	-0.4062	199	0.0441	-0.3437	51	0.0113	-0.4591	4,515	0.1292
2000	55	0.0123	-0.064	9	0.0020	-0.3795	465	0.1042	-0.0058	357	0.0800	0.1036	40	0.0090	0.5469	4,463	0.306
2001	576	0.1060	-0.4706	64	0.0118	-0.4816	426	0.0784	-0.3319	218	0.0401	-0.3168	36	0.0066	-0.4107	5,436	0.0413
2002	779	0.1075	-0.5257	75	0.0104	-0.4988	396	0.0547	-0.4332	235	0.0324	-0.4494	42	0.0058	-0.4731	7,246	-0.1262
2003	591	0.0745	-0.4741	29	0.0037	-0.491	294	0.0370	-0.3769	272	0.0343	-0.3818	24	0.0030	-0.3188	7,936	-0.0558
2004	527	0.0618	-0.5338	27	0.0032	-0.4976	356	0.0417	-0.3552	242	0.0284	-0.2692	13	0.0015	-0.3995	8,529	-0.0539
2005	667	0.0817	-0.5222	31	0.0038	-0.5501	298	0.0365	-0.4777	284	0.0348	-0.4803	29	0.0036	-0.4358	8,168	-0.1246
2006	752	0.1016	-0.5873	28	0.0038	-0.6057	306	0.0413	-0.4927	362	0.0489	-0.5305	35	0.0047	-0.6197	7,404	-0.1765
2007	637	0.0871	-0.5746	80	0.0109	-0.6591	352	0.0481	-0.5241	267	0.0365	-0.565	32	0.0044	-0.5636	7,314	-0.1747
2008	332	0.0622	-0.2856	20	0.0037	-0.1918	670	0.1254	0.0239	330	0.0618	0.0951	22	0.0041	0.1253	5,341	0.1951
2009	423	0.0832	-0.4168	52	0.0102	-0.4817	299	0.0588	-0.2013	248	0.0488	-0.2618	16	0.0031	-0.3354	5,084	0.1063
2010	609	0.1004	-0.4254	86	0.0142	-0.5437	326	0.0537	-0.3106	444	0.0732	-0.3679	26	0.0043	-0.4937	6,068	0.1115
2011	777	0.119	-0.3638	65	0.01	-0.517	242	0.0371	-0.3446	268	0.0411	-0.2413	14	0.0021	-0.4705	6,528	0.1084
2012	610	0.1268	-0.2833	20	0.0042	-0.2613	407	0.0846	-0.1342	611	0.127	-0.0067	29	0.006	-0.1164	4,812	0.3328
2013	570	0.1184	-0.433	23	0.0048	-0.5695	410	0.0852	-0.3696	395	0.0821	-0.3297	32	0.0066	-0.3474	4,814	-0.0346
2014	650	0.1766	-0.3922	38	0.0103	-0.4841	412	0.1119	-0.302	386	0.1049	-0.1426	49	0.0133	-0.1183	3,681	0.1062
2015	802	0.3227	-0.1027	93	0.0374	-0.2342	446	0.1795	0.0531	406	0.1634	0.3058	32	0.0129	0.1195	2,485	0.6685
2016	712	0.3153	0.8032	80	0.0354	0.6067	664	0.2941	1.1087	670	0.2967	1.1821	50	0.0221	0.9373	2,258	2.2357

Table C4. *Frequency Table for MSNBC's Broadcasts*

Year	Muslim n	Muslim Prop.	Muslim Std. Sent.	Muslim Am. n	Muslim Am. Prop.	Muslim Am. Std. Sent.	Black n	Black Prop.	Black Std. Sent.	Latino n	Latino Prop.	Latino Std. Sent.	Asian Am. n	Asian Am. Prop.	Asian Am. Std. Sent.	Total Trans. n	Total Trans. Std. Sent.
1999	10	0.0204	-0.6027	0	0	.	23	0.0469	-0.1979	19	0.0388	-0.0317	4	0.0082	-0.4115	490	-0.0042
2000	37	0.0151	-0.1072	1	0.0004	1.6627	241	0.0986	0.3693	190	0.0777	0.4774	32	0.0131	0.4614	2,444	0.323
2001	107	0.2215	-0.413	0	0	.	84	0.1739	0.6581	50	0.1035	0.4413	16	0.0331	0.5793	483	0.8707
2002	351	0.3385	-0.4184	37	0.0357	-0.5214	162	0.1562	0.0511	85	0.082	0.0214	25	0.0241	0.0065	1,037	0.1777
2003	450	0.2797	-0.1848	26	0.0162	-0.4219	215	0.1336	-0.1202	168	0.1044	0.0972	28	0.0174	0.1263	1,609	0.5648
2004	277	0.2113	-0.2089	18	0.0137	-0.2442	217	0.1655	0.6246	157	0.1198	0.8022	13	0.0099	0.3506	1,311	0.9687
2005	250	0.189	-0.0476	13	0.0098	-0.144	144	0.1088	-0.0025	126	0.0952	-0.0384	14	0.0106	-0.4223	1,323	0.679
2006	264	0.2167	-0.2155	12	0.0099	-0.3078	203	0.1667	0.0689	142	0.1166	-0.0072	30	0.0246	-0.1409	1,218	0.3715
2007	148	0.1504	0.0952	6	0.0061	-0.1281	201	0.2043	0.2942	112	0.1138	0.3254	12	0.0122	-0.1358	984	0.8018
2008	165	0.1653	0.3124	7	0.007	-0.2087	501	0.502	0.769	255	0.2555	0.9744	8	0.008	0.9035	998	1.7638
2009	184	0.1834	0.2068	11	0.011	0.3058	256	0.2552	0.428	180	0.1795	0.3364	10	0.01	0.4956	1,003	1.2831
2010	262	0.1617	0.1702	33	0.0204	-0.0126	311	0.192	0.3533	282	0.1741	0.2869	20	0.0123	0.1403	1,620	0.9719
2011	284	0.1311	0.2312	49	0.0226	0.0197	298	0.1376	0.2796	198	0.0914	0.3164	12	0.0055	0.2171	2,166	0.8078
2012	235	0.1191	0.3128	16	0.0081	0.0938	576	0.2919	0.6201	643	0.3259	0.6516	52	0.0264	1.0135	1,973	1.3658
2013	253	0.1257	0.1391	14	0.007	-0.1927	695	0.3453	0.4144	659	0.3274	0.432	81	0.0402	0.5033	2,013	0.9589
2014	271	0.162	-0.0342	12	0.0072	0.1288	694	0.4148	0.2527	521	0.3114	0.3873	65	0.0389	0.5583	1,673	1.0012
2015	387	0.3007	0.4323	74	0.0575	0.5297	540	0.4196	0.6028	443	0.3442	0.9019	46	0.0357	1.0439	1,287	1.7378
2016	459	0.4165	1.3234	77	0.0699	1.1256	490	0.4446	1.4436	482	0.4374	1.4306	46	0.0417	1.3914	1,102	3.0828

Table C5. Frequency Table for All Three News Outlets' Broadcasts

Year	Muslim n	Muslim Prop.	Muslim Std. Sent.	Muslim Am. n	Muslim Am. Prop.	Muslim Am. Std. Sent.	Black n	Black Prop.	Black Std. Sent.	Latino n	Latino Prop.	Latino Std. Sent.	Asian Am. n	Asian Am. Prop.	Asian Am. Std. Sent.	Total Trans. n	Total Trans. Std. Sent.
1992	503	0.0217	-0.5585	2	0.0001	-0.3817	496	0.0214	-0.3009	613	0.0264	-0.3334	137	0.0059	-0.4307	23,223	-0.1327
1993	1,354	0.0499	-0.499	12	0.0004	-0.7831	484	0.0178	-0.3315	504	0.0186	-0.3804	168	0.0062	-0.3731	27,146	-0.1127
1994	853	0.0362	-0.4552	8	0.0003	-0.3999	628	0.0267	-0.4881	330	0.014	-0.3831	91	0.0039	-0.3274	23,542	-0.157
1995	741	0.0271	-0.4509	11	0.0004	-0.4677	1,371	0.0502	-0.4526	436	0.016	-0.4036	182	0.0067	-0.4215	27,309	-0.1272
1996	449	0.0158	-0.5111	4	0.0001	-0.3122	766	0.0269	-0.3553	351	0.0123	-0.2479	144	0.0051	-0.1483	28,477	-0.1258
1997	423	0.0135	-0.3935	3	0.0001	-0.0884	764	0.0243	-0.3104	342	0.0109	-0.3012	253	0.0081	-0.2937	31,381	-0.1368
1998	439	0.0157	-0.4461	12	0.0004	-0.4203	641	0.0229	-0.2764	417	0.0149	-0.1652	148	0.0053	-0.2124	27,950	-0.1342
1999	814	0.0223	-0.3187	15	0.0004	-0.6141	992	0.0271	-0.2158	755	0.0206	-0.0995	203	0.0056	-0.2455	36,574	-0.0195
2000	1,034	0.0187	-0.248	40	0.0007	-0.163	2,725	0.0493	0.0896	1,949	0.0352	0.1996	321	0.0058	0.1993	55,295	0.1101
2001	2,147	0.0624	-0.3649	133	0.0039	-0.2915	1,394	0.0405	-0.1105	742	0.0216	-0.044	173	0.005	0.0322	34,392	0.0244
2002	2,469	0.079	-0.4087	190	0.0061	-0.4317	1,215	0.0389	-0.1646	726	0.0232	-0.179	121	0.0039	-0.2133	31,257	-0.0223
2003	2,555	0.0767	-0.304	83	0.0025	-0.4927	1,114	0.0334	-0.1344	838	0.0252	-0.1133	115	0.0035	-0.0905	33,306	0.028
2004	2,626	0.1298	-0.2785	112	0.0055	-0.322	1,488	0.0735	0.0629	1,067	0.0527	0.166	97	0.0048	0.0755	20,234	0.3101
2005	2,513	0.1383	-0.2468	90	0.005	-0.4342	1,234	0.0679	-0.0903	1,002	0.0551	-0.1613	102	0.0056	-0.3013	18,172	0.3395
2006	3,307	0.1982	-0.409	146	0.0087	-0.4625	1,374	0.0823	-0.1585	1,277	0.0765	-0.3044	159	0.0095	-0.3514	16,687	0.1451
2007	2,141	0.1411	-0.3578	193	0.0127	-0.5987	1,727	0.1138	-0.2204	1,252	0.0825	-0.2452	215	0.0142	-0.4566	15,171	0.1848
2008	1,357	0.1004	0.0877	66	0.0049	0.0522	3,542	0.262	0.4736	2,085	0.1542	0.6049	147	0.0109	0.5287	13,520	0.9945
2009	1,997	0.1504	0.0158	232	0.0175	-0.0342	2,300	0.1733	0.312	1,809	0.1363	0.257	192	0.0145	0.2506	13,275	0.8108
2010	2,072	0.1401	-0.0207	304	0.0206	-0.1071	1,860	0.1258	0.1787	1,822	0.1232	0.1257	134	0.0091	0.2074	14,788	0.7743
2011	2,595	0.157	-0.0753	332	0.0201	-0.1648	1,368	0.0827	0.0729	1,081	0.0654	0.0803	118	0.0071	0.3061	16,532	0.5645
2012	2,160	0.1451	-0.0909	71	0.0048	-0.1684	2,302	0.1547	0.2427	2,858	0.192	0.3072	224	0.015	0.3632	14,884	0.8378
2013	2,009	0.1131	-0.3124	70	0.0039	-0.4719	2,233	0.1257	-0.0628	1,954	0.11	0.0288	233	0.0131	0.0879	17,761	0.244
2014	2,262	0.1366	-0.402	73	0.0044	-0.4376	2,673	0.1614	-0.2045	1,700	0.1027	-0.0525	208	0.0126	-0.0742	16,560	0.1493
2015	3,929	0.2716	-0.2697	514	0.0355	-0.102	2,900	0.2005	-0.1115	2,144	0.1482	0.2561	198	0.0137	0.0517	14,465	0.3728
2016	4,785	0.2979	0.4972	684	0.0426	0.463	4,799	0.2988	0.7383	4,270	0.2659	0.8954	289	0.018	0.9061	16,060	1.6223

Table C6. *Regression Analysis: Examining Differences in Standardized Sentiment Score in CNN, Fox, and MSNBC Broadcasts*

	(1) CNN Hu and Liu Std. Sent.	(2) CNN Hu and Liu Std. Sent.	(3) FOX Hu and Liu Std. Sent.	(4) MSNBC Hu and Liu Std. Sent.
Black	0.123	0.0996***	0.0749**	0.0913*
	(0.0708)	(0.0198)	(0.0237)	(0.0415)
Latino	0.180*	0.142***	0.0869***	0.119**
	(0.0711)	(0.0200)	(0.0237)	(0.0418)
Muslim	0.00609	0.00284	0.0137	0.0119
	(0.0706)	(0.0190)	(0.0221)	(0.0405)
Asian	0.161*	0.0933***	0.0648	0.123*
American	(0.0727)	(0.0277)	(0.0366)	(0.0538)
Constant	−0.362***	−0.0108	−0.239***	0.375***
	(0.0702)	(0.0185)	(0.0216)	(0.0396)
n	22217	64365	21071	14505
adj. R^2	0.259	0.368	0.562	0.568
Pre-9/11 only?	✓			
Post-9/11 only?		✓	✓	✓

Note: Standard errors in parentheses.

* $p < 0.05$, ** $p < 0.01$, *** $p < 0.001$

Note: All models are fixed effect regressions, absorbed at the day level.

Table C7. *Standardized Mean Sentiment Scores of Alternative Black and Latino Corpuses Compared to Black and Latino Corpuses in Main Analysis*

Year	Alt. Black Std. Sent. Score	N	Black Std. Sent. Score	N	Difference	Alt. Latino Std. Sent. Score	N	Latino Std. Sent. Score	N	Difference
1992	−0.3337	1,746	−0.3009	496	0.033	−0.4070	486	−0.3334	613	0.074
1993	−0.3001	1,596	−0.3315	484	−0.031	−0.3893	756	−0.3804	504	0.009
1994	−0.3747	997	−0.4881	628	−0.113	−0.4329	385	−0.3831	330	0.050
1995	−0.3596	1,017	−0.4526	1,371	−0.093	−0.3744	465	−0.4036	436	−0.029
1996	−0.2612	1,091	−0.3553	766	−0.094	−0.3263	511	−0.2479	351	0.078
1997	−0.2745	965	−0.3104	764	−0.036	−0.2840	610	−0.3012	342	−0.017
1998	−0.2236	907	−0.2764	641	−0.053	−0.2081	435	−0.1652	417	0.043
1999	−0.1448	1,428	−0.2158	992	−0.071	−0.1405	808	−0.0995	755	0.041
2000	0.0893	2,799	0.0896	2,725	0.000	0.1455	1,246	0.1996	1,949	0.054
2001	−0.1299	1,537	−0.1105	1,394	0.019	−0.1851	857	−0.0440	742	0.141
2002	−0.2004	1,511	−0.1646	1,215	0.036	−0.3145	885	−0.1790	726	0.136
2003	−0.1153	1,683	−0.1344	1,114	−0.019	−0.2212	1,047	−0.1133	838	0.108
2004	0.0252	1,807	0.0629	1,488	0.038	−0.0719	1,267	0.1660	1,067	**0.238**
2005	−0.0109	2,042	−0.0903	1,234	−0.079	−0.2446	1,364	−0.1613	1,002	0.083
2006	−0.1510	1,691	−0.1585	1,374	−0.008	−0.2745	1,610	−0.3044	1,277	−0.030
2007	−0.2045	1,763	−0.2204	1,727	−0.016	−0.3102	1,763	−0.2452	1,252	0.065
2008	0.4198	2,094	0.4736	3,542	0.054	0.3039	2,094	0.6049	2,085	**0.301**
2009	0.2451	1,759	0.3120	2,300	0.067	0.1321	1,759	0.2570	1,809	0.125
2010	0.2785	1,513	0.1787	1,860	−0.100	0.0028	1,890	0.1257	1,822	0.123
2011	0.0250	1,591	0.0729	1,368	0.048	0.0400	1,164	0.0803	1,081	0.040
2012	0.3161	1,960	0.2427	2,302	−0.073	0.2920	1,446	0.3072	2,858	0.015
2013	−0.0671	1,738	−0.0628	2,233	0.004	−0.0274	1,342	0.0288	1,954	0.056
2014	−0.2194	1,752	−0.2045	2,673	0.015	−0.2292	1,868	−0.0525	1,700	0.177
2015	−0.0995	1,813	−0.1115	2,900	−0.012	0.1283	2,149	0.2561	2,144	0.128
2016	0.7507	2,785	0.7383	4,799	−0.012	0.7340	2,896	0.8954	4,270	0.161

CHAPTER 6 APPENDIX

Table D1. *Experiment 1 Template (Real) – Positive, Muslim American*

Sullivan, host: Kareem, you talk about Muslim Americans, and this is something you've been trying to bridge the gulf on this issue for decades now and trying to explain to people who Muslim Americans are, what they aren't, what they believe, what they don't believe. And very personally in your own case, what you believe and what you don't believe. In a passage in an article you wrote, you refer to something that happened where President Obama talked about Muslim Americans and Donald Trump tweeted about that. Let's first listen to what the president said.

Barack Obama, President of the United States: "Muslim Americans are our friends and our neighbors, our co-workers, our sports heroes. And yes, they are our men and women in uniform who are willing to die in defense of our country. We have to remember that."

Sullivan, host: Obviously, you know, when I heard him say that, you're the first name I thought of that he was talking about obviously, Muhammad Ali. But you can go on and on. It was real easy to come up with examples. But then, Donald Trump Tweeted:

Donald Trump, Tweet: "President Obama said in his speech that Muslim Americans are our sports heroes. What sport is he talking about and who?"

Kareem Abdul-Jabbar: So of course, Donald apparently had no memory of ever meeting me or knowing that I played basketball, despite publishing a picture of us we took together, which he now denies we ever took and claims it was Photo-shopped.

Sullivan, host: So, he's denying that he's – that that's him in the picture?

Kareem Abdul-Jabbar: Yes, he's denying that that's him in the picture.

Sullivan, host: But were you surprised in that moment we discovered that Donald Trump actually could not imagine Muslim Americans succeeding in any American sport on any level?

Kareem Abdul-Jabbar: Yes, I was very surprised at that, because Muslims have competed on many different sports here in America and done very well, along with a whole lot of other athletes. And, you know, it seems to me that he does not want to say anything positive about a person of color.

Sullivan, host: You wrote something about your experience as a Muslim American. And I got to say, this was really quite shocking to me about how some of your fans even treat you. You wrote,

"Some fans still call me Lew. I was born Lew Alcindor. Now I'm Kareem Abdul-Jabbar. The transition from Lew to Kareem was not merely a change in celebrity brand name – like Sean Combs to Puff Daddy to Diddy to P. Diddy – but a transformation of heart, mind, and soul... When you convert to an unfamiliar or unpopular religion, it invites criticism of one's intelligence, patriotism, and sanity. I should know. Even though I became a Muslim more than 40 years ago, I'm still defending that choice. Without really knowing the peaceful practices of most of the world's 1.6 billion Muslims, people see only the worst examples. Part of my conversion to Islam is accepting the responsibility to teach others about my religion, not to convert them but to coexist with them through mutual respect, support and peace. One world does not have to mean one religion, just one belief in living in peace."

Sullivan, host: And Kareem, you and I know that a person has to be 60 years old or older to know that your birth name was Lew Alcindor. It stunned me that some people would be out there clinging to that, and how can they not know that that's an offensive thing to do with you?

Kareem Abdul-Jabbar: I don't know how that's possible. Because, you know, change is part of our existence. You know, things change, people evolve, situations take a different turn and this is what has happened in my life, and it happens in everyone's life.

Sullivan, host: Thank you so much for joining us, Kareem, we really appreciate you being here.

Table D2. *Experiment 1 Template (Real) – Negative, Muslim American*

Sullivan, host: Just three weeks ago, we did a special called the "growing terror threat." And in it, we warned of future homegrown attacks and it didn't take long before it happened. An apparent radical Muslim, raised in America, has killed four marines in a terror attack on American soil. So, tonight, we will deconstruct what is happening and talk about what we should be doing to keep this country safe. The attack has prompted a federal domestic terror investigation and renewed concerns about America's vulnerabilities to Islamic terrorism by Muslims in America. [Miller], what do we know about the investigation so far?

Miller, chief intelligence correspondent: Federal law enforcement source tells us that so far there has been no evidence that's caused them to change their focus on terrorism – that's significant. So they continue to look at this shooting at the highest possible level in terms of investigative tools.

Sullivan, host: And [Miller], we noticed that he had a blog and there would be some, I guess that would be, maybe something like red flags on some of the things he was posting on his blog?

Miller, chief intelligence correspondent: Yes. He had a blog called "America the Vulnerable." Terrorism analysts have warned for years that the United States is susceptible to attacks on called soft targets and that ISIS is trying to inspire such attacks by connecting with Muslims in America and inspiring domestic terrorism.

Sullivan, host: If ISIS is involved even indirectly all hell is going to break loose in this country. For months those savages have been encouraging people on the net to attack Americans.

Smith, FBI special agent contributor: I agree. I have no doubt that it is traced to Islamic state. And this is very straightforward. As long as the Islamic state is an inspiration to would-be Muslim American jihadis, there are going to be more lone wolves and larger attacks here. We have got to stop playing defense. Stop living in fear. Make the terrorists afraid. Even those in this country. Religious fanaticism is meth. And until we go on the offensive, the terror will not end. You want to stop terrorism here? Obliterate the caliphate and show the would-be jihadis that Allah doesn't have their backs.

Miller, chief intelligence correspondent: Well – [Smith] is completely correct. And I'm tired of this parsing was this terror or not terror. This was terror. Within their culture the strong horse is the one that everybody wants to follow. So in a different metaphor, it's not necessarily meth, it's the strong horse. Same difference. We have got to show that we are in this to win it.

Sullivan, host: But guys, he was not watched. Why was he not on a terror watch list and more importantly, maybe we wiretap every single move he makes.

Miller, chief intelligence correspondent: Well, because we are more worried about civil liberties of terrorists than we are about civil defense of the American people. I mean terrorists don't have rights. Get over it. You know, look, we all love Lincoln. Lincoln – he suspended habeas corpus. We are in a war and we are pretending we are in a debate. This is not a debating society.

Sullivan, host: Well, okay, do we profile? Let me just put it out there. Is it time to start profiling?

Smith, FBI special agent contributor: Look, if someone – even if they are an American – is out there, saying that Hamas is a legitimate group despite their suicide bombings or that the caliphate in destroying Israel is a wonderful thing. That should be taken as indication that this Muslim guy is someone that you should watch even if you can't prosecute them for that speech.

Sullivan, host: So our final issue here: Does America have a growing Islamic extremism problem? Here's what I think, we have a growing concern in the United States over Islamic terror.

Miller, chief intelligence correspondent: Look 70% of Americans are concerned. We should be too.

Table D3. *Experiment 1 Template (Real) – Positive, Muslim*

Sullivan, host: A Muslim backlash is building in the world since the publication of the cartoon of Prophet Muhammad in a French magazine. In Algeria, Jordan, Pakistan, Iran, Turkey, and elsewhere, Muslims are rallying and Europe is rattled. Here to talk about all this, I'm joined by (Kay), an international affairs correspondent and (Smith) an international law expert. So, let me ask you about the response that we've seen in Europe and around the world by Muslims this week, what do you make of this strategically?

Kay, intelligence correspondent: I think what we see, you know, is, I think Europe has changed but is making a concerted effort to protect and respect its Muslim population.

Smith, international law expert: That's right. For example, last November, France implemented a law on hate speech. So, if someone is charged for the spoken word, then they can get potentially convicted up to five years in prison on $2,000 fine. If it's on the Internet, it's seven years and $120,000.

Sullivan, host: So what is the right balance for intelligence analysts?

Kay, intelligence correspondent: Well, it's a very fine line. We've been sort of talking about and debating and struggling with the balance of tolerance of religion, versus charging people for inciting hatred, extremism, or more violence. And, you know, the UK has been very prominent in that in their own Hyde Park, which is the biggest – one of the biggest parks in London – has Hyde Park Corner.

Sullivan, host: Interesting, so what is going on there?

Kay, intelligence correspondent: You have Hyde Park Corner. It's a speaker's corner on one of the corners in Hyde Park where people can come and they can talk freely about whatever they want. And that does include some Muslim people who want to talk about their diverse versions of Islam. And they've been allowed to do that as an outlet to express their concerns in society.

Smith, international law expert: Is this making it more complicated for the intelligence services to counter threats?

Sullivan, host: You know, a couple of months ago, six months ago, a year ago, there was this big debate in the U.S. about the NSA and the NSA's ability to troll e-mail accounts and look for that needle in the haystack. The intelligence community has a really difficult job. They damned if they do, they damned if they don't. But these people also need a peaceful outlet to be able to stand up for themselves and express themselves as well.

Sullivan, host: Right, what a fine line. Well thank you for joining us this morning.

Table D4. *Experiment Template (Real) – Negative, Muslim*

Sullivan, host: Dozens of schoolchildren have been slaughtered in a Taliban attack on a school in Pakistan. Gunmen roaming the halls, slaughtering children wherever they could find them, kids. The death toll now stands at 132 children murdered, ten staff members, and three Pakistani soldiers. Seven Islamic terrorists also died in the assault. Our chief intelligence correspondent (Scuitto) is with me here in the situation room. (Scuitto), this is brutal, what happened?

Scuitto, chief national security correspondent: No question about it. It was an attack so barbaric that even the Afghan branch of the Taliban condemned it today. I'm told by the Pakistani military that the attackers had ammunition and supplies to last for days and that this was certainly a suicide operation, that the Islamic terrorists intended both to kill and to die there. Recall that in 2009, one of their suicide bombers killed seven CIA officers and in 2010, the group claimed responsibility for the attempted car bombing of Times Square in New York City. And following the killing of Bin Laden in Pakistan in 2011, the group vowed more attacks on U.S. soil. But with the growth of ISIS, it has been unable to, and so they are trying to regain credibility.

Sullivan, host: And they think this gives them credibility by killing Muslim children?

Scuitto, chief national security correspondent: I mean, it's a sick, sick calculus the way these Islamist groups operate, right? They consider it a success when they capture your attention. They've certainly captured our attention today.

Sullivan, host: Brutal. All right. (Scuitto), thanks very much. Let's get some more now from Republican Congressman (Smith), who is joining us here today. Smith, what do you make of all this?

Smith, (R.) Congressman: These Islamic terrorist groups are going to be anti-American no matter what. To me, we have to stop using excuses. "Like if we do this, we're going to antagonize them." The fact is we did nothing to antagonize them, and they attacked us on 9/11.

Sullivan, host: Thank you, Congressman. New details are coming into the newsroom on the bloody siege in Sydney, Australia where a Muslim gunman, a self-styled Muslim cleric with a criminal record held hostages for more than 16 hours at a downtown café before a swat team moved in. The gunman and two hostages died. Authorities are still trying to piece together what exactly happened and why. Let's go live to Sydney. (McEnany), what is the latest?

McEnany, international correspondent: (Sullivan), it's hard to believe, but this gunman, a 50-year-old Muslim immigrant, was on the terror list here in Australia many years ago but recently he was taken off because it was deemed no longer to be a threat. So many here including the Australian prime minister questioning authorities as to how this man with a violent history with extremist views was known to police for so many years was allowed to walk the streets freely of Sydney. We're talking about somebody who was out on bail having been charged with serious offenses. We're talking about accessory to murder his ex-wife and sexual assault, 45 counts. But despite those charges, he was walking the streets of Sydney living his life, able to walk into this café with a gun.

Sullivan, host: Yes it's hard to believe. (McEnany), thanks for that report.

Table D5. *Experiment 2 Template (Manipulated) – Positive Treatments, Muslim and Muslim American*

Sullivan, host: Good evening to our viewers across the country and across the world. This is (Sullivan), and tonight we are examining the content of Facebook posts by (Muslim Americans/Muslims) around the world. Here with me is (Scuitto), our chief technology analyst. (Scuitto), welcome.

Scuitto, chief technology analyst: Thank you for having me.

Sullivan, host: So tell us – what did your research find?

Scuitto, chief technology analyst: Well as you know (Sullivan), (Muslim Americans/Muslims) are all over the news today. It seems you can't watch a regular broadcast segment without them popping up. But we know very little about them in general. So our team decided that one way to understand what is going on with them was to investigate what Muslims around the world are writing about on Facebook.

Strikingly one of the most active Facebook accounts we came across belonged to a man who is a (Muslim American of Jordanian background/recent immigrant from Jordan), who has graduated from college, and who is now living on the east coast. Just an average guy. But he has also been repeatedly and publicly denouncing ISIS and all forms of jihadi extremism in solidarity with the U.S. and our allies in the War on Terror. These posts really made us think that we need to reevaluate how we perceive Muslims around the world and that we need to understand their beliefs more carefully to make sure America knows what they think and who they are.

Note: Text in parentheses was experimentally manipulated.

Table D6. *Experiment 2 Template (Manipulated) – Negative Treatments, Muslim and Muslim American*

Sullivan, host: Good evening to our viewers across the country and across the world. This is (Sullivan), and tonight we are examining the content of Facebook posts by (Muslim Americans/Muslims) around the world. Here with me is (Scuitto), our chief technology analyst. (Scuitto), welcome.

Scuitto, chief technology analyst: Thank you for having me.

Sullivan, host: So tell us – what did your research find?

Scuitto, chief technology analyst: Well as you know (Sullivan), (Muslim Americans/Muslims) are all over the news today. It seems you can't watch a regular broadcast segment without them popping up. But we know very little about them in general. So our team decided that one way to understand what is going on with them was to investigate what Muslims around the world are writing about on Facebook.

Strikingly, one of the most active Facebook accounts we came across belonged to a man who is a (Muslim American of Jordanian background/recent immigrant from Jordan), who has graduated from college, and who is now living on the east coast. Just an average guy. But he has also been repeatedly and publicly supporting ISIS and all forms of jihadi extremism against the U.S. and our allies in the War on Terror. These posts really made us think that we need to reevaluate how we perceive Muslims around the world and that we need to understand their beliefs more carefully to make sure America knows what they think and who they are.

Note: Text in parentheses was experimentally manipulated.

Table D7. *Experiment 3: Treatment 1, Positive Muslim American*

Sullivan, host: Good evening to our viewers across the country and across the world. This is (Sullivan), and tonight we are examining the content of Facebook posts by Muslim Americans. Here with me is (Scuitto), our chief technology analyst. (Scuitto), welcome.

Scuitto, chief technology analyst: Thank you for having me.

Sullivan, host: So tell us – what did your research find?

Scuitto, chief technology analyst: Well as you know (Sullivan), Muslim Americans are all over the news today. It seems you can't watch a regular broadcast segment without them popping up. But we know very little about them in general. So our team decided that one way to understand what is going on with them was to investigate what Muslim Americans are writing about on Facebook.

Strikingly, one of the most active Facebook accounts we came across belonged to a Muslim American man, who has graduated from college, and who is now living on the east coast. Just an average guy. But he has also been repeatedly and publicly denouncing ISIS and all forms of jihadi extremism in solidarity with the U.S. and our allies in the War on Terror. These posts really made us think that we need to reevaluate how we perceive Muslim Americans and that we need to understand their beliefs more carefully to make sure America knows what they think and who they are.

Table D8. *Experiment 3: Treatment 2, Alternative Positive Muslim American*

Sullivan, host: Good evening to our viewers across the country and across the world. This is (Sullivan), and tonight we are examining the content of Facebook posts by Muslim Americans. Here with me is (Scuitto), our chief technology analyst. (Scuitto), welcome.

Scuitto, chief technology analyst: Thank you for having me.

Sullivan, host: So tell us – what did your research find?

Scuitto, chief technology analyst: Well as you know (Sullivan), Muslim Americans are all over the news today. It seems you can't watch a regular broadcast segment without them popping up. But we know very little about them in general. So our team decided that one way to understand what is going on with them was to investigate what Muslim Americans are writing about on Facebook.

Strikingly, one of the most active Facebook accounts we came across belonged to a Muslim American man, who has graduated from college, and who is now living on the east coast. Just an average guy. But he has also been repeatedly and actively participating in his community and serving the most marginalized, such as the homeless. These posts really made us think that we need to reevaluate how we perceive Muslim Americans and that we need to understand their beliefs more carefully to make sure America knows what they think and who they are.

Table D9. *Experiment 3: Treatment 3, Positive Muslim*

Sullivan, host: Good evening to our viewers across the country and across the world. This is (Sullivan), and tonight we are examining the content of Facebook posts by Muslims around the world. Here with me is (Scuitto), our chief technology analyst. (Scuitto), welcome.

Scuitto, chief technology analyst: Thank you for having me.

Sullivan, host: So tell us – what did your research find?

Scuitto, chief technology analyst: Well as you know (Sullivan), Muslims are all over the news today. It seems you can't watch a regular broadcast segment without them popping up. But we know very little about them in general. So our team decided that one way to understand what is going on with them was to investigate what Muslims around the world are writing about on Facebook.

Strikingly, one of the most active Facebook accounts we came across belonged to a Muslim man who is a recent immigrant from Jordan, who has graduated from college, and who is now living on the east coast. Just an average guy. But he has also been repeatedly and publicly denouncing ISIS and all forms of jihadi extremism in solidarity with the U.S. and our allies in the War on Terror. These posts really made us think that we need to reevaluate how we perceive Muslims around the world and that we need to understand their beliefs more carefully to make sure America knows what they think and who they are.

Table D10. *Experiment 3: Treatment 4, Negative Muslim American*

Sullivan, host: Good evening to our viewers across the country and across the world. This is (Sullivan), and tonight we are examining the content of Facebook posts by Muslim Americans. Here with me is (Scuitto), our chief technology analyst. (Scuitto), welcome.

Scuitto, chief technology analyst: Thank you for having me.

Sullivan, host: So tell us – what did your research find?

Scuitto, chief technology analyst: Well as you know (Sullivan), Muslim Americans are all over the news today. It seems you can't watch a regular broadcast segment without them popping up. But we know very little about them in general. So our team decided that one way to understand what is going on with them was to investigate what Muslim Americans are writing about on Facebook.

Strikingly, one of the most active Facebook accounts we came across belonged to a Muslim American man, who has graduated from college, and who is now living on the east coast. Just an average guy. But he has also been repeatedly and publicly supporting ISIS and all forms of jihadi extremism against the U.S. and our allies in the War on Terror. These posts really made us think that we need to reevaluate how we perceive Muslim Americans and that we need to understand their beliefs more carefully to make sure America knows what they think and who they are.

Table D11. *Examining Differences Between Control and Treatments on Policy Issues*

Condition	Policy Examined	Condition Mean	Control Mean	Diff.
T1. Muslim American pos.	Limit all imm.	2.8	2.82	−0.023 p = 0.805
T1. Muslim American pos.	Limit Muslim imm.	2.79	2.87	−0.073 p = 0.447
T1. Muslim American pos.	Limit MAM entry	2.46	2.61	−0.14 p = 0.109
T2. Muslim American alt. pos.	Limit all imm.	2.87	2.82	0.054 p = 0.571
T2. Muslim American alt. pos.	Limit Muslim imm.	2.84	2.87	−0.023 p = 0.814
T2. Muslim American alt. pos.	Limit MAM entry	2.49	2.61	0 −0.124 p = 0.190
T3. Muslim pos.	Limit all imm.	2.96	2.82	0.138 p = 0.145
T3. Muslim pos.	Limit Muslim imm.	2.91	2.87	0.040 p = 0.677
T3. Muslim pos.	Limit MAM entry	2.6	2.61	−0.013 p = 0.890
T4. Muslim American neg.	Limit all imm.	2.84	2.82	0.021 p = 0.825
T4. Muslim American neg.	Limit Muslim imm.	2.91	2.87	0.040 p = 0.676
T4. Muslim American neg.	Limit MAM entry	2.68	2.61	0.070 p = 0.457
T5. Muslim neg.	Limit all imm.	3.02	2.82	0.199 p = 0.039
T5. Muslim neg.	Limit Muslim imm.	3.08	2.87	0.215 p = 0.030
T5. Muslim neg.	Limit MAM entry	2.82	2.61	0.203 p = 0.033

Note: The policies above are measured on a 1–5 scale, with higher values indicating more support for the restrictive policy. Reported differences are between positive and negative conditions and the control.
Source: July 2018 Lucid survey.

Table D12. *Experiment 3: Treatment 5, Negative Muslim*

Sullivan, host: Good evening to our viewers across the country and across the world. This is (Sullivan), and tonight we are examining the content of Facebook posts by Muslims around the world. Here with me is (Scuitto), our chief technology analyst. (Scuitto), welcome.

Scuitto, chief technology analyst: Thank you for having me.

Sullivan, host: So tell us – what did your research find?

Scuitto, chief technology analyst: Well as you know (Sullivan), Muslims are all over the news today. It seems you can't watch a regular broadcast segment without them popping up. But we know very little about them in general. So our team decided that one way to understand what is going on with them was to investigate what Muslims around the world are writing about on Facebook.

Strikingly, one of the most active Facebook accounts we came across belonged to a Muslim man who is a recent immigrant from Jordan, who has graduated from college, and who is now living on the east coast. Just an average guy. But he has also been repeatedly and publicly supporting ISIS and all forms of jihadi extremism against the U.S. and our allies in the War on Terror. These posts really made us think that we need to reevaluate how we perceive Muslims around the world and that we need to understand their beliefs more carefully to make sure America knows what they think and who they are.

Table D13. *Experiment 3: Treatment 6, Positive Latino*

Sullivan, host: Good evening to our viewers across the country and across the world. This is (Sullivan), and tonight we are examining the content of Facebook posts by Latinos. Here with me is (Scuitto), our chief technology analyst. (Scuitto), welcome.

Scuitto, chief technology analyst: Thank you for having me.

Sullivan, host: So tell us – what did your research find?

Scuitto, chief technology analyst: Well as you know (Sullivan), Latinos are all over the news today. It seems you can't watch a regular broadcast segment without them popping up. But we know very little about them in general. So our team decided that one way to understand what is going on with them was to investigate what Latinos are writing about on Facebook.

Strikingly, one of the most active Facebook accounts we came across belonged to a Latino man who is of Mexican background, who has graduated from college, and who is now living on the east coast. Just an average guy. But he has also been repeatedly and publicly denouncing the MS-13 gang and all forms of criminal gang violence in solidarity with the U.S. in the War on Drugs. These posts really made us think that we need to reevaluate how we perceive Latinos and that we need to understand their beliefs more carefully to make sure America knows what they think and who they are.

Table D14. *Experiment 3: Treatment 7, Positive Immigrant*

Sullivan, host: Good evening to our viewers across the country and across the world. This is (Sullivan), and tonight we are examining the content of Facebook posts by immigrants. Here with me is (Scuitto), our chief technology analyst. (Scuitto), welcome.

Scuitto, chief technology analyst: Thank you for having me.

Sullivan, host: So tell us – what did your research find?

Scuitto, chief technology analyst: Well as you know (Sullivan), immigrants are all over the news today. It seems you can't watch a regular broadcast segment without them popping up. But we know very little about them in general. So our team decided that one way to understand what is going on with them was to investigate what immigrants are writing about on Facebook.

Strikingly, one of the most active Facebook accounts we came across belonged to an immigrant man, who has graduated from college, and who is now living on the east coast. Just an average guy. But he has also been repeatedly and publicly denouncing illegal immigration into the U.S. and all forms of law breaking in solidarity with U.S. policy. These posts really made us think that we need to reevaluate how we perceive immigrants around the world and that we need to understand their beliefs more carefully to make sure America knows what they think and who they are.

Table D15. *Experiment 3: Treatment 8, Negative Latino*

Sullivan, host: Good evening to our viewers across the country and across the world. This is (Sullivan), and tonight we are examining the content of Facebook posts by Latinos. Here with me is (Scuitto), our chief technology analyst. (Scuitto), welcome.

Scuitto, chief technology analyst: Thank you for having me.

Sullivan, host: So tell us – what did your research find?

Scuitto, chief technology analyst: Well as you know (Sullivan), Latinos are all over the news today. It seems you can't watch a regular broadcast segment without them popping up. But we know very little about them in general. So our team decided that one way to understand what is going on with them was to investigate what Latinos are writing about on Facebook.

Strikingly, one of the most active Facebook accounts we came across belonged to a Latino man who is of Mexican background, who has graduated from college, and who is now living on the east coast. Just an average guy. But he has also been repeatedly and publicly supporting the MS-13 gang and all forms of criminal gang violence against the U.S. in the War on Drugs. These posts really made us think that we need to reevaluate how we perceive Latinos and that we need to understand their beliefs more carefully to make sure America knows what they think and who they are.

Table D16. *Experiment 3: Treatment 9, Negative Immigrant*

Sullivan, host: Good evening to our viewers across the country and across the world. This is (Sullivan), and tonight we are examining the content of Facebook posts by immigrants. Here with me is (Scuitto), our chief technology analyst. (Scuitto), welcome.

Scuitto, chief technology analyst: Thank you for having me.

Sullivan, host: So tell us – what did your research find?

Scuitto, chief technology analyst: Well as you know (Sullivan), immigrants are all over the news today. It seems you can't watch a regular broadcast segment without them popping up. But we know very little about them in general. So our team decided that one way to understand what is going on with them was to investigate what immigrants are writing about on Facebook.

Strikingly, one of the most active Facebook accounts we came across belonged to an immigrant man, who has graduated from college, and who is now living on the east coast. Just an average guy. But he has also been repeatedly and publicly supporting illegal immigration into the U.S. and all forms of law breaking in opposition to U.S. policy. These posts really made us think that we need to reevaluate how we perceive immigrants around the world and that we need to understand their beliefs more carefully to make sure America knows what they think and who they are.

Table D17. *Experiment 3: Treatment 10, Control*

Sullivan, host: Good evening to our viewers across the country and across the world. This is (Sullivan), and tonight we are examining the content of Facebook posts. Here with me is (Scuitto), our chief technology analyst. (Scuitto), welcome.

Scuitto, chief technology analyst: Thank you for having me.

Sullivan, host: So tell us – what did your research find?

Scuitto, chief technology analyst: Well as you know (Sullivan), Facebook is all over the news today. It seems you can't watch a regular broadcast segment without the company popping up. But we know very little about their users in general. So our team decided that one way to understand what is going on with them was to investigate what users are writing about on Facebook.

Strikingly, some of the most active Facebook accounts we came across belonged to ordinary Americans; they have graduated from college and they typically live away from where they grew up. Just average guys and gals. They stay in touch with their friends, write about their day-to-day experiences, and post pictures of their lives. These posts really made us think that we need to reevaluate how we perceive the Facebook company and that we need to understand how useful the platform is to ordinary American users.

Table D18. *Balance Table for Real Frames (Experiment 1)*

Variable	T1 Positive MAM	T2 Positive Muslim	T3 Negative MAM	T4 Negative Muslim
Age (mean, years)	43.84	44.7	44.33	45.79
% Female	55.31%	54.94%	44.56%	56.04%
% Dem.	36.17%	35.16%	28.26%	28.57%
% Rep.	30.85%	27.47%	36.96%	24.18%
% Ind.	29.79%	35.16%	32.61%	38.46%
Educ. (mean, 1–6 scale)	3.84	3.94	3.84	3.86
Income (mean, 1–6 scale)	3.48	3.30	3.84	3.46
Pre-MAR (mean, 1–7 scale)	3.57	3.40	3.61	3.63

Table D19. *Balance Table for Manipulated Frames (Experiment 2)*

Variable	T1 Positive MAM	T2 Positive Muslim	T3 Negative MAM	T4 Negative Muslim
Age (mean, years)	44.24	44.98	45.52	44.64
% Female	55.32%	55.91%	54.83%	45.74%
% Dem.	36.17%	35.16%	28.08%	27.95%
% Rep.	30.85%	27.47%	24.71%	37.63%
% Ind.	29.79 %	35.16%	40.45%	32.25%
Educ. (mean, 1–6 scale)	3.84	3.92	3.79	3.84
Income (mean, 1–6 scale)	3.48	3.27	3.46	3.85
Pre-MAR (mean, 1–7 scale)	3.57	3.38	3.65	3.62

Table D20. *Balance Table for July 2018 Lucid Survey across Experimental Conditions*

Variable	T1 Positive MAM	T2 Positive MAM (Alt)	T3 Positive Muslim	T4 Negative MAM	T5 Negative Muslim
Age (mean, years)	45.06	45.41	44.28	45.12	46.21
% Female	57.92	53.61	54.98	56.66	60.98
% Dem.	39.48	38.33	39.89	38.71	39.01
% Rep.	31.94	31.94	29.66	32.82	30.23
% Ind.	28.57	29.72	30.43	28.46	30.74
Educ. (mean, 1–6 scale)	3.44	3.41	3.40	3.4	3.43
Income (mean, 1–6 scale)	2.83	2.93	2.76	2.86	2.81
Married	45.45	47.22	44.50	46.66	47.54
Have children	54.80	56.94	60.86	63.84	58.91
Pre-MAR (mean, 1–5 scale)	2.59	2.60	2.60	2.63	2.64
Observations	n = 385	n = 360	n = 391	n = 390	n = 387

Variable	T6 Positive Latino	T7 Positive Immigrant	T8 Negative Latino	T9 Negative Immigrant	T10 Control –
Age (mean, years)	46.77	45.05	44.93	46.96	44.27
% Female	54.26	57.97	55.96	55.20	54.02
% Dem.	39.27	38.48	36.60	38.54	41.29
% Rep.	33.33	29.87	32.89	35.41	27.27
% Ind.	27.39	31.64	30.50	26.04	31.42
Educ. (mean, 1–6 scale)	3.38	3.36	3.22	3.43	3.38
Income (mean, 1–6 scale)	2.82	2.72	2.64	2.84	2.72
Married	49.35	44.30	46.94	45.83	43.37
Have children	59.68	56.70	57.82	57.81	55.06
Pre-MAR (mean, 1–5 scale)	2.56	2.61	2.60	2.67	2.55
Observations	n = 387	n = 395	n = 377	n = 384	n = 385

Table D21. *Validation of the MAR Scale, Factor Analysis*

Dataset	Factor Range	CFI	TLI	RMSEA	Cronbach's Alpha
6/2016 SSI	0.251702–.8885576	0.724	0.632	0.202	0.8404
7/2018 Lucid	0.392474–0.837274	0.796	0.728	0.166	0.8543

Table D22. *Predictors of MAR in Experiments 1 and 2, and in July 2018 Robustness Experiment*

	DV: Pre-MAR Experiment 1 June 2016	DV: Pre-MAR Experiment 2 June 2016	DV: Pre-MAR Experiment 3 July 2018
Age	−0.001	0.004	0.003**
	(0.883)	(0.269)	(0.001)
Income	−0.054	0.080	−0.044***
	(0.171)	(0.052)	(0.000)
Gender: Male	0.276*	0.278*	0.091***
	(0.017)	(0.017)	(0.000)
Education	−0.064	−0.198***	−0.085***
	(0.128)	(0.000)	(0.000)
Married			0.134***
			(0.000)
Have children			0.092**
			(0.001)
Black			−0.1t18**
			(0.003)
Hispanic			−0.096
			(0.396)
Asian American			0.003
			(0.968)
Other race			−0.101
			(0.179)
Native American			0.047
			(0.641)
Constant	3.879***	3.763***	2.762***
	(0.000)	(0.000)	(0.000)
n	367	371	3802
R^2	0.028	0.062	0.050

Note: p-values in parentheses.

* p < 0.05, ** p < 0.01, *** p < 0.001

Note: In Experiments 1 and 2, the DV is measured on a 1–7 Likert scale. In experiment 3, the DV is measured on a 1–5 Likert scale. Increasing values across all three experiments indicate greater resentment.

Note: The three models above are all OLS regressions.

Table D23. *Descriptive Statistics for Individual Scale Items Measuring Muslim American Resentment for Respondents Randomly Exposed to Real and Manipulated Treatments*

Item	Mean Pre-Treatment	Mean Post-Treatment	SD Pre-Treatment	SD Post-Treatment
Most Muslim Americans integrate successfully into American culture.	Exp. 1 = 3.43 Exp. 2 = 3.43 Exp. 3 = 2.78	Exp. 1 = 3.90 Exp. 2 = 3.86 Exp. 3 = 2.69	Exp. 1 = 1.60 Exp. 2 = 1.59 Exp. 3 = 1.16	Exp. 1 = 1.58 Exp. 2 = 1.53 Exp. 3 = 1.10
Muslim Americans sometimes do not have the best interests of Americans at heart.	Exp. 1 = 4.22 Exp. 2 = 4.30 Exp. 3 = 2.98	Exp. 1 = 4.23 Exp. 2 = 4.27 Exp. 3 = 2.99	Exp. 1 = 1.63 Exp. 2 = 1.59 Exp. 3 = 1.17	Exp. 1 = 1.62 Exp. 2 = 1.61 Exp. 3 = 1.18
Muslims living in the U.S. should be subject to more surveillance than others.	Exp. 1 = 3.92 Exp. 2 = 3.86 Exp. 3 = 2.62	Exp. 1 = 3.88 Exp. 2 = 3.79 Exp. 3 = 2.61	Exp. 1 = 1.74 Exp. 2 = 1.71 Exp. 3 = 1.23	Exp. 1 = 1.75 Exp. 2 = 1.73 Exp. 3 = 1.24
Muslim Americans, in general, tend to be more violent than other people.	Exp. 1 = 3.38 Exp. 2 = 3.41 Exp. 3 = 2.43	Exp. 1 = 3.40 Exp. 2 = 3.48 Exp. 3 = 2.48	Exp. 1 = 1.78 Exp. 2 = 1.72 Exp. 3 = 1.20	Exp. 1 = 1.65 Exp. 2 = 1.71 Exp. 3 = 1.19
Most Muslim Americans reject jihad and violence.	Exp. 1 = 3.33 Exp. 2 = 3.39 Exp. 3 = 2.64	Exp. 1 = 3.43 Exp. 2 = 3.40 Exp. 3 = 2.59	Exp. 1 = 1.62 Exp. 2 = 1.66 Exp. 3 = 1.12	Exp. 1 = 1.59 Exp. 2 = 1.64 Exp. 3 = 1.12
Most Muslim Americans lack basic English-language skills.	Exp. 1 = 3.62 Exp. 2 = 3.55 Exp. 3 = 2.61	Exp. 1 = 3.62 Exp. 2 = 3.58 Exp. 3 = 2.65	Exp. 1 = 1.60 Exp. 2 = 1.60 Exp. 3 = 1.16	Exp. 1 = 1.69 Exp. 2 = 1.58 Exp. 3 = 1.16
Most Muslim Americans are not terrorists.	Exp. 1 = 2.63 Exp. 2 = 2.66 Exp. 3 = 2.09	Exp. 1 = 2.79 Exp. 2 = 2.81 Exp. 3 = 2.15	Exp. 1 = 1.47 Exp. 2 = 1.52 Exp. 3 = 1.10	Exp. 1 = 1.48 Exp. 2 = 1.52 Exp. 3 = 1.07
Wearing headscarves should be banned in all public places.	Exp. 1 = 3.21 Exp. 2 = 3.22 Exp. 3 = 2.34	Exp. 1 = 3.23 Exp. 2 = 3.18 Exp. 3 = 2.37	Exp. 1 = 1.91 Exp. 2 = 1.92 Exp. 3 = 1.32	Exp. 1 = 1.94 Exp. 2 = 1.95 Exp. 3 = 1.31
Muslim Americans do a good job of speaking out against Islamic terrorism.	Exp. 1 = 4.21 Exp. 2 = 4.10 Exp. 3 = 2.93	Exp. 1 = 4.30 Exp. 2 = 4.18 Exp. 3 = 2.89	Exp. 1 = 1.70 Exp. 2 = 1.70 Exp. 3 = 1.12	Exp. 1 = 1.58 Exp. 2 = 1.62 Exp. 3 = 1.11

Note: Higher values on the scale indicate greater resentment. The statements in Experiments 1 and 2 were measured on a seven-point Likert scale. The statements in Experiment 3 were measured on a five-point Likert scale. Items 1, 5, 7, and 9 were recoded. Increasing values indicate greater resentment.

Table D24. *Heterogeneous Effects of News Coverage Sentiment on Within-Subject MAR and Differences by Party – June 2016 Study*

Condition	Pre-MAR	Post-MAR	Diff.
Among Republicans			
			0.0306
T1. Muslim American positive (n = 29)	3.83	3.80	p = 0.735
			0.04
T2. Muslim positive (n = 25)	3.84	3.8	p = 0.649
			0.085
T3. Muslim American negative (n = 21)	4.58	4.49	p = 0.303
			−0.219
T4. Muslim negative (n = 35)	3.57	3.79	p = 0.010
Among Democrats			
			−0.003
T1. Muslim American positive (n = 34)	3.24	3.25	p = 0.960
			−0.156
T2. Muslim positive (n = 32)	2.82	2.97	p = 0.119
			−0.191
T3. Muslim American negative (n = 25)	3.33	3.52	p = 0.119
			0.094
T4. Muslim negative (n = 26)	3.59	3.50	p = 0.433
Among Independents/Other Party			
			0.036
T1. Muslim American positive (n = 31)	3.68	3.65	p = 0.722
			0.049
T2. Muslim positive (n = 34)	3.62	3.57	p = 0.520
			−0.268
T3. Muslim American negative (n = 41)	3.31	3.58	p = 0.000
			−0.201
T4. Muslim negative (n = 31)	3.63	3.83	p = 0.044

Note: MAR is measured on a 1–7 scale, and reported differences are between respondent's pre- and post-MAR by party.
Source: June 2016 SSI survey.

Table D25. *Heterogeneous Effects of News Coverage Sentiment on Within-Subject MAR and Differences by Party – July 2018 Study*

Condition	Pre-MAR	Post-Mar	Diff.
Among Republicans			
T1. Muslim American positive (n = 123)	2.90	2.82	0.074 p = 0.024
T2. Muslim American positive (alt.) (n = 115)	3.00	2.97	0.035 p = 0.249
T3. Muslim positive (n = 128)	3.00	2.92	0.081 p = 0.009
T4. Muslim American negative (n = 116)	2.98	3.04	−0.055 p = 0.105
T5. Muslim negative (n = 117)	2.89	3.00	−0.111 p = 0.001
Among Democrats			
T1. Muslim American positive (n = 152)	2.35	2.30	0.043 p = 0.153
T2. Muslim American positive (alt.) (n = 138)	2.31	2.29	0.014 p = 0.679
T3. Muslim positive (n = 151)	2.35	2.29	0.059 p = 0.030
T4. Muslim American negative (n = 156)	2.34	2.39	−0.052 p = 0.038
T5. Muslim negative (n = 151)	2.41	2.45	−0.039 p = 0.185
Among Independents/Other Party			
T1. Muslim American positive (n = 110)	2.58	2.58	−0.003 p = 0.906
T2. Muslim American positive (alt.) (n = 107)	2.56	2.47	0.091 p = 0.001
T3. Muslim positive (n = 111)	2.57	2.60	−0.027 p = 0.434
T4. Muslim American negative (n = 119)	2.58	2.68	−0.100 p = 0.007
T5. Muslim negative (n = 119)	2.67	2.73	−0.061 p = 0.069

Note: MAR is measured on a 1–5 scale, and reported differences are between respondent's pre- and post-MAR by party.
Source: July 2018 Lucid survey.

Table D26. *Heterogeneous Effects of News Coverage Sentiment on MAR by Party ID – June 2016 Study*

Among Republicans, n = 111				
Positive Condition	**Post-MAR**	**Negative Condition**	**Post-MAR**	**Diff.**
T1. Muslim American	3.80	T3. Muslim American	4.497	−0.696 p = 0.032
T2. Muslim	3.8	T4. Muslim	3.79	0.009 p = 0.970
Aggregate	4.05	Aggregate	3.80	0.255 p = 0.205
Among Democrats, n = 117				
Positive Condition	**Post-MAR**	**Negative Condition**	**Post-MAR**	**Diff.**
T1. Muslim American	3.24	T3. Muslim American	3.52	−0.276 p = 0.356
T2. Muslim	2.97	T4. Muslim	3.5	−0.520 p = 0.058
Aggregate	3.51	Aggregate	3.12	0.394 p = 0.051
Among Independents/Other Party, n = 159				
Positive Condition	**Post-MAR**	**Negative Condition**	**Post-MAR**	**Diff.**
T1. Muslim American	3.65	T3. Muslim American	3.57	0.075 p = 0.767
T2. Muslim	3.57	T4. Muslim	3.82	−0.252 p = 0.334
Aggregate	3.68	Aggregate	3.61	0.073 p = 0.684

Note: MAR is measured on a 1–7 scale, and reported differences of Post-MAR are within-subject differences by the respondent's party identification.
Source: June 2016 SSI survey.

Table D27. *Heterogeneous Effects of News Coverage Sentiment on MAR by Party ID – July 2018 Study*

Among Republicans, n = 704				
Positive Condition	**Post-MAR**	**Negative Condition**	**Post-MAR**	**Diff.**
T1. Muslim American	2.82	T4. Muslim American	3.04	−0.218 p = 0.021
T2. Muslim American (alt.)	2.96	T4. Muslim American	3.04	−0.074 p = 0.447
T3. Muslim	2.92	T5. Muslim	2.99	−0.075 p = 0.461
Aggregate	2.90	Aggregate	3.02	−0.116 p = 0.069
Among Democrats, n = 907				
Positive Condition	**Post-MAR**	**Negative Condition**	**Post-MAR**	**Diff.**
T1. Muslim American	2.30	T4. Muslim American	2.38	−0.086 p = 0.359
T2. Muslim American (alt.)	2.29	T4. Muslim American	2.39	−0.094 p = 0.321
T3. Muslim	2.29	T5. Muslim	2.45	−0.165 p = 0.069
Aggregate	2.29	Aggregate	2.42	−0.125 p = 0.036
Among Independents/Other Party, n = 687				
Positive Condition	**Post-MAR**	**Negative Condition**	**Post-MAR**	**Diff.**
T1. Muslim American	2.58	T4. Muslim American	2.68	−0.095 p = 0.349
T2. Muslim American (alt.)	2.47	T4. Muslim American	2.68	−0.212 p = 0.0456
T3. Muslim	2.60	T5. Muslim	2.73	−0.132 p = 0.174
Aggregate	2.553	Aggregate	2.70	−0.154 p = 0.016

Note: MAR is measured on a 1–5 scale, and reported differences of post-MAR are within-subject differences by the respondent's party identification.
Source: July 2018 SSI survey.

Table D28. *T-Tests for Immigration Policy Positions by Disaggregated Treatments*

	Limit All Imm. (Mean)	Sig.	Limit Muslim Imm. (Mean)	Sig.	Limit Musl. Am. from Reentering (Mean)	Sig.
Experiment 1: Real Frames						
Positive Treatments						
T1. Muslim American positive	3.99		4.19		3.45	
T2. Muslim positive	3.83		4.21		3.611	
(Aggregate)	3.91		4.20		3.53	
Negative Treatments						
T3. Muslim American negative	4.17	p = 0.519	4.36	p = 0.577	4	p = 0.057
T4. Muslim negative	4.22	p = 0.167	4.22	p = 0.964	3.64	p = 0.893
(Aggregate)	4.20	p = 0.154	4.29	p = 0.660	3.82	p = 0.146
Experiment 2: Manipulated Frames						
Positive Treatments						
T1. Muslim American positive	3.75		3.97		3.49	
T2. Muslim positive	3.69		3.91		3.315	
(Aggregate)	3.72		3.94		3.40	
Negative Treatments						
T3. Muslim American negative	4.26	p = 0.069	4.53	p = 0.045	4.31	p = 0.002
T4. Muslim negative	4.42	p = 0.006	4.69	p = 0.003	4.06	p = 0.003
(Aggregate)	4.34	p = 0.001	4.61	p = 0.0005	4.18	p = 0.000

Table D29. *Effect of Sentiment on MAR at the Individual Level*

Condition	Obvs.	Pre-MAR	Post-MAR	Diff.
Positive Treatments				
T1. Muslim American	n = 385	2.589	2.549	0.0401 p = 0.0225
T2. Muslim American (alt.)	n = 360	2.605	2.561	.04382 p = 0.0171
T3. Muslim	n = 390	2.627	2.585	0.0418 p = 0.0177
Negative Treatments				
T4. Muslim American	n = 391	2.603	2.671	0.0682 p = 0.0002
T5. Muslim	n = 387	2.636	2.704	0.0674 p = 0.0002
Control	n = 385	2.555	2.552	0.0031 p = 0.8535

Note: MAR is measured on a 1–5 scale, and reported differences are between pre- and post-MAR at the individual level.
Source: July 2018 Lucid survey.

Notes

CHAPTER 1

1 https://bit.ly/341k1MB
2 www.colorlines.com/articles/state-rep-muslims-are-cancer-must-be-cut-american-society
3 https://www.bbc.com/news/world-us-canada-34864814
4 https://bit.ly/35hlfUa
5 https://bit.ly/2XdEZ8m
6 For example, the SPLC reports that a woman at San Jose State University was grabbed by her hijab, while in Nashville a man in a truck hurled racial slurs at a woman wearing a hijab as she waited for the bus with her son, saying, "Go back to your fucking country and take your terrorist son with you" (SPLC, 2016).
7 https://bit.ly/2Xt8suZ
8 https://bit.ly/2Kqx8Pq
9 https://ucr.fbi.gov/hate-crime/2017/tables/table-1.xls
10 CAIR has a feature on their website, where individuals can post bias incidents. For more detail, please see: https://www.cair.com/report.
11 https://bit.ly/2qtUjl7
12 Only in very rare instances do U.S. courts consult religious law.
13 According to the Pew Research Center, there are 1.6 billion Muslims in the world today. The CIA Factbook lists the largest religions of the world in the following order: Christian 33.39%, Muslim 22.74%, Hindu 13.8%, Buddhist 6.77%, Sikh 0.35%, Jewish 0.22%, Baha'i 0.11%, other religions 10.95%, nonreligious 9.66%, atheists 2.01% (2010 est.). See https://pewrsr.ch/2qtnchh.
14 https://pewrsr.ch/2Ot2ia6
15 https://pewrsr.ch/2O1asHN
16 Some estimates place this figure at over 12 million. See https://wapo.st/341Hzkf.
17 See http://www.usreligioncensus.org/compare.php and https://bit.ly/2qiNFyi.
18 https://pewrsr.ch/2pxfl1X

19 https://pewrsr.ch/2pxfl1X

20 https://pewrsr.ch/2pxfl1X

21 https://pewrsr.ch/2pxfl1X

22 This category can be misleading as it captures much racial and ethnic variation, with Pew writing that this category includes those who identify as, for example, Arab, Middle Eastern, and Persian/Iranian:

> it is sometimes difficult for respondents to select from the Census Bureau's options. For example, immigrants and the children of immigrants from the Middle East-North Africa region and from Iran have no explicit option to identify as Arab, Persian, Kurdish, etc., or to identify with a particular place of origin (e.g., Egypt, Palestine, Morocco) in place of a racial category. In the census, respondents who specify a country or region of origin in the Middle East-North Africa region instead of a specific racial category generally are counted as white; historically, the U.S. government has classified people as white if they have "origins in any of the original peoples of Europe, the Middle East or North Africa."

See: https://pewrsr.ch/2pxfl1X.

23 https://pewrsr.ch/2pxfl1X

24 https://pewrsr.ch/2KxPLRt

25 https://pewrsr.ch/37kbmH3

26 https://pewrsr.ch/341xbZV

27 https://pewrsr.ch/341xbZV

CHAPTER 2

1 https://pewrsr.ch/2QuZWtU

2 See Pew 2017 dataset on Muslim Americans and https://pewrsr.ch/2O0jvbQ.

3 https://to.pbs.org/2KByBCA

4 https://s.si.edu/37cObOK

5 See https://s.si.edu/37ng8Dx.

6 In fact, the National Museum of African American History & Culture maintains a video of this ritual dance observed at minute 42:50 on the website listed in this footnote. See https://s.si.edu/2KvC4mj and https://to.pbs.org/35fNCBV.

7 https://to.pbs.org/35fNCBV

8 https://to.pbs.org/35fNCBV

9 https://to.pbs.org/35fNCBV

10 https://to.pbs.org/35fNCBV

11 Maghbouleh (2017) identifies the following cases: *In re Najour* in 1909, *In re Halladjian* in 1909, and *In re Balsara* in 1909, *Ex parte Dow* in 1914, *In re Dow* in 1914, and *Dow v. United States* in 1915.

12 *Dow v. United States*, 226 F. 145 (4th Cir. 1915).

13 *Dow v. United States*, 226 F. 145 (4th Cir. 1915).

14 Muslims are considered affluent relative to other groups in the United States. See https://on.cfr.org/2OuvUUH.

15 Support among U.S. Muslims for the Republican nominee went from 28% in June 2000 to 40% in September 2000, and finally to 72% by the time of election (Findley, 2001). Moreover, Findley (2001) finds that 15% of Black Muslims voted for Bush in 2000, which amounts to double the support Bush received from Black Christians (Barreto and Bozonelos, 2009; Findley, 2001).

16 The national threat assessment was conveyed through the following colors: Green = low, blue = guarded, yellow = elevated, orange = high, red = severe.

17 https://bit.ly/2Xi8nKx

18 https://bit.ly/2QzcAIo

CHAPTER 3

1 https://pewrsr.ch/2O1EJWY

2 https://pewrsr.ch/2O1EJWY

3 About 75% of respondents in the face-to-face portion placed Muslims at 50 or higher on the 2016 ANES.

4 Even when excluding the items measuring policy attitudes, the results typically still hold (e.g. removing the policy-related questions in Lajevardi and Oskooii (2018) did not hamper the MAR scale's predictive capabilities on policy-related dependent variables).

5 https://pewrsr.ch/2QEanM5

6 https://pewrsr.ch/32Y1gIj

7 https://pewrsr.ch/2QEanM5

8 https://pewrsr.ch/2QEanM5

9 https://pewrsr.ch/2QEanM5

10 The surveys were fielded on the following platforms: (1) 5/2016 Amazon Mechanical Turk, (2) 10/2016 Cooperative Campaign Analysis Project, (3)

12/2016 Survey Sampling International, (4) 1/2017 Amazon Mechanical Turk, (5) 6/2017 Amazon Mechanical Turk, (6) 7/2018 Lucid Academia, (7) 10/2018 Cooperative Congressional Election Study, (8) 10/2018 Lucid Academia, (9) 3/2019 Lucid Academia, and (10) 6/2019 Lucid Academia.

11 Berinsky, Huber, and Lenz (2012) provide evidence of the validity and comparability of surveys conducted on online convenience samples, such as on MTurk, with surveys conducted on representative samples.

12 The following variables were used in each of the datasets: 5/2016 (MTurk): support for Trump in the 2016 primary; 10/2016 (CCAP): Trump vote in 2016; 12/2016 (SSI): support for Trump in 2016 election; 1/2017 (MTurk): Trump approval; 6/2017 (MTurk): Trump vote in 2016; 10/2018 (CCES): Trump approval; 10/2018 (Lucid): Trump support in 2016; 3/2019 (Lucid): Trump approval; and 6/2019 (Lucid) Trump vote in 2016. Each question was rescaled to range from 0 to 1 for ease of interpretation, with mean values ranging from 0.263 in the June 2017 MTurk survey to 0.553 in the January 2017 MTurk sample.

13 When available in a dataset, racial resentment is measured by using the following items: (1) Over the past few years, Blacks have gotten less than they deserve (reverse coded); (2) Irish, Italian, Jewish, and many other minorities overcame prejudice and worked their way up. Blacks should do the same without any special favors; (3) It's really a matter of some people not trying hard enough; if Blacks would only try harder they could be just as well off as Whites; and (4) Generations of slavery and discrimination have created conditions that make it difficult for Blacks to work their way out of the lower class.

14 Table A15 follows and expands on the analyses in Lajevardi and Abrajano (2019), and includes indicators for education, age, gender, income, race, and partisanship, as well as the MAR scale and any other available resentment or attitudinal questions.

15 https://bit.ly/2KvDuNF; https://bit.ly/2KvDuNF

16 The October 2016 CCAP, January 2017 MTurk, June 2017 MTurk, and October 2018 CCES did not ask this question and are excluded from these analyses.

17 For ease of interpretation both the dependent variables (the policy variables) and the main independent variables (MAR and other attitudinal measures) have been rescaled to range from 0 to 1 across each survey. As support for a policy position is being explored, the alternative MAR scale, which excludes items 3 and 8, is used.

18 https://cnn.it/2pB5h88
19 https://on.nyc.gov/35f7rcx
20 https://bit.ly/37tFnV0
21 https://bit.ly/37tFnV0
22 https://bit.ly/333JKCy
23 https://bit.ly/37iOpE7
24 https://bit.ly/2O0aIXn

CHAPTER 4

1 https://bit.ly/2XCK8XT
2 https://bit.ly/2XCKbmx
3 Using the same pictures addresses cross-partisan comparisons, though it does not address any cross-racial comparisons. For instance, the pictures may be racially distinctive but may also differ on nonracial dimensions such as demeanor or attractiveness.
4 The development of these blurbs was finalized with the assistance of participants in the UCSD American Politics workshop in May 2015.
5 https://bit.ly/2Qm1E0P
6 This is not a nationally representative survey. To assess low, medium, and high levels of MAR, I subsetted the sample to those with low levels of resentment (those below the 25th percentile), medium levels of resentment (those between the 25th and 75th percentiles), and high levels of resentment (those above the 75th percentile).
7 One limitation, however, is that there is no manipulation check to ensure that the Arab American candidate was perceived as such.
8 https://bit.ly/2NYOxB5

CHAPTER 5

1 https://bit.ly/330RfdB
2 Basic Sentiment Analysis in R. See https://sites.google.com/site/miningtwitter/questions/sentiment/analysis.
3 Sentiment analysis does not come without its limitations, including bias (Hopkins and King, 2010). While my approach does not use supervised learning, or classify documents, sentiment analysis must be validated to ensure that it is in fact measuring the tone of a given document.
4 Table C2 presents the raw figures.
5 See Table C3 for raw figures.

6 See Table C4 for raw figures.

7 See also www.people-press.org/2009/10/29/fox-news-viewed-as-most-ideological-network/.

8 See Table C6 for these regressions.

9 Please see Models 2 (CNN), 3 (Fox), and 4 (MSNBC) in Table C6.

CHAPTER 6

1 www.pewforum.org/2014/07/16/how-americans-feel-about-religious-groups/

2 California (272,814 Muslims), Florida (164,846 Muslims), Illinois (359,264 Muslims), Michigan (120,351 Muslims), New Jersey (160,666 Muslims), New York (392,953 Muslims), Texas (421,972 Muslims), and Virginia (213,032 Muslims). See www.usreligioncensus.org/compare.php and http://rcms2010.org/compare.php?confirm2=confirm&sel_denom=267&sel_list_option2=3&sel_year2=2010&source=form2.

3 For the real Muslim American negative treatment, the third most negative transcript was selected as the first and second most negative broadcasts were not substantially about Muslim Americans. For the real Muslim positive treatment, the sixth most positive transcript was selected as the top five either did not discuss Muslims as a group or were not in fact very positive in tone. The real Muslim American positive treatment featured an African American who converted to Islam many years ago, and thus differs from the other transcripts in context. Finally, for the real Muslim negative treatment, the most negative treatment from 2014 was selected, as the most negative Muslim treatments from 2015 were too tied in subject matter to the presidential election.

4 It is also worth noting the text of the manipulated treatment was altered slightly to correct for a typo and to insert a reference to the relevant "negative" group in the paragraph beginning "Strikingly."

5 One limitation with measuring MAR pre- and post-test should be noted. Because respondents were asked about group attitudes toward Muslim Americans prior to the treatment, it is possible that their attitudes toward the group were primed. This was mitigated in two ways. First, respondents across all conditions were asked this question before randomization, thereby ensuring that if in fact group attitudes were activated, this was the case across the board. Second, balance tables for each of the experiments (see Tables D18, D19, and D20) reveal very little variation in pre-MAR levels.

6 Ogan et al. (2014), for instance, analyze Fox News viewers' reported anti-Muslim feelings and find that 60% of Republicans who trusted Fox News the most also believed that Muslims were attempting to establish sharia law in the United States. Moreover, the researchers describe a study that found that those who trust Fox News the most also tend to believe that Islamic values are incompatible with American values (68%). Conversely, this percentage is much lower for those who trust CNN the most (37%). Ogan et al.'s (2014) research also confirms that Democratic viewers are much more likely to watch more liberal networks, such as MSNBC, which tend to portray Muslim Americans more positively.

7 The difference in mean ratings between the Muslim positive and negative treatments approaches significance for the Limit All Muslim Immigration treatment.

CHAPTER 7

1 In fact, Michigan – a key battleground state in the 2016 presidential election – is home to one of the oldest and largest concentrations of Muslims in America.

2 www.theatlantic.com/politics/archive/2016/02/muslim-voters-2016/458691/

3 The Pew "Muslim Americans: No Signs of Growth in Alienation or Support for Extremism" report indicates that those with higher family incomes are more likely than those at the lower end of the scale to say they are registered. It also finds that 78% of those with family incomes of $75,000 or more say they are certain they are registered, compared with 60% among those with incomes of less than $30,000. See www.people-press.org/2011/08/30/section-5-political-opinions-and-social-values/.

4 www.hillaryclinton.com/briefing/factsheets/2016/09/21/stronger-together-hillary-clintons-vision-for-muslim-americans/

5 For instance, many state legislatures go so far as to insist that potential applicants for internships contact their representatives directly and ask for applications by email. See the Massachusetts State Assembly page for an example: https://malegislature.gov/StateHouse/EducationalOpportunities/Internships.

6 www.ncsl.org/research/about-state-legislatures/full-and-part-time-legislatures.aspx

7 (1) Idaho (R House, R Senate); (2) Kansas (R House, R Senate); (3) Maine (D House, D Senate); (4) Mississippi (R House, R Senate); (5) Montana

(R House, R Senate); (6) New Hampshire (D House, D Senate); (7) New Mexico (D House, D Senate); (8) North Dakota (R House, R Senate); (9) Rhode Island (D House, D Senate); (10) South Dakota (R House, R Senate); (11) Utah (R House, R Senate); (12) Vermont (D House, D Senate); (13) West Virginia (R House, R Senate); and (14) Wyoming (R House, R Senate).

8   https://ballotpedia.org/Partisan_composition_of_state_legislatures

9   Of course, the inability to contact the full universe of legislators may introduce some bias into the results.

10 Block random assignment is a procedure whereby subjects are partitioned into subgroups (called blocks) and complete random assignment of each treatment and control occurs within each block (Gerber and Green, 2008). It ensures that equal numbers of covariates will be assigned to each experimental condition and has the advantage of reducing sample variability, as well as eliminating the possibility of rogue randomizations (Gerber and Green, 2008).

11 See NCSL Full and Part Time Legislatures Map on Gold Legislatures for more details. www.ncsl.org/research/about-state-legislatures/full-and-part-time-legislatures.aspx.

12 Because the intercoder reliability between the two coders was high (yielding a Cohen's Kappa score of: 0.8963), the rest of the analysis focuses on Coder 1's results.

13 See Costa (2017a) for information on average response rates across a wide range of audit studies.

14 www.people-press.org/2011/08/30/section-5-political-opinions-and-social-values/

15 In 2014, Pew reported that 38% of Americans say they know someone who is Muslim, compared to 61% who know a Jewish person, or 59% who know an atheist. See www.pewforum.org/2014/07/16/how-americans-feel-about-religious-groups/.

CHAPTER 8

1   http://buffalonews.com/1993/05/02/arab-americans-suffering-with-guilt-by-unfair-association/ and www.nytimes.com/1993/03/07/nyregion/twin-towers-backlash-muslims-united-states-fear-upsurge-hostility.html

2   www.nytimes.com/2012/08/06/us/shooting-reported-at-temple-in-wisconsin.html

3 www.nytimes.com/2014/04/16/nyregion/police-unit-that-spied-on-muslims-is-disbanded.html?_r=0

4 www.nytimes.com/2014/04/16/nyregion/police-unit-that-spied-on-muslims-is-disbanded.html?_r=0

5 https://theintercept.com/2014/07/09/under-surveillance/

6 www.wired.com/2011/09/fbi-muslims-radical/

7 www.wired.com/2011/09/fbi-muslims-radical/

8 www.reuters.com/article/us-usa-muslims/polling-calls-to-u-s-muslims-raise-surveillance-fears-idUSKBN13I2PK

9 www.census.gov/topics/population/race/about.html

10 www.reuters.com/article/us-usa-muslims-idUSKBN13I2PK

11 www.pewforum.org/2017/07/26/demographic-portrait-of-muslim-americans/

12 www.pewresearch.org/fact-tank/2017/07/26/american-muslims-are-concerned-but-also-satisfied-with-their-lives/

13 www.pewforum.org/2017/07/26/the-muslim-american-experience-in-the-trump-era/

Chapter 9

1 https://theintercept.com/2018/10/22/2018-midterms-muslim-candidates-islamophobia/

2 https://theintercept.com/2018/10/22/2018-midterms-muslim-candidates-islamophobia/

Bibliography

Abdo, Geneive. 2005. "Islam in America: Separate but Unequal." *Washington Quarterly* 28(4):5–17.

Abrajano, Marisa A., Christopher S. Elmendorf, and Kevin M. Quinn. 2018. "Labels vs. Pictures: Treatment-Mode Effects in Experiments about Discrimination." *Political Analysis* 26(1):20–33.

Abrajano, Marisa, and Zoltan L. Hajnal. 2017. *White Backlash: Immigration, Race, and American Politics.* Princeton University Press.

Abrajano, Marisa, and Simran Singh. 2009. "Examining the Link between Issue Attitudes and News Source: The Case of Latinos and Immigration Reform." *Political Behavior* 31(1):1–30.

Abramson, John R., and John Aldrich David Rohde. 2002. *Change and Continuity in the 2000 Elections.* Washington D.C.: CQ Press.

Adida, Claire L., David D. Laitin, and Marie-Anne Valfort. 2010. "Identifying Barriers to Muslim Integration in France." *Proceedings of the National Academy of Sciences* 107(52):22,384–22,390.

Agirdag, Orhan, Mieke van Houtte, and Patrick Loobuyck. 2012. "Determinants of Attitudes Toward Muslim Students among Flemish Teachers: A Research Note." *Journal for the Scientific Study of Religion* 51:368–376.

Allen, Christopher, and Jørgen S. Nielsen. 2002. "Summary Report on Islamophobia in the EU after 11 September 2001." European Monitoring Centre on Racism and Xenophobia, Vienna. https://bit.ly/2Qyg6my

Alsultany, Evelyn. 2012. *Arabs and Muslims in the Media: Race and Representation after 9/11.* New York University Press.

Alvarez, R. Michael, and Jonathan Nagler. 1995. "Economics, Issues, and the Perot Candidacy: Voter Choice in the 1992 Election." *American Journal of Political Science* 39:714–744.

Austin, Allan D. 1984. *African Muslims in Antebellum America: A Sourcebook,* Vol. 5. New York: Garland Publishing.

Ayers, John W. 2007. "Changing Sides: 9/11 and the American Muslim Voter." *Review of Religious Research* 49(2):187–198.

Aziz, Sahar F. 2009. "Sticks and Stones, the Words that Hurt: Entrenched Stereotypes Eight Years after 9/11." *New York City Law Review* 13:33.

Aziz, Sahar. 2012. "Racial Profiling by Law Enforcement Is Poisoning Muslim Americans' Trust." https://bit.ly/2CTuDkH

Aziz, Sahar F. 2017. "A Muslim Registry: The Precursor to Internment." *Brigham Young University Law Review* 101:779.

Bagby, Ihsan. 2009. "The American Mosque in Transition: Assimilation, Acculturation and Isolation." *Journal of Ethnic and Migration Studies* 35(3):473–490.

Bagby, Ihsan. 2012. "The American Mosque 2011: Report Number 1 from the US Mosque Study 2011." *Islamic Society of North America* 1(2):1–58.

Bail, Christopher A. 2012. "The Fringe Effect: Civil Society Organizations and the Evolution of Media Discourse about Islam since the September 11th Attacks." *American Sociological Review* 77(6):855–879.

Bakalian, Anny, and Medhi Bozorgmehr. 2009. *Backlash 9/11: Middle Eastern and Muslim Americans Respond*. Berkeley: University of California Press.

Baker, Lee D. 1998. *From Savage to Negro: Anthropology and the Construction of Race, 1896–1954*. Berkeley: University of California Press.

Barberá, Pablo. 2014. "Birds of the Same Feather Tweet Together: Bayesian Ideal Point Estimation Using Twitter Data." *Political Analysis* 23(1):76–91.

Barreto, Matt A. 2007. "¡Sí Se Puede! Latino Candidates and the Mobilization of Latino Voters." *American Political Science Review* 101(3):425–441.

Barreto, Matt A. 2010. *Ethnic Cues: The Role of Shared Ethnicity in Latino Political Participation*. Ann Arbor: University of Michigan Press.

Barreto, Matt A., and Dino N. Bozonelos. 2009. "Democrat, Republican, or None of the Above? The Role of Religiosity in Muslim American Party Identification." *Politics and Religion* 2(2):200–229.

Barreto, Matt A., and Karam Dana. 2010. "The American Muslim Voter: What Explains Voting When Nobody Cares?" APSA 2010 Annual Meeting Paper. https://bit.ly/2qhFL8n

Barreto, Matt A., and Karam Dana. 2019. "Best Practices for Gathering Public Opinion Data among Muslim Americans." In Brian R. Calfano and Nazita Lajevardi (eds.), *Understanding Muslim Political Life in America: Contested Citizenship in the Twenty-First Century*, Vol. 12, Religious Engagement in Democratic Politics. Philadelphia, PA: Temple University Press.

Barreto, Matt A., Karam Dana, and Kassra A. R. Oskooii. 2013. "No Mosque, No Sharia: Orientalist Notions of Islam and Intolerance toward Muslim-Americans." Presented at Midwest Political Science Association Annual Conference. Chicago, Illinois.

Barreto, Matt A., Natalie Masuoka, and Gabriel Sanchez. 2008. "Religiosity, Discrimination and Group Identity among Muslim Americans." Presented at Western Political Science Association Annual Conference, San Diego, California.

Barreto, Matt A., and Nathan D. Woods. 2005. "The Anti-Latino Political Context and Its Impact on GOP Detachment and Increasing Latino Voter Turnout in Los Angeles County." In Gary M. Segura and Shaun Bowler (eds.), *Diversity in Democracy: Minority Representation in the United States.* Charlottesville: University of Virginia Press, pp. 148–169.

Bartels, Larry M. 1998. "Where the Ducks Are: Voting Power in a Party System." In John G. Geer (ed.), *Politicians and Party Politics.* Baltimore, MD: Johns Hopkins University Press, pp. 43–79.

Bartels, Larry M. 2016. *Unequal Democracy: The Political Economy of the New Gilded Age.* Princeton University Press.

Baum, Matthew A. 2003. "Soft News and Political Knowledge: Evidence of Absence or Absence of Evidence?" *Political Communication* 20(2):173–190.

Behm-Morawitz, Elizabeth, and Michelle Ortiz. 2013. "Race, Ethnicity, and the Media." In Karen Dill-Shackleford (ed.), *The Oxford Handbook of Media Psychology.* Oxford University Press, pp. 252–266.

Berinsky, Adam J., Gregory A. Huber, and Gabriel S. Lenz. 2012. "Evaluating Online Labor Markets for Experimental Research: Amazon.com's Mechanical Turk." *Political Analysis* 20(3):351–368.

Bevelander, Pieter, and Jonas Otterbeck. 2010. "Young People's Attitudes towards Muslims in Sweden." *Ethnic and Racial Studies* 33(3):404–425.

Beydoun, Khaled A. 2018. *American Islamophobia: Understanding the Roots and Rise of Fear.* Berkeley: University of California Press.

Bhonde, Reshma, Binita Bhagwat, Sayali Ingulkar, and Apeksha Pande. 2015. "Sentiment Analysis Based on Dictionary Approach." *International Journal of Emerging Engineering Research and Technology* 3(1):51–55.

Bobo, Lawrence. 1983. "Whites' Opposition to Busing: Symbolic Racism or Realistic Group Conflict?" *Journal of Personality and Social Psychology* 45(6):1196.

Bobo, Lawrence. 2001. "Racial Attitudes and Relations at the Close of the Twentieth Century." In Neil Smelser and William Julius Wilson (eds.), *America Becoming: Racial Trends and Their Consequences,* Vol. 1. Washington D.C.: The National Academies Press, pp. 264–301.

Bobo, Lawrence, and James Kluegel. 1997. "Status, Ideology, and Dimensions of Whites' Racial Beliefs and Attitudes: Progress and Stagnation." In Steven A. Tuch and Jack Martin (eds.), *Racial Attitudes in the 1990s: Continuity and Change.* Westport, CN: Praeger, pp. 93–120.

Bobo, Lawrence, James R. Kluegel, and Ryan A. Smith. 1997. "Laissez-Faire Racism: The Crystallization of a Kinder, Gentler, Antiblack Ideology." In Steven A. Tuch and Jack Martin (eds.), *Racial Attitudes in the 1990s: Continuity and Change.* Westport, CN: Praeger, pp. 15–42.

Bowler, Shaun, and Gary Segura. 2011. *The Future Is Ours: Minority Politics, Political Behavior, and the Multiracial Era of American Politics.* Thousand Oaks, CA: SAGE.

Brady, Henry E., and Paul M. Sniderman. 1985. "Attitude Attribution: A Group Basis for Political Reasoning." *American Political Science Review* 79(4): 1061–1078.

Braman, Eileen, and Abdulkader H. Sinno. 2009. "An Experimental Investigation of Causal Attributions for the Political Behavior of Muslim Candidates: Can a Muslim Represent You?" *Politics and Religion* 2(2):247–276.

Branscombe, Nyla R., Michael T. Schmitt, and Richard D. Harvey. 1999. "Perceiving Pervasive Discrimination among African Americans: Implications for Group Identification and Well-Being." *Journal of Personality and Social Psychology* 77(1):135.

Branton, Regina, and Johanna Dunaway. 2008. "English- and Spanish-Language Media Coverage of Immigration: A Comparative Analysis." *Social Science Quarterly* 89(4):1006–1022.

Brennan Center. 2017. "Countering Violent Extremism." https://bit.ly/37fZqpD

Broockman, David E. 2013. "Black Politicians Are More Intrinsically Motivated to Advance Blacks Interests: A Field Experiment Manipulating Political Incentives." *American Journal of Political Science* 57(3):521–536.

Brummett, Barry. 2014. *Rhetoric in Popular Culture.* Los Angeles: SAGE.

Bruyneel, Kevin. 2007. *The Third Space of Sovereignty: The Postcolonial Politics of US–Indigenous Relations.* Minneapolis: University of Minnesota Press.

Bukhari, Zahid H., and Sulayman S. Nyang. 2004. "Muslims in the American Public Square: Shifting Political Winds & Fallout from 9/11, Afghanistan and Iraq." In M.i.t.A.P.S.Z. International (ed.), *Project MAPS: Muslims in the American Public Square.* Washington D.C.: Georgetown University & Zogby International.

Burrell, Barbara. 1994. *A Women's Place is in the House: Campaigning for Congress in the Electoral Arena.* Ann Arbor: University of Michigan Press.

Butler, Daniel M. 2014. *Representing the Advantaged: How Politicians Reinforce Inequality.* Cambridge University Press.

Butler, Daniel M., and David E. Broockman. 2011. "Do Politicians Racially Discriminate Against Constituents? A Field Experiment on State Legislators." *American Journal of Political Science* 55(3):463–477.

Butler, Daniel M., Christopher F. Karpowitz, and Jeremy C. Pope. 2012. "A Field Experiment on Legislators' Home Styles: Service Versus Policy." *Journal of Politics* 74(2):474–486.

Butler, Katharine I., and Richard Murray. 1989. "Minority Vote Dilution Suits and the Problem of Two Minority Groups: Can a Rainbow Coalition Claim the Protection of the Voting Rights Act." *Pacific Law Journal* 21:619.

CAIR. 2016a. "American Muslim Voters and the 2016 Election: A Demographic Profile and Survey of Attitudes." www.cair.com/american_muslim_voters_and_the_2016_election

CAIR. 2016b. "Confronting Fear: Islamophobia and Its Impact in the U.S. 2013–2015." https://bit.ly/37meAJVhttps://bit.ly/2KCwj6h

CAIR. 2017. "Civil Rights Data Quarter Two Update: Anti-Muslim Bias Incidents April–June 2017." https://bit.ly/2KCwj6h

CAIR. 2018. "Civil Rights Data Quarter Two Update: Anti-Muslim Bias Incidents April–June 2018." https://bit.ly/32Xh6mB

Calfano, Brian. 2018. *Muslims, Identity, and American Politics*. London: Routledge.

Calfano, Brian R., and Nazita Lajevardi (eds.). 2019. *Understanding Muslim Political Life in America: Contested Citizenship in the Twenty-First Century*, Vol. 12, Religious Engagement in Democratic Politics. Philadelphia, PA: Temple University Press.

Calfano, Brian R., Nazita Lajevardi, and Melissa R. Michelson. 2019. "Trumped Up Challenges: Limitations, Opportunities, and the Future of Political Research on Muslim Americans." *Politics, Groups, and Identities* 7(2): 477–487.

Campbell, Angus, Philip Converse, Warren Miller, and Donald E. Stokes. 1960. *The American Voter*. University of Chicago Press.

Canon, David T., Matthew M. Schousen, and Patrick J. Sellers. 1996. "The Supply Side of Congressional Redistricting: Race and Strategic Politicians, 1972–1992." *Journal of Politics* 58(3):846–862.

Carmines, Edward, and James Stimson. 1980. "The Two Faces of Issue Voting." *American Political Science Review* 74:78–91.

Carnes, Nicholas, and John Holbein. 2015. "Unequal Responsiveness in Constituent Services? Evidence from Casework Request Experiments in North Carolina." https://bit.ly/330gjRR. Unpublished Paper.

Chauhan, D. S. 1978. "Education for Public Service: Managing Internship Programs." *State & Local Government Review* 10(3):100–105.

Chin, Michelle L., Jon R. Bond, and Nehemia Geva. 2000. "A Foot in the Door: An Experimental Study of PAC and Constituency Effects on Access." *Journal of Politics* 62(2):534–549.

Chomsky, Noam. 1997. "What Makes Mainstream Media Mainstream." *Z Magazine* 10(10):17–23.

Chouhoud, Youssef, Karam Dana, and Matt Barreto. 2019. "American Muslim Political Participation: Between Diversity and Cohesion." *Politics and Religion* 12(4):736–765.

Citrin, Jack, Beth Reingold, and Donald P. Green. 1990. "American Identity and the Politics of Ethnic Change." *Journal of Politics* 52(4):1124–1154.

Citrin, Jack, Cara Wong, and Brian Duff. 2001. "The Meaning of American National Identity." *Social Identity, Intergroup Conflict, and Conflict Reduction* 3:71.

Collingwood, Loren, Nazita Lajevardi, and Kassra A. R. Oskooii. 2018. "A Change of Heart? Why Individual-Level Public Opinion Shifted against Trump's Muslim Ban." *Political Behavior* 40(4): 1035–1072.

Coppock, Alexander. 2018. "Avoiding Post-Treatment Bias in Audit Experiments." *Journal of Experimental Political Science* 6(1):1–4.

Costa, Mia. 2017a. "How Responsive Are Political Elites? A Meta-analysis of Experiments on Public Officials." *Journal of Experimental Political Science* 4(3):241–254.

Costa, Mia. 2017b. "Improving Measures of Responsiveness for Elite Audit Experiments." Unpublished Paper.

Crocker, Jennifer, and Brenda Major. 1989. "Social Stigma and Self-Esteem: The Self-Protective Properties of Stigma." *Psychological Review* 96(4):608.

Dana, Karam, and Matt A. Barreto. 2019. "American Muslims and the State: Contexts and Contentions." In Brian R. Calfano and Nazita Lajevardi (eds.), *Understanding Muslim Political Life in America: Contested Citizenship in the Twenty-First Century*, Vol. 12, Religious Engagement in Democratic Politics. Philadelphia, PA: Temple University Press, pp. 21–36.

Dana, Karam, Matt A. Barreto, and Kassra A. R. Oskooii. 2011. "Mosques as American Institutions: Mosque Attendance, Religiosity and Integration into the Political System among American Muslims." *Religions* 2(4):504–524.

Dana, Karam, Nazita Lajevardi, Kassra A. R. Oskooii and Hannah L. Walker. 2018. "Veiled Politics: Experiences with Discrimination among Muslim Americans." *Politics and Religion* 12(4):629–677.

Dana, Karam, Bryan Wilcox-Archuleta, and Matt Barreto. 2017. "The Political Incorporation of Muslims in the United States: The Mobilizing Role of Religiosity in Islam." *Journal of Race, Ethnicity and Politics* 2(2):170–200.

Darcy, R., Susan Welch, and Janet Clark. 1994. *Women, Elections, and Representation*. Lincoln: University of Nebraska Press.

Distelhorst, Greg, and Yue Hou. 2014. "Ingroup Bias in Official Behavior: A National Field Experiment in China (May 5, 2014)." *Quarterly Journal of Political Science* 9(2):203–230. https://bit.ly/330RAx1. Unpublished Paper.

Djupe, Paul A., and John C. Green. 2007. "The Politics of American Muslims." In J. Matthew Wilson (ed.), *From Pews to Polling: Faith and Politics in the American Religious Mosaic*. Washington, D.C.: Georgetown University Press, pp. 213–250.

Donovan, Barbara. 2007. "Minority Representation in Germany." *German Politics* 16(4):455–480.

Dower, John W. 1986. *War without Mercy: Race & Power in the Pacific War*. Ann Arbor, MI: Pantheon Books.

Dwyer, Claire, Bindi Shah, and Gurchathen Sanghera. 2008. "From Cricket Lover to Terror Suspect: Challenging Representations of Young British Muslim Men." *Gender, Place & Culture* 15(2):117–136.

Einstein, Katherine Levine, and David M. Glick. 2017. "Does Race Affect Access to Government Services? An Experiment Exploring Street-level Bureaucrats and Access to Public Housing." *American Journal of Political Science* 61(1): 100–116.

Elver, Hilal. 2012. "Racializing Islam before and after 9/11: From Melting Pot to Islamophobia." *Transnational Law & Contemporary Problems* 21:119.

Entman, Robert M. 1990. *Democracy without Citizens: Media and the Decay of American Politics*. Oxford University Press.

Entman, Robert M., and Andrew Rojecki. 2001. *The Black Image in the White Mind: Media and Race in America*. University of Chicago Press.

Epstein, David, and Sharyn O'Halloran. 1999. *Delegating Powers: A Transaction Cost Politics Approach to Policy Making under Separate Powers*. Cambridge University Press.

Esposito, John L. 1999. *The Islamic Threat: Myth or Reality?* New York: Oxford University Press.

Esposito, John L. and Yvonne Yazbeck Haddad. 1998. *Muslims on the Americanization Path?* Oxford University Press.

Ewing, Katherine Pratt. 2008a. *Being and Belonging: Muslims in the United States since 9/11*. New York: Russell Sage Foundation.

Ewing, Katherine Pratt. 2008b. *Stolen Honor: Stigmatizing Muslim Men in Berlin*. Stanford University Press.

Fenno, Richard F. 1978. *Home Style: House Members in their Districts*. Glenview, IL: HarperCollins.

Findley, Paul. 2001. *Silent No More: Confronting America's False Images of Islam*. Beltsville, MD: Amana Books.

Finnegan, Lisa. 2006. *No Questions Asked: News Coverage since 9/11*. Westport, CN: Praeger.

Firebaugh, Glenn, and Kenneth E. Davis. 1988. "Trends in Antiblack Prejudice, 1972–1984: Region and Cohort Effects." *American Journal of Sociology* 94(2):251–272.

Fitch, Brad, Kathy Goldschmidt, Ellen Fulton, and Nicole Griffin. 2005. *How Capitol Hill Is Coping with the Surge in Citizen Advocacy.* Washington D.C.: Congressional Management Foundation. https://bit.ly/37couOi

Fleras, Augie. 2011. *The Media Gaze: Representations of Diversities in Canada.* Vancouver: UBC Press.

Frymer, Paul. 1999. *Uneasy Alliances.* Princeton University Press.

Gadarian, Shana Kushner. 2010. "The Politics of Threat: How Terrorism News Shapes Foreign Policy Attitudes." *Journal of Politics* 72(2):469–483.

Gaertner, Samuel L., and John F. Dovidio. 1986. *The Aversive Form of Racism.* New York: Academic Press.

Garcia-Rios, Sergio, and Angela X. Ocampo. 2018. "A Novel Approach and New Measure of Latino Ethno-racial Resentment." Presented at the Annual Meeting of the American Political Science Association, Boston, MA.

Gerber, Alan S., and Donald P. Green. 2008. "Field experiments and natural experiments." In Janet M. Box-Steffensmeier, Henry E. Brady, and David Collier (eds.), *The Oxford Handbook of Political Methodology.* Oxford University Press.

GhaneaBassiri, Kambiz. 2013. "Islamophobia and American History." In C. W. Ernst (ed.), *Islamophobia in America.* New York: Palgrave Macmillan, pp. 53–74.

Gilens, Martin. 1999. *Why Americans Hate Welfare: Race, Media, and the Politics of Antipoverty Policy,* University of Chicago Press.

Gilens, Martin. 2005. "Inequality and Democratic Responsiveness." *Public Opinion Quarterly* 69(5):778–796.

Gilliam Jr., Franklin D., and Karen M. Kaufmann. 1998. "Is There an Empowerment Life Cycle? Long-term Black Empowerment and Its Influence on Voter Participation." *Urban Affairs Review* 33(6):741–766.

Gilliam Jr., Franklin D., and Shanto Iyengar. 2000. "Prime Suspects: The Influence of Local Television News on the Viewing Public." *American Journal of Political Science* 44(3):560–573.

Gilliam Jr., Franklin D., Shanto Iyengar, Adam Simon, and Oliver Wright. 1996. "Crime in Black and White: The Violent, Scary World of Local News." *Harvard International Journal of Press/Politics* 1(3):6–23.

Gillum, Rachel M. 2019. "Muslim Expectations of U.S. Law Enforcement Behavior." In Brian R. Calfano and Nazita Lajevardi (eds.), *Understanding Muslim Political Life in America: Contested Citizenship in the Twenty-First*

Century, Vol. 12, Religious Engagement in Democratic Politics. Philadelphia, PA: Temple University Press, pp. 87–113.

Goff, Phillip Atiba, Jennifer L. Eberhardt, Melissa J. Williams, and Matthew Christian Jackson. 2008. "Not Yet Human: Implicit Knowledge, Historical Dehumanization, and Contemporary Consequences." *Journal of Personality and Social Psychology* 94(2):292.

González-Bailón, Sandra, and Georgios Paltoglou. 2015. "Signals of Public Opinion in Online Communication: A Comparison of Methods and Data Sources." *ANNALS of the American Academy of Political and Social Science* 659(1):95–107.

Gotanda, Neil. 2011. "The Racialization of Islam in American Law." *ANNALS of the American Academy of Political and Social Science* 637(1):184–195.

Greenberg, Bradley S., Dana Mastro, and Jeffrey E. Brand. 2002. "Minorities and the Mass Media: Television into the 21st Century." In Jennings Bryant and Dolf Zillmann (eds.), *Media Effects: Advances in Theory and Research*. Mahwah, NJ: Lawrence Erlbaum, pp. 333–351.

Griffin, John D., and Brian Newman. 2008. *Minority Report: Evaluating Political Equality in America*. University of Chicago Press.

Grose, Christian R., Neil Malhotra, and Robert Parks van Houweling. 2015. "Explaining Explanations: How Legislators Explain Their Policy Positions and How Citizens React." *American Journal of Political Science* 59(3): 724–743.

Gryski, Gerard S., Gerald W. Johnson, and Laurence J. O'Toole. 1987. "Undergraduate Internships: An Empirical Review." *Public Administration Quarterly* 11(2):150–170.

Gustavsson, Gina. 2017. "National Attachment – Cohesive, Divisive or Both?: The Divergent Links to Solidarity from National Identity, National Pride, and National Chauvinism." Presented at "Liberal Nationalism and Its Critics: Normative and Empirical Questions," June 20–21. Nuffield College, Oxford.

Gutterman, David S., and Andrew R. Murphy. 2014. "The Ground Zero Mosque: Sacred Space and the Boundaries of American Identity." *Politics, Groups, and Identities* 2(3):368–385.

Haddad, Yvonne Yazbeck, and Adair T. Lummis. 1987. *Islamic Values in the United States: A Comparative Study*. New York: Oxford University Press.

Haddad, Yvonne Yazbeck, and Jane I. Smith. 1993. *Mission to America: Five Islamic Sectarian Communities in North America*. Gainesville: University Press of Florida.

Hainmueller, Jens, and Daniel J. Hopkins. 2014. "Public Attitudes toward Immigration." *Annual Review of Political Science* 17:225–249.

Hainmueller, Jens, Daniel J. Hopkins, and Teppei Yamamoto. 2013. "Causal Inference in Conjoint Analysis: Understanding Multidimensional Choices via

Stated Preference Experiments." *Political Analysis* 22(1):1–30.

Hamamoto, Darrell Y. 1994. *Monitored Peril: Asian Americans and the Politics of TV Representation.* Minneapolis: University of Minnesota Press.

Hardy-Fanta, Carol, Pei-te Lien, Christine Marie Sierra, and Dianne Pinderhughes. 2007. "A New Look at Paths to Political Office: Moving Women of Color from the Margins to the Center." Presented at Annual Meeting of the American Political Science Association, Boston, Chicago.

Harwood, Jake, Miles Hewstone, Yair Amichai-Hamburger, and Nicole Tausch. 2013. "Intergroup Contact: An Integration of Social Psychological and Communication Perspectives." *Annals of the International Communication Association* 36(1):55–102.

Haynes, Chris, Jennifer Merolla, and S. Karthick Ramakrishnan. 2016. *Framing Immigrants: News Coverage, Public Opinion, and Policy.* New York: Russell Sage Foundation.

Hedlund, Ronald D. 1973. "Reflections on Political Internships." *PS: Political Science & Politics* 6(1):19–25.

Heitmeyer, Wilhelm, and Andreas Zick. 2004. "Anti-Semitism, Islamophobia and Groupfocused Enmity in Germany. A Research Note." Bielefield, Germany: Institute for Interdisciplinary Research on Conflict and Violence.

Helson, Harry. 1964. *Adaptation-Level Theory: An Experimental and Systematic Approach to Behavior.* New York: Harper & Row.

Hennessy, Bernard C. 1970. *Political Internships: Theory, Practice, Evaluation.* Pennsylvania State University Studies, Number 28. University Park: Pennsylvania State University.

Highton, Benjamin. 2004. "White Voters and African American Candidates for Congress." *Political Behavior* 26(1):1–25.

Hobbs, William, and Nazita Lajevardi. 2019. "Effects of Divisive Political Campaigns on the Day-to-Day Segregation of Arab and Muslim Americans." *American Political Science Review* 113(1):270–276.

Hopkins, Peter E. 2004. "Young Muslim Men in Scotland: Inclusions and Exclusions." *Children's Geographies* 2(2):257–272.

Hopkins, Daniel J., and Gary King. 2010. "A Method of Automated Nonparametric Content Analysis for Social Science." *American Journal of Political Science* 54(1):229–247.

Huddy, Leonie. 2001. "From Social to Political Identity: A Critical Examination of Social Identity Theory." *Political Psychology* 22(1):127–156.

Huddy, Leonie. 2015. "Group Identity and Political Cohesion." In *Emerging Trends in the Social and Behavioral Sciences: An Interdisciplinary, Searchable, and Linkable Resource.* Wiley Online Library.

Huddy, Leonie, and Nadia Khatib. 2007. "American Patriotism, National Identity, and Political Involvement." *American Journal of Political Science* 51(1): 63–77.

Human Rights Watch. 2005. "Witness to Abuse: Human Rights Abuses under the Material Witness Law since September 11." https://bit.ly/342Wuux

Huntington, Samuel P. 1997. *The Clash of Civilizations and the Remaking of World Order*. New Delhi: Penguin Books India.

Hutchings, Vincent L., and Nicholas A. Valentino. 2004. "The Centrality of Race in American Politics." *Annual Review Political Science* 7:383–408.

Hyman, Herbert H., and Paul B. Sheatsley. 1956. "Attitudes toward Desegregation." *Scientific American* 195(6):35–39.

ISPU. 2017. "American Muslim Poll 2017: Muslims at the Crossroads." https://bit.ly/341g62l

Iyengar, Shanto, James Curran, Anker Brink Lund, Inka Salovaara-Moring, Kyu S. Hahn, and Sharon Coen. 2010. "Cross-National versus Individual-Level Differences in Political Information: A Media Systems Perspective." *Journal of Elections, Public Opinion and Parties* 20(3):291–309.

Iyengar, Shanto, Mark D. Peters, and Donald R. Kinder. 1982. "Experimental Demonstrations of the Not-So-Minimal Consequences of Television News Programs." *American Political Science Review* 76(4):848–858.

Jalalzai, Farida. 2009. "The Politics of Muslims in America." *Politics and Religion* 2(2):163–199.

Jamal, Amaney. 2005. "The Political Participation and Engagement of Muslim Americans: Mosque Involvement and Group Consciousness." *American Politics Research* 33(4):521–544.

Jamal, Amaney. 2009. "The Racialization of Muslim Americans." In Abdulkader H. Sinno (ed.), *Muslims in Western Politics*. Bloomington: Indiana University Press, pp. 200–215.

Juchtmans, Goedroen, and Ides Nicaise. 2013. "Religion and Immigration: The Acculturation Attitudes of Muslim Primary School Children attending Flemish Schools." In Emer Smyth, Maureen Lyons, and Merike Darmody (eds.), *Religious Education in a Multicultural Europe: Children, Parents and Schools*. London: Palgrave Macmillan, pp. 132–163.

Kalin, Michael, and Nazita Lajevardi. 2017. "Breathing While Muslim in the Age of Trump." Political Violence at a Glance. https://bit.ly/332BGSw

Kalkan, Kerem Ozan, Geoffrey C. Layman, and John C. Green. 2018. "Will Americans Vote for Muslims? Cultural Outgroup Antipathy, Candidate Religion, and US Voting Behavior." *Politics and Religion* 11(4):798–829.

Kalkan, Kerem Ozan, Geoffrey C. Layman, and Eric M. Uslaner. 2009. "Bands of Others? Attitudes toward Muslims in Contemporary American Society." *Journal of Politics* 71(3):847–862.

Kalmoe, Nathan P., and Spencer Piston. 2013. "Is Implicit Prejudice against Blacks Politically Consequential? Evidence from the AMP." *Public Opinion Quarterly* 77(1):305–322.

Kam, Cindy D. 2007. "Implicit Attitudes, Explicit Choices: When Subliminal Priming Predicts Candidate Preference." *Political Behavior* 29(3):343–367.

Karam, Nicoletta. 2012. *The 9/11 Backlash: A Decade of US Hate Crimes Targeting the Innocent*. Berkeley, CA: Beatitude Press.

Katz, Irwin. 1981. *Stigma: A Social-Psychological Perspective*. Hillsdale, NJ: Erlbaum.

Kaufmann, Karen M. 2003. "Cracks in the Rainbow: Group Commonality as a Basis for Latino and African-American Political Coalitions." *Political Research Quarterly* 56(2):199–210.

Kellstedt, Paul M. 2000. "Media Framing and the Dynamics of Racial Policy Preferences." *American Journal of Political Science* 44(2):245–260.

Kellstedt, Paul M. 2003. *The Mass Media and the Dynamics of American Racial Attitudes*. Cambridge University Press.

Kellstedt, Paul M. 2005. "Media Frames, Core Values, and the Dynamics of Racial Policy Preferences." In Karen Callaghan and Frauke Schnell (eds.), *Framing American Politics*. University of Pittsburgh Press, pp. 167–178.

Khan, Mohommed A. Muqtedar. 1998. "Muslims and Identity Politics in America." In Y. Y. Haddad and J. L. Esposito (eds.), *Muslims on the Americanization Path*. New York: Oxford University Press, pp. 107–125.

Khan, Mussarat, and Kathryn Ecklund. 2013. "Attitudes toward Muslim Americans Post-9/11." *Journal of Muslim Mental Health* 7(1).

Kim, Claire Jean. 1999. "The Racial Triangulation of Asian Americans." *Politics & Society* 27(1):105–138.

Kinder, Donald R., and Lynn M. Sanders. 1996. *Divided by Color: Racial Politics and Democratic Ideals*. University of Chicago Press.

Kinder, Donald R., and David O. Sears. 1981. "Prejudice and Politics: Symbolic Racism versus Racial Threats to the Good Life." *Journal of Personality and Social Psychology* 40(3):414.

Kluegel, James R., and Eliot R. Smith. 1986. *Beliefs about Inequality: Americans' Views of What Is and What Ought to Be*. Piscataway, NJ: Transaction Publishers.

Kreppel, Amie, and George Tsebelis. 1999. "Coalition Formation in the European Parliament." *Comparative Political Studies* 32(8):933–966.

Kteily, Nour, Emile Bruneau, Adam Waytz, and Sarah Cotterill. 2015. "The Ascent of Man: Theoretical and Empirical Evidence for Blatant Dehumanization." *Journal of Personality and Social Psychology* 109(5):901.

Lajevardi, Nazita. 2017. "A Comprehensive Study of Muslim American Discrimination by Legislators, the Media, and the Masses." Doctoral Dissertation. University of California, San Diego.

Lajevardi, Nazita, and Marisa Abrajano. 2019. "How Negative Sentiment toward Muslim Americans Predicts Support for Trump in the 2016 Presidential Election." *Journal of Politics* 81(1):296–302.

Lajevardi, Nazita, and Kassra A. R. Oskooii. 2018. "Old-Fashioned Racism, Contemporary Islamophobia, and the Isolation of Muslim Americans in the Age of Trump." *Journal of Race, Ethnicity and Politics* 3(1):112–152.

Lajevardi, Nazita, Marianne M. Marrar, and Melissa R. Michelson. 2014. "The Unbearable Whiteness of Being Middle Eastern." Presented at the 37th meeting of the Politics of Race, Immigration, and Ethnicity Consortium (PRIEC), University of California, San Diego.

Larson, Stephanie Greco. 2006. *Media & Minorities: The Politics of Race in News and Entertainment.* Lanham, MD: Rowman & Littlefield.

Lau, Richard R. 1982. "Negativity in Political Perception." *Political Behavior* 4(4):353–377.

Lau, Richard R. 1985. "Two Explanations for Negativity Effects in Political Behavior." *American Journal of Political Science* 29:119–138.

Lavergne, Michael, and Sendhil Mullainathan. 2004. "Are Emily and Greg More Employable than Lakisha and Jamal? A Field Experiment on Labor Market Discrimination." *The American Economic Review* 94(4):991–1013.

Layman, Geoffrey C., Kerem Ozan Kalkan, and John C. Green. 2014. "A Muslim President? Misperceptions of Barack Obama's Faith in the 2008 Presidential Campaign." *Journal for the Scientific Study of Religion* 53(3): 534–555.

Lee, Cynthia. 2008. "Hate Crimes and the War on Terror." Barbara Perry, ed., 2008; GWU Legal Studies Research Paper No. 442; GWU Law School Public Law Research Paper No. 442. https://ssrn.com/abstract=1268355

Lee, Taeku. 2000. "Racial Attitudes and the Color Line(s) at the Close of the Twentieth Century." In Paul M. Ong (ed.), *The State of Asian Pacific Americans: Race Relations*, Vol. IV. Los Angeles: LEAP Asian Pacific American Public Policy Institute and UCLA Asian American Studies Center, pp. 457–478.

Lerman, Amy E., Katherine T. McCabe, and Meredith L. Sadin. 2015. "Political Ideology, Skin Tone, and the Psychology of Candidate Evaluations." *Public Opinion Quarterly* 79(1):53–90.

Lopez, Ian Haney. 1997. *White by Law: The Legal Construction of Race*. New York University Press.

Lopez, Ian F. Haney. 2009. *Racism on Trial: The Chicano Fight for Justice*. Cambridge, MA: Harvard University Press.

Lublin, David. 1999. *The Paradox of Representation: Racial Gerrymandering and Minority Interests in Congress*. Princeton University Press.

MacLeod, Colin, and Andrew Mathews. 1988. "Anxiety and the Allocation of Attention to Threat." *Quarterly Journal of Experimental Psychology Section A* 40(4):653–670.

Madonna, Anthony J., and Ian Ostrander. N.d. "Getting the Congress You Pay For: The Influence of Staff on Legislative Productivity." https://bit.ly/2r7MNfE

Maghbouleh, Neda. 2017. *The Limits of Whiteness: Iranian Americans and the Everyday Politics of Race*. Stanford University Press.

Mansbridge, Jane. 1999. "Should Blacks Represent Blacks and Women Represent Women? A Contingent 'Yes'." *Journal of Politics* 61(3):628–657.

Marcus, George E., and Michael B. MacKuen. 1993. "Anxiety, Enthusiasm, and the Vote: The Emotional Underpinnings of Learning and Involvement during Presidential Campaigns." *American Political Science Review* 87(3):672–685.

Markham, James W., and Crispin Maslog. 1971. "Images and the Mass Media." *Journalism Quarterly* 48(3):519–525.

Martin, Gregory J., and Ali Yurukoglu. 2017. "Bias in Cable News: Persuasion and Polarization." *American Economic Review* 107(9):2565–2599.

Martin, Shane. 2009. "The Congressional Representation of Muslim-American Constituents." *Politics and Religion* 2(2):230–246.

Mastro, Dana. 2009. "Effects of Racial and Ethnic Stereotyping." *Media Effects: Advances in Theory and Research* 3:325–341.

Mastro, Dana E., and Maria A. Kopacz. 2006. "Media Representations of Race, Prototypicality, and Policy Reasoning: An Application of Self-Categorization Theory." *Journal of Broadcasting & Electronic Media* 50(2):305–322.

Masuoka, Natalie, and Jane Junn. 2013. *The Politics of Belonging: Race, Public Opinion, and Immigration*. University of Chicago Press.

Mayhew, David R. 1974. *Congress: The Electoral Connection*. New Haven, CT: Yale University Press.

McCarus, Ernest Nasseph. 1994. *The Development of Arab-American Identity*. Ann Arbor: University of Michigan Press.

McCloud, Aminah Beverly. 1995. *African American Islam*. London: Routledge.

McConahay, John B. 1986. "Modern Racism, Ambivalence, and the Modern Racism Scale." In John F. Dovidio and Samuel L. Gaertner (eds.), *Prejudice, Discrimination, and Racism: Historical Trends and Contemporary Approaches*. Orlando FL: Academic Press, pp. 91–125.

McConahay, John B., and Joseph C. Hough. 1976. "Symbolic Racism." *Journal of Social Issues* 32(2):23–45.

McConnaughy, Corrine M., Ismail K. White, David L. Leal, and Jason P. Casellas. 2010. "A Latino on the Ballot: Explaining Coethnic Voting among Latinos and the Response of White Americans." *Journal of Politics* 72(4):1199–1211.

Meier, Kenneth J., and Joseph Stewart Jr. 1991. "Cooperation and Conflict in Multiracial School Districts." *Journal of Politics* 53(4):1123–1133.

Mendelberg, Tali. 2001. *The Race Card: Campaign Strategy, Implicit Messages, and the Norm of Equality*. Princeton University Press.

Merolla, Jennifer, S. Karthick Ramakrishnan, and Chris Haynes. 2013. "Illegal, Undocumented, or Unauthorized: Equivalency Frames, Issue Frames, and Public Opinion on Immigration." *Perspectives on Politics* 11(3):789–807.

Merolla, Jennifer L., and Elizabeth J. Zechmeister. 2009. *Democracy at Risk: How Terrorist Threats Affect the Public*. University of Chicago Press.

Merolla, Jennifer L., and Elizabeth J. Zechmeister. 2018. "Threat and Information Acquisition: Evidence from an Eight Country Study." *Journal of Experimental Political Science* 5(3):167–181.

Modood, Tariq, and Riva Kastoryano. 2006. "Secularism and the Accommodation of Muslims in Europe." In Tariq Modood, Anna Triandafyllidou, and Ricard Zapata-Barrero (eds.), *Multiculturalism, Muslims and Citizenship: A European Approach*. New York: Routledge, pp. 162–178.

Müller, Karsten, and Carlo Schwarz. 2019. "From Hashtag to Hate Crime: Twitter and Anti-minority Sentiment." https://papers.ssrn.com/sol3/papers.cfm?abstract_id=3149103

Muslim Advocates. 2018. *Running on Hate: 2018 Pre Election Report*. www.politico.com/f/?id=00000166-9304-d166-a77e-9f8c488b0001

Nacos, Brigitte. 2016. *Mass-Mediated Terrorism: Mainstream and Digital Media in Terrorism and Counterterrorism*. Lanham, MD: Rowman & Littlefield.

Nacos, Brigitte L., and Oscar Torres-Reyna. 2002. "Muslim Americans in the News before and after 9–11." Presented at the symposium "Restless Searchlight: Terrorism, the Media & Public Life," Harvard University.

Nacos, Brigitte Lebens, and Oscar Torres-Reyna. 2007. *Fueling Our Fears: Stereotyping, Media Coverage, and Public Opinion of Muslim Americans*. Lanham, MD: Rowman & Littlefield.

Naff, Alixa. 1993. *Becoming American: The Early Arab Immigrant Experience*. Carbondale: Southern Illinois University Press.

Ngai, Mae M. 2014. *Impossible Subjects: Illegal Aliens and the Making of Modern America*. Princeton University Press.

Nyang, Sulayman Sheih. 1999. *Islam in the United States of America*. Chicago: Kazi Publications Incorporated.

Ocampo, Angela X., Karam Dana, and Matt A. Barreto. 2018. "The American Muslim Voter: Community Belonging and Political Participation." *Social Science Research* 72:84–99.

Ogan, Christine, Lars Willnat, Rosemary Pennington, and Manaf Bashir. 2014. "The Rise of Anti-Muslim Prejudice: Media and Islamophobia in Europe and the United States." *International Communication Gazette* 76(1):27–46.

Olivola, Christopher Y., and Alexander Todorov. 2010. "Elected in 100 Milliseconds: Appearance-Based Trait Inferences and Voting." *Journal of Nonverbal Behavior* 34(2):83–110.

Omi, Michael, and Howard Winant. 2004. "Racial Formations." *Race, Class, and Gender in the United States* 6:13–22.

Omi, Michael, and Howard Winant. 2014. *Racial Formation in the United States*. New York: Routledge.

Oskooii, Kassra A. R. 2016. "How Discrimination Impacts Sociopolitical Behavior: A Multidimensional Perspective." *Political Psychology* 37(5):613–640.

Oskooii, Kassra A. R. 2018. "Perceived Discrimination and Political Behavior." *British Journal of Political Science* pp. 1–26.

Oskooii, Kassra A. R., and Karam Dana. 2018. "Muslims in Great Britain: The Impact of Mosque Attendance on Political Behaviour and Civic Engagement." *Journal of Ethnic and Migration Studies* 44(9):1479–1505.

Oskooii, Kassra A. R., Karam Dana, and Matthew A. Barreto. 2019. "Beyond Generalized Ethnocentrism: Islam-specific Beliefs and Prejudice toward Muslim Americans." *Politics, Groups, and Identities* pp. 1–28.

Oskooii, Kassra A. R., Nazita Lajevardi, and Loren Collingwood. 2019. "Opinion Shift and Stability: The Information Environment and Long-Lasting Opposition to Trump's Muslim Ban." *Political Behavior* pp. 1–37.

Pager, Devah, Bart Bonikowski, and Bruce Western. 2009. "Discrimination in a Low-Wage Labor Market: A Field Experiment." *American Sociological Review* 74(5):777–799.

Palmer, Barbara, and Dennis Simon. 2010. *Breaking the Political Glass Ceiling: Women and Congressional Elections*. New York: Routledge.

Panagopoulos, Costas. 2006. "The Polls-Trends: Arab and Muslim Americans and Islam in the Aftermath of 9/11." *Public Opinion Quarterly* 70(4):608–624.

Pantoja, Adrian D., Ricardo Ramirez, and Gary M. Segura. 2001. "Citizens by Choice, Voters by Necessity: Patterns in Political Mobilization by Naturalized Latinos." *Political Research Quarterly* 54(4):729–750.

Parker, Christopher S. 2009. "When Politics Becomes Protest: Black Veterans and Political Activism in the Postwar South." *Journal of Politics* 71(01):113–131.

Pettigrew, Thomas F. 1982. *Prejudice*. Cambridge, MA: Harvard University Press.

Pew. 2011. "Muslim Americans: No Signs of Growth in Alienation or Support for Extremism." https://pewrsr.ch/2r3Z2dk

Pew. 2017. "U.S. Muslims Concerned about Their Place in Society, but Continue to Believe in the American Dream." Pew Research Center. https://pewrsr.ch/2Qy2V4N

Philpot, Tasha S., and Hanes Walton. 2007. "One of Our Own: Black Female Candidates and the Voters Who Support Them." *American Journal of Political Science* 51(1):49–62.

Pitkin, Hanna F. 1967. *The Concept of Representation.* Berkeley: University of California Press.

Plous, Scott, and Tyrone Williams. 1995. "Racial Stereotypes from the Days of American Slavery: A Continuing Legacy." *Journal of Applied Social Psychology* 25(9):795–817.

Popkin, Samuel L. 1994. *The Reasoning Voter: Communication and Persuasion in Presidential Campaigns.* University of Chicago Press.

Powell, Kimberly A. 2011. "Framing Islam: An Analysis of US Media Coverage of Terrorism since 9/11." *Communication Studies* 62(1):90–112.

Prior, Markus. 2005. "News vs. Entertainment: How Increasing Media Choice Widens Gaps in Political Knowledge and Turnout." *American Journal of Political Science* 49(3):577–592.

Ramakrishnan, Subramanian Karthick. 2005. *Democracy in Immigrant America: Changing Demographics and Political Participation.* Stanford: Stanford University Press.

Ramasubramanian, Srividya. 2011. "The Impact of Stereotypical versus Counterstereotypical Media Exemplars on Racial Attitudes, Causal Attributions, and Support for Affirmative Action." *Communication Research* 38(4): 497–516.

Ramírez, Ricardo. 2007. "Segmented Mobilization Latino Nonpartisan Get-Out-the-Vote Efforts in the 2000 General Election." *American Politics Research* 35(2):155–175.

Read, Jennan Ghazal. 2008. "Discrimination and Identity Formation in a Post-9/11 Era." In Amaney Jamal and Nadine Naber (eds.), *Race and Arab Americans before and after 9/11.* New York: Syracuse University Press, pp. 305–317.

Reeves, Keith. 1997. *Voting Hopes or Fears?: White Voters, Black Candidates & Racial Politics in America.* Oxford University Press on Demand.

Rippy, Alyssa E., and Elana Newman. 2006. "Perceived Religious Discrimination and Its Relationship to Anxiety and Paranoia among Muslim Americans." *Journal of Muslim Mental Health* 1(1):5–20.

Romzek, Barbara S. 2000. "Accountability of Congressional Staff." *Journal of Public Administration Research and Theory* 10(2):413–446.

Romzek, Barbara S., and Jennifer A. Utter. 1996. "Career Dynamics of Congressional Legislative Staff: Preliminary Profile and Research Questions." *Journal of Public Administration Research and Theory* 6(3):415–442.

SAALT. 2017. "Report: Communities on Fire: Confronting Hate Violence and Xenophobic Political Rhetoric." https://bit.ly/2KvvXOT

Said, Edward. 1979. *Orientalism: Western Representations of the Orient.* New York: Pantheon.

Said, Edward W. 2003. *Orientalism (25th Anniversary Edition).* New York: Vintage Books.

Salaita, Steven George. 2005. "Ethnic Identity and Imperative Patriotism: Arab Americans before and after 9/11." *College Literature* 32(2):146–168.

Saleem, Muniba, Grace S. Yang, and Srividya Ramasubramanian. 2016. "Reliance on Direct and Mediated Contact and Public Policies Supporting Outgroup Harm." *Journal of Communication* 66(4):604–624.

Savelkoul, Michael, Peer Scheepers, Jochem Tolsma, and Louk Hagendoorn. 2010. "Anti-Muslim Attitudes in the Netherlands: Tests of Contradictory Hypotheses Derived from Ethnic Competition Theory and Intergroup Contact Theory." *European Sociological Review* 27(6):741–758.

Schoettmer, Patrick. 2015. "Mobilization and the Masjid: Muslim Political Engagement in Post-9/11 America." *Politics, Groups, and Identities* 3(2):255–273.

Schulman, Kevin A., Jesse A. Berlin, William Harless, Jon F. Kerner, Shyrl Sistrunk, Bernard J. Gersh, Ross Dube, Christopher K. Taleghani, Jennifer E. Burke, Sankey Williams et al. 1999. "The Effect of Race and Sex on Physicians' Recommendations for Cardiac Catheterization." *New England Journal of Medicine* 340(8):618–626.

Schuman, Howard, Charlotte Steeh, and Lawrence Bobo. 1985. *Racial Trends in America: Trends and Interpretations.* Cambridge, MA: Harvard University Press.

Sears, David O. 1988. "Symbolic Racism." In P. A. Katz and D. A. Taylor (eds.), *Eliminating Racism: Perspectives in Social Psychology.* Boston: Springer, pp. 53–84.

Sears, David O., and Patrick J. Henry. 2003. "The Origins of Symbolic Racism." *Journal of Personality and Social Psychology* 85(2):259–275.

Sears, David O., and Donald R. Kinder. 1971. *Racial Tension and Voting in Los Angeles,* Vol. 156, Los Angeles: Institute of Government and Public Affairs, University of California.

Sears, David O., P. J. Henry, and Rick Kosterman. 2000. "Egalitarian Values and Contemporary Racial Politics." In David O. Sears, Jim Sadanius, and Lawrence Bobo (eds.), *Racialized Politics: The Debate about Racism in America.* University of Chicago Press, pp. 75–117.

Segura, Gary M., and Luis R. Fraga. 2008. "Race and the Recall: Racial and Ethnic Polarization in the California Recall Election." *American Journal of Political Science* 52(2):421–435.

Selod, Saher. 2015. "Citizenship Denied: The Racialization of Muslim American Men and Women Post-9/11." *Critical Sociology* 41(1):77–95.

Shah, Hemant, and Michael C. Thornton. 1994. "Racial Ideology in US Mainstream News Magazine Coverage of Black–Latino Interaction, 1980–1992." *Critical Studies in Media Communication* 11(2):141–161.

Shaheen, Jack G. 2003. "Reel Bad Arabs: How Hollywood Vilifies a People." *Annals of the American Academy of Political and Social Science* 588(1):171–193.

Shamas, Diala, and Nermeen Arastu. 2010. *Mapping Muslims: NYPD Spying and Its Impact on America Muslims*. Long Island City, NY: CLEAR Project, with MACLC and AALDEF. https://bit.ly/35fnt6j

Sides, John, and Kimberly Gross. 2013. "Stereotypes of Muslims and Support for the War on Terror." *Journal of Politics* 75(3):583–598.

Sigelman, Carol K., Lee Sigelman, Barbara J. Walkosz, and Michael Nitz. 1995. "Black Candidates, White Voters: Understanding Racial Bias in Political Perceptions." *American Journal of Political Science* 39(1):243–265.

Simpson, George Eaton, and J. Milton Yinger. 2013. *Racial and Cultural Minorities: An Analysis of Prejudice and Discrimination*. Medford, MA: Springer Science & Business Media.

Smith, Rogers M. 1993. "Beyond Tocqueville, Myrdal, and Hartz: The Multiple Traditions in America." *American Political Science Review* 87(3):549–566.

Sniderman, Paul M., and Aloysius Hagendoorn. 2007. *When Ways of Life Collide: Multiculturalism and Its Discontents in the Netherlands*. Princeton University Press.

Sniderman, Paul, Louk Hagendoorn, and Markus Prior. 2003. "De moeizame acceptatie van moslims in Nederland." *Mens & Maatschappij* 78(3):199.

SPLC. 2016. "Ten Days After: Harassment and Intimidation in the Aftermath of the Election." https://bit.ly/332Vkhc

Steeh, Charlotte, and Howard Schuman. 1992. "Young White Adults: Did Racial Attitudes Change in the 1980s?" *American Journal of Sociology* 98(2):340–367.

Steet, Linda. 2000. *Veils and Daggers: A Century of National Geographic's Representation of the Arab World*. Philadelphia: Temple University Press.

Stephens, LaFleur Nadiyah. 2013. "The Effectiveness of Implicit and Explicit Racial Appeals in a 'Post-Racial' America." PhD Dissertation. University of Michigan.

Strabac, Zan, and Ola Listhaug. 2008. "Anti-Muslim Prejudice in Europe: A Multilevel Analysis of Survey Data from 30 Countries." *Social Science Research* 37(1):268–286.

Suleiman, Michael W. 1999. "Islam, Muslims and Arabs in America: The Other of the Other of the Other..." *Journal of Muslim Minority Affairs* 19(1): 33–47.

Swain, Carol Miller. 1995. *Black Faces, Black Interests: The Representation of African Americans in Congress*. Cambridge, MA: Harvard University Press.

Tan, Alexis, Yuki Fujioka, and Gerdean Tan. 2000. "Television Use, Stereotypes of African Americans and Opinions on Affirmative Action: An Affective Model of Policy Reasoning." *Communications Monographs* 67(4):362–371.

Taylor, D. Garth, Paul B. Sheatsley, and Andrew M. Greeley. 1978. "Attitudes toward Racial Integration." *Scientific American* 238(6):42–49.

Tehranian, John. 2007. "Selective Racialization: Middle-Eastern American Identity and the Faustian Pact with Whiteness." *Connecticut Law Review* 40:1201.

Tehranian, John. 2008. *Whitewashed: America's Invisible Middle Eastern Minority*, Critical America, Vol. 46. New York University Press.

Tekelioglu, Ahmet Selim. 2019. "Muslim American Debates on Engagement with Law Enforcement." In Brian R. Calfano and Nazita Lajevardi (eds.), *Understanding Muslim Political Life in America: Contested Citizenship in the Twenty-First Century*, Vol. 12, Religious Engagement in Democratic Politics. Philadelphia, PA: Temple University Press, pp. 69–86.

Terkildsen, Nayda. 1993. "When White Voters Evaluate Black Candidates: The Processing Implications of Candidate Skin Color, Prejudice, and Self-Monitoring." *American Journal of Political Science* 37:1032–1053.

Terman, Rochelle. 2017. "Islamophobia and Media Portrayals of Muslim Women: A Computational Text Analysis of US News Coverage." *International Studies Quarterly* 61(3):489–502.

Tesler, Michael. 2012. "The Return of Old-Fashioned Racism to White Americans' Partisan Preferences in the Early Obama Era." *Journal of Politics* 75(1): 110–123.

Tesler, Michael. Forthcoming. "President Obama and the Emergence of Islamophobia in Mass Partisan Preferences." *Political Research Quarterly* 3(1): 153–155.

Tesler, Michael. 2018. "Islamophobia in the 2016 Election." *Journal of Race, Ethnicity and Politics* pp. 1–3.

Thernstrom, Stephan, and Abigail Thernstrom. 2009. *America in Black and White: One Nation, Indivisible*. New York: Simon & Schuster.

Thomsen, Danielle M. 2015. "Why So Few (Republican) Women? Explaining the Partisan Imbalance of Women in the US Congress." *Legislative Studies Quarterly* 40(2):295–323.

Tyler, Tom R., Stephen Schulhofer, and Aziz Z. Huq. 2010. "Legitimacy and Deterrence Effects in Counterterrorism Policing: A Study of Muslim Americans." *Law and Society Review* 44(2):365–402.

van Dijk, Teun A. et al. 1995. "Power and the News Media." *Political Communication and Action* 6(1):9–36.

van Horn, Carl E. 1989. "The Entrepreneurial States." In C. van Horn (ed.), *The State of the States*. Washington, D.C.: Congressional Quarterly Press, pp. 209–221.

Verkuyten, Maykel. 2005. "Ethnic Group Identification and Group Evaluation among Minority and Majority Groups: Testing the Multiculturalism Hypothesis." *Journal of Personality and Social Psychology* 88(1):121.

Verkuyten, Maykel. 2007. "Religious Group Identification and Inter-religious Relations: A Study among Turkish-Dutch Muslims." *Group Processes & Intergroup Relations* 10(3):341–357.

Visalvanich, Neil. 2017. "When Does Race Matter? Exploring White Responses to Minority Congressional Candidates." *Politics, Groups, and Identities* 5(4):618–641.

Wald, Kenneth D. 2008. "Homeland Interests, Hostland Politics: Politicized Ethnic Identity among Middle Eastern Heritage Groups in the United States." *International Migration Review* 42(2):273–301.

Weaver, Vesla M. 2012. "The Electoral Consequences of Skin Color: The 'Hidden' Side of Race in Politics." *Political Behavior* 34(1):159–192.

Westfall, Aubrey, Özge Çelik Russell, Bozena Welborne, and Sarah Tobin. 2017. "Islamic Headcovering and Political Engagement: The Power of Social Networks." *Politics and Religion* 10(1):3–30.

Westfall, Aubrey, Bozena Welborne, Sarah Tobin, and Özge Çelik Russell. 2016. "The Complexity of Covering: The Religious, Social, and Political Dynamics of Islamic Practice in the United States." *Social Science Quarterly* 97(3):771–790.

White, Ariel R., Noah L. Nathan, and Julie K. Faller. 2015. "What Do I Need to Vote? Bureaucratic Discretion and Discrimination by Local Election Officials." *American Political Science Review* 109(1):129–142.

Wilkins, Karin G. 1995. "Middle Eastern Women in Western Eyes: A Study of US Press Photographs of Middle Eastern Women." In Yahya R. Kamalipor (ed.), *The US Media and the Middle East: Image and Perception*. Westport, CN: Praeger, pp. 50–61.

Winter, Nicholas J. G. 2006. "Beyond Welfare: Framing and the Racialization of White Opinion on Social Security." *American Journal of Political Science* 50(2):400–420.

Winter, Nicholas J. G. 2008. *Dangerous Frames: How Ideas about Race and Gender Shape Public Opinion*. University of Chicago Press.

Wormser, Richard. 1994. *American Islam: Growing Up Muslim in America*. New York: Walker.

Wortley, Scot, John Hagan, and Ross Macmillan. 1997. "Just Des(s)erts? The Racial Polarization of Perceptions of Criminal Injustice." *Law and Society Review* 31(4):637–676.

Yadon, Nicole, and Spencer Piston. 2019. "Examining Whites' Anti-Black Attitudes after Obama's Presidency." *Politics, Groups, and Identities* 7(4): 794–814.

Zoll, Rachel. 2008. "US Muslim Voters Are Election Year Outcasts." *USA Today.* https://bit.ly/37tweMa

Index